STUDIA **PHILO**LOGICA PRAGENSIA

Martin Humpál and
Helena Březinová,
editors

Migration and Identity in Nordic Literature

CHARLES UNIVERSITY
KAROLINUM PRESS
2022

KAROLINUM PRESS
Karolinum Press is a publishing department of Charles University
Ovocný trh 560/5, 116 36 Prague 1, Czech Republic
www.karolinum.cz

This work was supported by the European Regional Development Fund project
"Creativity and Adaptability as Conditions of the Success of Europe
in an Interrelated World" (reg. no.: CZ.02.1.01/0.0/0.0/16_019/0000734) implemented
at Charles University, Faculty of Arts. The project is carried out under the ERDF Call
"Excellent Research" and its output is aimed at employees of research organizations
and Ph.D. students.

EUROPEAN UNION
European Structural and Investment Funds
Operational Programme Research,
Development and Education

MINISTRY OF EDUCATION,
YOUTH AND SPORTS

© Karolinum Press, 2022
Edited by Martin Humpál and Helena Březinová
Texts © Helena Březinová, Petra Broomans, Jan Dlask, Satu Gröndahl,
Jon Helt Haarder, Martin Humpál, Annika Bøstein Myhr, Elisabeth Oxfeldt,
Sylwia Izabela Schab, Radka Stahr, 2022
Cover by Markéta Baťková
Graphic design by Zdeněk Ziegler
Set and printed in the Czech Republic by Karolinum Press
First edition

Cataloguing-in-Publication Data is available from the National Library
of the Czech Republic

The original manuscript was peer-reviewed by Margita Gáborová (Comenius University,
Bratislava) and Jiří Munzar (Masaryk University, Brno).

ISBN 978-80-246-4731-9
ISBN 978-80-246-4932-0 (pdf)

Contents

Preface

Martin Humpál and Helena Březinová 7

PART I – Tracing Approaches and Rethinking Concepts

1. **Autobiographical Narratives in an Era of Migration: To What Extent Is the Idea of Individual and National Identity Still Viable Today?**
Annika Bøstein Myhr 10

2. **Creating (Im)migrant Literature in Sweden since the 1970s**
Satu Gröndahl 27

PART II – Migration, Identity, and Literature

3. **Andersen, Ibsen, and Strindberg as Migrant Writers**
Helena Březinová 46

4. **Emigration and the Image of the USA in Henrik Ibsen's**
Samfundets støtter (*Pillars of Society*)
Martin Humpál 64

5. **Christer Kihlman's Autobiography** *Alla mina söner* (*All My Sons*)
in the Perspective of *Orientalism* **by Edward W. Said**
Jan Dlask 73

6. **Playing with Identities: Variants of Biography and the Sylleptic 'I'**
in Bronisław Świderski's Migration Novels
Sylwia Izabela Schab 90

7. ***"Det här är en märklig plats"*: Space as a Reflection of Identity**
in Golnaz Hashemzadeh Bonde's Novel *Hon är inte jag*
Radka Stahr 97

8. ***Dulce de Leche*: Translingualism, Laughter and Sweet Stickiness**
in Veronica Salinas's *Og – En argentinsk au pairs ordbok*
Elisabeth Oxfeldt 112

5

9. **Migration and Loss of Identity in Linnea Axelsson's *Ædnan: Epos* (2018)**
   Petra Broomans 129

10. **"The Ugly Grey-White Blocks of Concrete": Class, Gender, and Ethnicity
    in Danish "Ghetto Literature"**
    Jon Helt Haarder 142

Notes on Contributors 158

Summary 160

Preface

Martin Humpál and Helena Březinová

Migration is a frequent topic of debates nowadays, whether it concerns refugees from war-torn areas or the economic pros and cons of the mobility of multinational corporations and their employees. We live in an era of globalization, after all, and one could argue that we are witnessing a greater intermingling of people from different cultures than the world has ever seen before. Yet we must not overestimate the scope of the current phenomenon. Migration has been here since time immemorial, and its dimensions were sometimes larger than we can imagine today. Its nature, manifestations, and consequences, however, have not always been the same. It is therefore important to take into account the historical and sociological aspects when we speak of migration and its character.

In our book we focus on migration as it has manifested itself in literature and culture in nineteenth, twentieth, and early twenty-first century Northern Europe, more concretely, in Denmark, Norway, Sweden, Finland, and Iceland. We have chosen to examine the theme of migration in relation to the questions of identity, both national and individual. We believe that migration almost always leads to a disturbance of identity and creates a potential for conflicts between individuals as well as between groups of people. The present book therefore concentrates on such cases of disturbance, disruption, and hybridization of identity, as they are represented in literary works linked to the European North.

The book opens with two chapters that have broader implications. While some critics doubt the usefulness of the notion of identity these days because, allegedly, identity is always a fluid and hybrid phenomenon, Annika Bøstein Myhr's contribution, "Autobiographical Narratives in an Era of Migration: To What Extent Is the Idea of Individual and National Identity Still Viable Today?", shows that the concept of identity is still relevant. She ties her arguments to the existence of nation states and to the power relationships between and within them. Satu Gröndahl's chapter "Creating (Im)migrant Literature in Sweden since the 1970s" provides the reader with an overview of scholarly approaches to (im)migrant literature in Sweden during the past several decades. The text focuses on Sweden, but some of the general observations about the development of the critical discourse are also valid for discussions in other Nordic countries.

The remaining part of the book consists of contributions on the migration aspects in Scandinavian literature from the nineteenth century until today. Helena Březinová's chapter "Andersen, Ibsen, and Strindberg as Migrant Writers" deals with an interesting paradox: while the world-famous authors H. C. Andersen, Henrik Ibsen, and August

Strindberg are often described as the essential component of, respectively, Danish, Norwegian, and Swedish national literature, they spent many years abroad, and this migrant aspect of their work is usually disregarded, or at least underplayed. In his chapter "Emigration and the Image of the USA in Henrik Ibsen's *Samfundets støtter* (*Pillars of Society*)," Martin Humpál discusses Ibsen's *Pillars of Society* as part of the playwright's criticism of Norwegian society and points to a surprising aspect of the drama: while many people assume that migration leads to a split identity, Ibsen claims the opposite – those Norwegians who have emigrated to the USA have been able to remain true to themselves, whereas those who stay in Norway end up with split personalities, because they have to conform to the enormous pressure of conventions and false morals.

Jan Dlask's contribution, "Christer Kihlman's Autobiography *Alla mina söner* (*All My Sons*) in the Perspective of *Orientalism* by Edward W. Said," examines an autobiographical text which tells the story of a relationship between a Finland-Swedish intellectual and an Argentinian homosexual prostitute as an encounter of two different worlds and value systems. The chapter shows the usefulness of some of Said's concepts for discussing the differences between Europe and South America. In her chapter "Playing with Identities: Variants of Biography and the Sylleptic "I" in Bronisław Świderski's Migration Novels," Sylwia Izabela Schab analyzes the manner in which the Polish-Danish writer Bronisław Świderski's novels deal with the question of (auto)biography. The protagonists of the novels are emigrants with unstable identities, and Schab shows that the *self* in these texts is intentionally "double-coded": both authentic and fictional at the same time.

The remaining four chapters deal with the most recent literary works. The first one concerns Sweden and Iran: Radka Stahr analyzes spatial representation in relation to migration in her contribution "'Det här är en märklig plats.' Space as a Reflection of Identity in Golnaz Hashemzadeh Bonde's Novel *Hon är inte jag*." In her chapter, "*Dulce de Leche*: Translingualism, Laughter and Sweet Stickiness in Veronica Salinas's *Og – En argentinsk au pairs ordbok*," Elisabeth Oxfeldt examines a book of autobiographic free-verse poems about an Argentinian refugee's first year in Norway. Oxfeldt describes the text as tied to the project of developing a new hybrid identity and uses, among other analytic tools, Kristeva's notion of being a "subject in process." In "Migration and Loss of Identity in Linnea Axelsson's *Ædnan: Epos* (2018)," Petra Broomans analyzes Axelsson's epic poem *Ædnan* which deals with the history of forced migration of Sámi people, as depicted by representatives of different generations. Finally, Jon Helt Haarder's chapter "'The ugly grey-white blocks of concrete': Class, Gender, and Ethnicity in Danish 'Ghetto Literature,'" ties the issue of migration to the questions of social and ethnic segregation, as they manifest themselves in a specific phenomenon of contemporary Denmark, so-called "ghetto literature."

The initial ideas for the individual chapters of this book were developed in a workshop which took place at Charles University in Prague on March 5 and 6, 2020. The workshop was sponsored by *KREAS*, a project of the Operational Program "Research, Development and Education," whose financial support we gratefully acknowledge here.

PART I
Tracing Approaches and Rethinking Concepts

1. Autobiographical Narratives in an Era of Migration: To What Extent Is the Idea of Individual and National Identity Still Viable Today?

Annika Bøstein Myhr

We have long since grown accustomed to authors of postcolonial literature challenging Eurocentric ideas about what constitutes a nation's identity. In the last few years, authors without traditional postcolonial experiences have begun doing the same. This chapter compares three such works, namely Bergsveinn Birgisson's *Den svarte vikingen* (2013, The Black Viking), Maja Lee Langvad's *Hun er vred: Et vidnesbyrd om transnational adoption* (2014, She Is Angry: A Testimony of Transnational Adoption), and Mikhail Shishkin's *Venerin volos* (2005, *Maidenhair* 2012).[1] The works, set in the national contexts of Iceland, Denmark, and Switzerland, respectively, explore the problems of belonging certain individuals face in these nations – both today and historically. The books are partially, but not exclusively, autobiographical, and the life stories of their authors are therefore relevant to the analysis. To begin with, I will define some terms in the chapter's title and suggest three answers to the chapter's central question: to what extent is the idea of individual and national identity still viable today?

Some Definitions

All three books combine autobiographical and fictional elements. Not all of them, however, fit the description of a "narrative," understood as a fictional or non-fictional report of connected events. Although the events in a narrative may be told out of sequence, underneath the surface is a plot that ties the events together in a chronological order. Usually, we actively look for ways in which to put the events in both fictional and autobiographical works together in a way that would fit the works' plot (Brooks). Not being able to re-create such a storyline, plan, scheme, or main story may leave us feeling unfulfilled, and therefore the lack of a plot is, in fact, quite a powerful literary device. The lack of a plot in a literary or autobiographical work could, for instance, reflect a person's inability to structure a coherent life story and a disturbed relationship between an individual's life story and the societal conditions framing that story.

---

[1] Since the first two books have not been translated into English, I will use my own translations of both their titles and content. *Maidenhair* was originally published as *Venerin volos* in Russian in 2005, but I will be quoting from Marian Schwartz's English translation from 2012.

The word "identity" commonly refers to (1) "who someone is: the name of a person or group," and (2) "the qualities, beliefs, etc., that make a particular person or group different from others" (*Merriam-Webster Dictionary*). Both of these meanings are important to understanding the three chosen works. When referring to individuals, we need to be aware that the word identity may indicate the formal, or official, identity that we find, for instance, in a passport or a birth certificate and not just to our own or others' ideas about who we are. Also, we should keep in mind that identity is created over time, through encounters between different persons and groups. This is also obvious from the etymology of the word identity, which in Latin means "the same." The question is not only if I am the same as the others in my group – it is also if I am the same today as I was yesterday, five, ten, or thirty years ago. It is true of individuals as well as of groups that we are both the same and different over time. Thus, in contrast to an essentialist notion of identity as something given that does not change, the constructivist notion of identity as flexible and negotiable would seem to pave the way for the inclusion of the "other" into the national "self."

But although it is important to be aware of the fact that both individuals and nations change over time, we should also bear in mind that we cannot talk about a nation's identity in the same way we do about an individual's identity. A nation is not a body, and it does not have *one* mind. A nation consists of many people, its population changes over time, and the geographical borders of the national space may also change. Over the last few decades, the populace of European countries has been changing more noticeably than before because of migration. Europe's recent migration history and the current prevalence of the idea that identity is a construct are factors that raise the question of whether the ideas of individual and national identity are at all viable today.

The word *viable* comes from the French "viable," meaning 'capable of life.' The term originally comes from the disciplines of biology and botany. Defined as "the ability of a thing (a living organism, an artificial system, an *idea*, etc.) to maintain itself or recover its potentialities" ("Viability"),[2] the term can, however, also pertain to the field of literary studies – broadly understood as including studies of both fiction and life writings – since the borders between these genres are becoming increasingly blurred. Translated into the field of literary studies, the question is to what extent the idea of individual and national identities lives on in such literature today: Can we understand literary works better by reading them with an eye to the idea of individual and national identity in our postmodern and post-national times? And can reading such works tell us something new about the idea of individual and national identity?

In order to investigate these issues, I will propose three answers to the article's central question. First, I will argue that the idea of individual and national identity is viable to the extent that citizens of certain nation states are discriminated against because of their country's place in the global hegemony of power. Second, the idea of individual and national identity is viable if non-white individuals are not recognised as equals to white individuals within Western European nations like Iceland, Denmark, or Switzerland. Third, the idea of individual and national identity is viable if a country's official

---

[2] I cite *Wikipedia* as a source here. I have also checked other sources but have come to the conclusion that *Wikipedia* has the best definition for my purposes.

national narrative – propagated, for instance, in school curricula today – does not include the story of the nation's heterogeneous past. The third premise is particularly important in connection with Birgisson's book *Den svarte vikingen* which is the first work I will discuss. In my analysis of the three books I have chosen to focus on, I will deliberate whether or not the premises I have put up are reflected in their form, content, and genres.

Birgisson: *Den svarte vikingen* (The Black Viking)

Birgisson was born in Iceland in 1971 and lives in Norway. He is a philologist and author of fiction, poetry, and non-fiction prose in Icelandic and Norwegian. *Den svarte vikingen* was originally published in Norwegian. Although the book's narrative is made possible by Birgisson's use of fictional devices, the book was nominated for the Brage Prize for the best non-fiction book in 2013. This was possible, because one of the book's two main plots is a historical investigation, which depicts the story of Geirmund Heljarskinn, a Viking born in Norway around 850 A.D. to one Norwegian and one Mongol-looking parent from the Russian North. The structure of the book mirrors Heljarskinn's lifeline: He was born in Rogaland (Ch. 2) but in his early teens moved for some time to Bjarmaland in the North of Russia (Ch. 3). He then spent some years in Ireland (Ch. 4) before ending up in Iceland in the period of settlement at the end of the ninth century (Ch. 5). The book's second plot describes Birgisson's quest for Heljarskinn's life story. Birgisson tells us how, as a little boy in Iceland, he heard stories about this great black Viking who was also his 26th great grandfather. As Birgisson gets older, it puzzles him that so little is known about Heljarskinn, and he asks himself: Why did no one write his saga?

The book *Den svarte vikingen* can be read as Birgisson's attempt to write the never-before-written saga of Heljarskinn.[3] Birgisson confesses to the reader that he is not at all certain about what his approach to this should be. As the book's first-person narrator and historical author, he asks himself: "Hvordan skal jeg formidle stoffet slik at noen orker å lese? Skal jeg formidle fragmentene uten å trekke for vidtfavnende konklusjoner, eller skal jeg heller forsøke å lage en historie ut av det hele?" (84). ["How should I impart the material in a way that will make it bearable for people to read? Should I convey the fragments without drawing conclusions that are too wide-ranging, or should I try to make a story out of it all?"] Birgisson describes his project and method in Chapter 1. He chooses to create a coherent narrative but knows that even though he provides the book with 32 pages of references to his source material and 52 pages of notes, he will not be able to convince the reader, let alone himself, that his story tells the *truth* about Heljarskinn. Therefore, he may as well lay his cards on the table. As he puts it: "Men der de gamle sagamestrene helt og holdent skjuler sitt håndverk, prøver jeg å gjøre leseren oppmerksom på mitt" (27). ["Whereas the old saga masters were hiding their devices entirely, I try to make the reader aware of mine."] For instance, he explains to the reader how he fills in the parts of the stories that the sagas do *not* tell. He may spend more than

---

[3]   Since publishing *Den svarte vikingen*, Birgisson has also written *Geirmundar saga Heljarskinns*, a book about the (fictional) discovery of Geirmund Heljarskinn's saga.

two pages describing "noe som en saga ikke ville spandert mer enn en setning på" (86) ["something that a saga would not have spent more than a sentence on"].

"Sagaskriverne" ["The authors of the sagas"], he explains, "hadde begrenset interesse for praktiske forhold, og de foretrakk å berette om store hendelser i få ord" (86) ["had only a limited interest in practicalities and preferred to depict great events in few words"]. This of course makes it very difficult to reconstruct "hverdagslivet [til vikingene] på bakgrunn av norrøne tekster" (86) ["the Vikings'] everyday life based on Norse texts"], and Birgisson, therefore, needs other sources apart from texts. He explains that he has to use scientific methods in order to be able to interpret these sources – place names, archaeological findings, DNA samples, and the like. He defines his role as that of a "fortolker" ["interpreter"] and "en røst som kaster lys over det mørklagte" (28) ["a voice illuminating what lies in darkness"]. His method is what he calls "kunnskapsbasert fantasi" (28) ["knowledge-based imagination"]: As the narrator of Heljarskinn's story, Birgisson is clear about what it is that we know, and what we have to assume.

In his assumptions, Birgisson relies both on his philological skills and on his bodily experiences. For instance, he tests the saying that men get an erection when passing Snorraskjól in Iceland – and when he finds that the saying is true, he starts imagining Heljarskinn and his *harem* at Kvenhóll. As Birgisson sees it, the fact that Heljarskinn *had* a harem is one of several reasons why Geirmund's saga was never written. Geirmund simply did not fit into the Icelandic founding myth. Such a myth, says Birgisson, "viser oss gjerne ideelle forhold" (28) ["is likely to show us ideal conditions"]. And this ideal reveals "det samtida mangler" (28) ["what is missing in the present time"]. When the history of the founding of Iceland was written down, Iceland was in a state of civil war, and Birgisson explains that it was, therefore, "fornuftig å minnes det motsatte – de gode, gamle dager da alle var likestilt og noen få høvdinger ikke hadde all makt, slik situasjonen var på Island da sagaene ble skrevet" (28) ["sensible to recall the opposite – the good old days when everyone was equal [...], as was the case in Iceland at the time the sagas were written"].

The story Birgisson composes from the fragments about Heljarskinn *contradicts* the myth of all Icelanders being equals since it shows Heljarskinn as

en aristokrat som strategisk la under seg store deler av Nordvest- og Vest-Island [...]. Han var en økonomisk motivert viking som ikke bare hersket over mange andre norrøne menn, han var også en grossistaktig importør av et uønsket element i det islandske samfunnet: irske treller. [...] I tillegg har han røtter blant fremmede folkeslag i nord [i Bjarmeland] (217).

[an aristocrat, who strategically conquered large parts of northwestern and western Iceland [...]. He was a financially motivated Viking, who not only ruled over many other Norse men but was also a large-scale importer of an unwanted element in the Icelandic society, namely the Irish thralls. [...] In addition, he was biologically related to some unknown peoples from the north [in Bjarmaland]].

The name Heljarskinn means dark skin, and Geirmund acquired this name because of his dark complexion. As Birgisson sees it, both egalitarianism and xenophobia have played a role in the *forgetting* of Heljarskinn's story. Since the saga of Geirmund

Heljarskinn was never written, his story never became a part of what Aleida Assmann calls a *functional memory* – that is, a memory that members of the Icelandic national community identify with (*Erinnerungsräume* & *Cultural Memory and Western Civilization*).

One might speculate that perhaps Iceland's contemporary history could have taken a different turn, had the saga of Geirmund Herljarskinn been written and introduced into school curricula. For Heljarskinn's story strongly resonates with the story of the Icelandic bank crisis of 2008 to 2011. The crisis resulted in part from the implementation of reforms in the 1990s, which gradually made Icelanders develop *away* from their traditional egalitarianism and inspired Birgisson to write *Den svarte vikingen*. The book shows how part of Iceland's heterogeneous past was forgotten because it did not fit the national founding myth. By reintroducing something that has been repressed into the Icelandic national narrative, Birgisson shows that the forgetting of Iceland's historical "other" was essential to the development of the country's national identity – and has perhaps made the country vulnerable to such events as the 2008–2011 financial crisis. One might also ask if the discrepancy between Birgisson's narrative and the narratives of school textbooks is the reason why Birgisson wrote *Den svarte vikingen* in Norwegian rather than in Icelandic. Birgisson's more prosaic explanation for his choice of language was that the book was funded mainly from Norwegian sources (Birgisson 2014).

Den svarte vikingen shows how the writing of a book may be triggered by what Homi Bhabha calls "the distracting presence of another temporality that disturbs the contemporaneity of the national present" (205). The silencing of his 26th great grandfather's story disturbed Birgisson so much that he invested years of his life writing the tale of Heljarskinn. In doing so, he found a place for himself as an author of a book in a semi-academic, semi-autobiographical, and semi-fictional genre. For the autobiographical plot in *Den svarte vikingen* tells the story of how Birgisson, who holds a doctoral degree in Norse philology, creates a professional identity on the side of what he calls "mer beskrivende enn engasjerende" (27) ["descriptive rather than captivating"] academic objectivity. And this, he knows, is controversial for the more traditional historians. In the book's afterword, Birgisson says that he has found "en mellomvei mellom forskeren og forfatteren" (303) ["a middle way between researcher and author"]. The professional identity of the historical author Birgisson is thus neither a stable nor a final one. From this middle path, Birgisson also reminds us that ours is not the *only* age of migration – Iceland was in fact founded by immigrants, and at least one of them visibly stood out.

Birgisson has continued to write about the Middle Ages. He presents the book *Soga om Geirmund Heljarskinn* (2016, The Saga of Geirmund Heljarskinn) as a restoration of Heljarskinn's saga based on, recently discovered manuscripts, which are fictional in reality. In this book, Birgisson reveals neither his doubts nor his method, and thus he becomes rather an author of fiction, pretending to write nonfictional prose. Two recently published novels – *Reisen til livsvannet* (2020, The Journey to the Waters of Life) and *Mannen fra middelalderen* (2020, The Man from the Middle Ages) – seem to confirm that Birgisson has embraced the professional identity of a more clear-cut fiction writer.

Langvad: Hun er vred (She Is Angry)

In Maja Lee Langvad's book *Hun er vred: Et vidnesbyrd om transnational adoption* (She Is Angry: A Testimony of Transnational Adoption), the *visual* aspect of standing out amongst white Danes is important. The name of the protagonist of Langvad's book is identical to the author's, both in Danish and Korean (Maja Lee and Chun Bok, 107, 108, see also Høgh). In order to avoid confusion, I will refer to Langvad the author as "she/her" and to the book's protagonist as "She/Her." The latter grows up feeling She stands out as an adopted South Korean girl in Denmark. In Her early twenties, She goes to Seoul, where She meets with adoption criticism, something She never came across in Denmark. The reader is told that "[hun er vred over, at hun er vokset op med et hvidt, vestlig skønhedsideal" (27) ["she is angry because she grew up with a white, Western ideal of beauty"], and "[hun er vred over, at hun ikke har haft mulighed for at spejle sig i asiatiske kroppe i sin opvækst. Det er derfor, at hun kan bruge timer på at betragte kvindernes kroppe, når hun er i jimjilbang" (28) ["she is angry that she did not have the chance to reflect herself in Asian bodies as she was growing up. This is the reason she can spend hours studying women's bodies when she is at a jimjilbang"]. A jimjilbang, note 15 of 159 in the back of the book explains, is "et stort, offentligt badehus i Syd-korea" (240) ["a large public bathhouse in South Korea"]. When She is at a jimjilbang, She studies "[bryster, maver, hofter, numser, lår, fødder, tær, hudfarve. Alt skal nøje studeres" (28) ["breasts, tummies, hips, butts, thighs, feet, toes, skin colour. Everything is subjected to close scrutiny"]. She is, however, not only looking at people, but also searching for historical and scientifically provable *facts* that might explain and justify her anger.

Just like Birgisson, Langvad the author lists her sources. But whereas Birgisson aims to reconstruct a life that was lived but not recorded, Langvad is providing the reader with facts that may substantiate Her anger at the fact that She was adopted – as well as at the fact that She is angry at herself for being angry at the fact that She was adopted, as well as at the fact that She is angry at herself for being angry at herself for being angry at the fact that She was adopted, and so on. The cycles of outrage sometimes assume comical proportions, since in Her anger, She is quite contradictory. For instance: "Hun er vred på dem, der mener, at abort er at foretrække for adoption" ["She is angry at those who think abortion is preferable to adoption"], as well as "på dem, der mener, at adoption er at foretrække for abort" (59) ["at those who think adoption is preferable to abortion"]. And, indeed, how can one choose which of these options is better or worse? Because of Her biographical background and Her life story, She is confronted with impossible choices, and these choices are, in turn, tied to global injustice.

In one sense, *Hun er vred* is a 237-page long list of information on and criticism of transnational adoption, which She sees as a modern form of colonialism, as an industry, often run by missionaries, and as misguided aid (115–118). All the entries in the list also function to characterise Her. Indeed, every single passage in the book starts with the words "hun er vred" ["she is angry"]. The other characters that appear are listed throughout five pages at the beginning of the book, but they are present merely as points of reference that She can manoeuvre around and position herself in relation to. None of these 92 people become characters of their own, and they are never represented in their own voice. Instead, She paraphrases what they have said and speaks only of what they have done or will do that angers Her. The repetitive and formulaic structure of the book in fact prevents Her from talking about what others are doing in the present and from including these others in a dialogue. Since we only get to know other individuals through Her eyes, the book is very monologic (Bakhtin): Everything and everyone is reduced to being the sources of Her anger.

The others in the book may be significant – like the biological and adoptive parents – but the fact that they never enter into the book's present, or the time of narration, but remain in the time of the narrated, reflects the emotional and psychological distance that She feels towards them. She longs to belong but does not feel at home anywhere, or with anyone, and the form of the book reflects the content in this regard. Unlike Birgisson's story of *Den svarte vikingen* [The Black Viking], *Hun er vred* does not bring all the pieces together in a coherent narrative. Birgisson struggles but manages to shape Heljarskinn's story into a journey, with a beginning and an end, and even structures his book according to this chronology. As for Langvad's text, the question is if it is really a narrative at all, or if it is rather a *non*-narrative.

A non-narrative does not unfold as a story but can instead be organised – for instance, as a dictionary with alphabetical listings or state a main idea complete with supporting details. With its structure of a list providing supporting evidence for the idea that transnational adoption is a detrimental practice, *Hun er vred* may indeed be characterised as a non-narrative. It is, however, possible to identify a plot of sorts in the description of the protagonist's development. I would therefore define the book as a semi-narrative – that is, something in between a narrative and a non-narrative. The question is to what extent is the semi-narrative *autobiographical*. The subtitle of the book claims that it is *Et vidnesbyrd om transnational adoption* ("A Testimony of Transnational Adoption"). A "testimony" in law, religion and literary studies is a term used to describe the action of giving a "solemn attestation as to the truth of a matter" ("Testimony"). The Latin word the term originates from, *testis*, refers to the notion of a third person, a disinterested witness. The use of the third person "she" in Langvad's text certainly fits this original meaning, but She is far from being a *disinterested* third party. Curiously, She seems to think that writing about adoption cannot be made legitimate by interest alone – as She sees it, one *has to be* adopted in order to write about adoption, and especially if one writes in the first person, one has to have a personal experience of adoption.

She argues that for a certain Marie Myung-Ok Lee to have written a book in the first person with an adopted Korean woman as a narrator is unethical, both because Lee is not herself adopted, and because Lee is making money from writing about adoption. The last point here comes across as ironic, given that Langvad herself has written about adoption in more than one book; one could even argue that she has made an entire career based on writing about adoption (Langvad, *Hun er vred*; *Find Holger Danske*; and *Find Holger Danske: Appendix, Dage med galopperende hjertebanken*). In *Hun er vred*, Langvad does not write in the first person, *although* she is adopted, and she clearly uses her own story – for example, the book's protagonist *and* Langvad both found out in their early twenties that they were not found on the street and that their biological family is still

16

alive (190; Schmidt). Also, both the protagonist and Langvad went to Seoul and stayed there for several years as members of the adoption criticism community (9; Langvad, "Læserne spørger," Schmidt). Just like Langvad, She does not speak Korean well (169, 213; Schmidt), and both are lesbian (151–152; Tetzlaff). We are also told that the protagonist is writing a book that is more or less autobiographical (196).

Still, it can be argued that it is no less morally dubious for an adopted person to write about transnational adoption in the third person than it is for a non-adopted person to write about the topic in the first person. For by writing in the third person, Langvad the (historical) author, or She, the narrator – the key idea here is that the book is written and narrated by one person – makes her story *more general* than what a first-person narrative would have been. It thus becomes a story about the anger of people, or at least girls and women, who are adopted from Korea *in general* instead of the anger of one individual speaking only for herself. In stating that "HUN ER VRED over, at hun ikke har nogen barndomsminder fra Syd-korea" (capitalised letters in original, 51) ["SHE IS ANGRY at not having any childhood memories from South Korea"], Langvad lets the protagonist speak not only for herself, as the character or narrator, but for the thousands of South Korean girls who have been adopted in the West since the Second World War. Thus, when She describes how She finds herself caught in a hierarchy of national identities, She metonymically speaks not only for herself but for other adopted Korean women in Denmark too:

Hun er vred over den forestilling, mange gør sig om thailandske kvinder i Danmark.
Hun er vred på Mette over at være bange for at blive set på som en thailandsk kvinde i Danmark.
Hun er vred på sig selv over at være bange for at blive set på som en thailandsk kvinde i Danmark. […]
Hun er vred på sig selv over at synes, at det er finere at være koreaner end kineser.
Hun er vred på sig selv over at synes, at det er finere at være japaner end koreaner.
Hun er vred over, at hun ikke er japaner.
Hun er vred over, at hun er koreaner. (105)

[She is angry at the idea that many people have of Thai women in Denmark.
She is angry with Mette for being afraid of being taken for a Thai woman in Denmark.
She is angry with herself for being afraid of being taken for a Thai woman in Denmark.
She is angry with herself for being afraid of being taken for a Chinese immigrant in Denmark. […]
She is angry with herself for thinking that it is better to be Korean than Chinese.
She is angry with herself for thinking that it is better to be Japanese than Korean.
She is angry that she is not Japanese.
She is angry that she is Korean.]

Langvad and She look Korean, but their language and culture are Danish. By using the third person "she," Langvad also makes the point that it is difficult to integrate these differences into a personal identity in the first-person "I." The book's lack of a coherent narrative reflects this difficulty.

It is hard to place the entries of the list in Langvad's book in chronological order, but it can be noted that in them, She is always *positioning* herself in relation to others

17

and feels rejected everywhere and always. The fact that She is rejected, or at least not warmly and openly received by Her Korean family who, for instance, keep Her existence a secret from the spouses of Her sisters, contributes to the impression that Her story has no beginning and no ending – only ever new beginnings and endings. She has to look for a sense of belonging outside both Her biological and Her adoptive family.

Whereas the biographer Birgisson explicitly makes the reader aware of his using a set of more or less scholarly methods in order to gloss over inconsistencies in Heljarskinn's story, Langvad lets the reader know that she does not intend to cover up inaccuracies or to tell a coherent story. Given the many biographical similarities between the author and protagonist of *Hun er vred*, one might think that it would be easier for Langvad to tell a coherent story about her own life than it is for Birgisson to construct a coherent narrative about a historical figure, whose life we know little about. But as a matter of fact, in his book, Birgisson captures another person's story in a coherent narrative, whereas the coherence in the story of Langvad's protagonist is always slipping away – and due to a lack of coherence in Her life story, it is also difficult to state the significance of Her experiences and relationships. Also, the fact that She belongs biologically in South Korea and culturally and linguistically in Denmark, makes it extremely hard, if not impossible, for Her to define *where* She belongs. Unfortunately, without a sense of belonging, sorting out what is important and what is not becomes challenging, and for this reason, She never reaches a sense of coherent identity. In this respect, the formal and linguistic rendering of what She is angry about in Langvad's book may be said to represent a realistic impression of the fragmented sense of self that She experiences and the central constituent of this self, the feeling of anger.

Interestingly, in an e-mail to the newspaper *Politiken*, published on 12 February 2015, Langvad says that the book *Hun er vred* has become her ticket *home*; her bridge from South Korea back to Denmark (Langvad, "Interviewtræt Maja Lee Langvad"). Her e-mail was sent from the Canary Islands where she had gone because a psychologist, to whom she turned when her life seemed "completely empty" when the book *Hun er vred* had "left her," recommended she take half a year away from it all. Because projects always end – writing the book did not provide Langvald a permanent identity. The connections between *Hun er vred* and Langvad's life are not only to be found in the past but, to Langvad, continue into the future, as she has had to find other projects and put herself in new places of non-belonging – such as the Canary Islands. Like Birgisson, Langvad, too, constructs a professional identity as a writer through her texts, but hers seems more ephemeral, an identity that is tightly bound to a sense of being preoccupied with a project – a sense of self-oblivion found in being caught up in a creative process. As she puts it in her last book, *Dage med galopperende hjertebanken* (2017, Days of Galloping Heartbeat): "Jeg trives bedst, når jeg er i en skabelsesproces […] HUN ER VRED er ikke længere den bog, der skaber mening i mit liv" (85–86). ["I feel the best when I'm in a process of creation […] SHE IS ANGRY is no longer the book that creates meaning in my life.]

Shishkin: *Venerin volos* (*Maidenhair*)

Whereas all of Langvad's books are unmistakably autobiographical and even contain pictures of Langvad and her biological parents, Mikhail Shishkin's works involve more fiction yet still often include autobiographical features. The 2005 novel *Venerin volos* (trans. *Maidenhair* 2012) presents a collection of different life stories. We encounter asylum seekers from post-Soviet countries whose aim is to obtain permanent refugee status in Switzerland where the novel's protagonist works as an interpreter for the Swiss Immigration Office. Shishkin himself had this very job for several years until he left it to become a full-time writer. Here, again, life and literature are interlinked. The interpreter in *Venerin volos* is also a writer of sorts who was, before emigrating from Russia, commissioned to write a biography of the opera singer Izabella Iurieva (1899–2000). He writes letters to his son about his divorce from the boy's mother and about reading the diaries of Iurieva and the *Anabasis* (ca. 370 BC) – one of the first known autobiographies – by the Greek mercenary and philosopher Xenophon. Similarly as in Langvad's book, the different narrative strands in *Venerin volos* do not join to form a coherent plot. Instead, they are framed within the mind of the book's protagonist, who is simply called the interpreter.

The task of the Swiss Immigration Office is to give people asylum if they are entitled to receive it – as the interpreter puts it:

Для того чтобы не пустить в рай, очень важно узнать то, что было на самом деле. Но как выяснишь, если люди здесь становятся рассказанными ими историями. Никак не выяснишь. Значит, все просто: раз нельзя выяснить правду, то нужно выяснить хотя бы не-правду. (25)

[In order to keep them out of paradise, we have to ferret out what really happened. But how can you if people become the stories they tell? You just can't. That means it's all very simple. Since you can't clarify the truth, you at least need to clarify the lie.] (21)

This is a reasonably realistic description of the logic the immigration offices abide by: They look for inconsistencies – and these are often to be found in the details. As the interpreter puts it: "По инструкции, неправдоподобие в показаниях дает основание поставить вот этот самый штамп [отказа]. Так что получше придумывайте себе легенду и не забывайте, что самое главное – мелкие детали, подробности" (25). ["According to our instructions, improbability in statements is grounds for affixing this very stamp {of rejection}. So you'll have to come up with a better legend for yourself and not forget what is most important: the minor details, the trivia" (21).] But if we are to believe the interpreter, what really determines the asylum seekers' cases is the personality of the case officer:

До Петра столоначальницей была Сабина. Она, наоборот, всем верила. И не задавала вопросов из всезнающей книжицы. И никогда не ставила штамп «Prioritätsfall». Вот ее и уволили. А Петр ставит почти каждому. В досье на первой страничке. Это означает ускоренное рассмотрение дела ввиду очевидного отказа. (19)

[Before Peter, Sabina was our chief. She, on the contrary, believed everyone. And didn't ask questions from the omniscient book. And never used her stamp 'Prioritätsfall.' So, she was fired. But Peter lets nearly everyone have it. On the first page of their file. This means an expedited review of the case in view of its obvious rejection.] (16)

It is possible that Shishkin, with his past as an interpreter of asylum interviews, exaggerates to underline the tendencies in European and Swiss treatment of asylum seekers. But before we start passing judgement on the interviewer for rejecting everyone or on the asylum seekers for making up "легенду" (25) ["a legend" (21)] for themselves, we first have to evaluate the credibility of the interpreter. For in the last five of the novel's ten interviews, so many unrealistic things start happening that it becomes hard to believe that the asylum seekers or interviewers would actually say what we read.

In interview number seven (36–108; 30–94), for example, the story of a Chechen asylum seeker becomes increasingly sensational when motifs from the interpreter's letters to his son start appearing. The asylum seeker, amongst other fantastic things, claims in the words of the interviewer: "Вас спас капитан Немо на своем «Наутилусе» и высадил на берег уже в Романсхорне" (54) ["You were saved by Captain Nemo in his *Nautilus* and put to shore at Romanshorn" (46).] It is hard to understand why the asylum seeker would make his story unbelievable by employing motifs from the Jules Verne novels *Twenty Thousand Leagues under the Sea* (1870) and *The Mysterious Island* (1874). But then again, the fact that the story of the asylum seeker is told by the interviewer, and not the asylum seeker himself, could imply a critique of the use of so-called *leading questions*. This could be Shishkin the author parodying this lousy technique of interviewers. Still, although we may read this interview as a critique of both the asylum seekers as well as the interviewers, we should turn our attention to yet another clue in order to figure out what is going on. For already quite early on in the novel, the narrator-interpreter explains how he struggles to fall asleep at night, since he hears the interviews he interpreted during the day over and over again in his head: "Будто разговариваешь сам с собой. Сам себе задаешь вопросы. Сам себе отвечаешь" (30). ["It's like talking to yourself. You ask yourself the questions. And answer them" (25).]

From this piece of information, we can infer that there is a meta-level here that has to be taken into account in the analysis of the asylum seeker interviews: for if the interviews we read take place only in the mind of the interpreter, it is *he* (who is otherwise supposed to serve as a neutral medium in the communication between the interviewer and the asylum seeker) who does all the talking – and thinking. If we think of the absurdities in the interviews as of the interpreter's own experiences, emotions and readings that cross paths, so to speak, with his memories of the interviews, it suddenly makes more sense that motifs from Jules Verne's stories, for instance, find their way from letters into interviews, seeing that the motifs and stories have a common frame in the *mind* of the interpreter, who is digesting his different experiences.

When we take this metaperspective into consideration, the other characters who are described in the novel seem a bit less unprofessional and unreliable. Yet we still do not know which of the interpreter's memories are only the products of his imagination and which of them are representative of something that has really happened. One of the questions the novel raises is whether one's "real" story can possibly be told. When the interpreter says about the asylum seekers that "[пусть говорящие фиктивны, но говоримое реально" (29) ["those speaking may be fictitious, but what they say is real" (24)], it sounds quite enigmatic. But if we consider the process that asylum seekers go through – in which they are given only one interview, which is turned into a report, which in turn becomes the basis for the case officers in charge of their cases – the following actually makes sense: "Хорошо, люди не настоящие, но истории, истории-то настоящие! […] Мы есть то, что мы говорим. […] Мы станем тем, что будет занесено в протокол. Словами" (29). ["Fine, the people aren't real but the stories, oh, the stories are! […] We are what we say. […] We *become* what gets written in the transcript. The words" (24).]

If we want to dispute this claim, history tells us that we know the autobiographies of remarkably few individuals from, for instance, Xenophon's time. Our understanding of Xenophon today is based on what was written in his "протокол" (29) ["transcript" (24)] – that is his autobiographical *Anabasis* – or in sources that we can interpret his life story from, just like Birgisson wrote Heljarskinn's story based on sources about his life. But whereas Birgisson used sources other than texts, Shishkin focuses on words – as is indicated as early as in the novel's epigraph from the apocryphal Revelation of Baruch ben Neriah: "Ибо словом был создан мир, и словом воскреснем" (5). ["For by the word was the world created, and by the word shall we be resurrected" (3).] *Venerin volos* is a novel in which the battle against death and oblivion is being fought through the word (Kochetkova). By underlining that our knowledge of the historical past is dependent on sources like Xenophon's *Anabasis*, Shishkin underlines that narration as a survival strategy concerns not only asylum seekers or others, who tell stories in order to transport or translate their identities across physical and cultural borders; narratives are also crucial for the preservation, or translation, of identity and culture across *temporal* borders.

Xenophon and the Chechen asylum seekers meet in the same space in *Venerin volos* (351; *Maidenhair* 309), and this happens, because the interpreter has read Xenophon's *Anabasis* and heard the asylum seekers from Chechnya. In the interpreter's *mind*, borders between different times and places are broken down. He even sees his childhood Russian schoolteacher in contemporary Rome, and she, understandably, reproaches him for mixing things up: "Ты все путаешь! Ты все на свете перепутал! Ты путаник. […] Древние греки – одно, чеченцы – другое" (552). ["You're mixing everything up! You always mixed everything up! You're a bungler. […] The ancient Greeks are one, the Chechens another" (486).] But ultimately the teacher gives in to the interpreter's worldview:

А теперь понимаю, что все просто. Все всегда происходит одновременно. Вот ты сейчас пишешь эту строчку, а я ее как раз читаю. Ты вот сейчас поставишь в конце этого предложения точку, а я до нее как раз в то же самое время доберусь. (565)

["But now I understand that it's all simple. Everything is always happening simultaneously. Here you are writing this line now, while I'm reading it. Here you are putting a period at the end of this sentence, while I reach it at the very same time."] (497)

This makes sense, if one focuses on the consciousness through which the writer and the reader of the sentence experience it. Still, the contexts that the sentence is written or read in vary, and it is peculiar that *Venerin volos* rejects this difference.

By mirroring different narratives in one another, and by refuting the chronology of historical time, Shishkin presents an image of a world in which the borders between minds, and between different times and cultures, are porous. This porousness makes it difficult to discern between the thoughts of the interpreter-narrator and the people's whose stories he hears, tells, reads, translates, and contemplates. An explanation for why the borders that stand between different people are broken down in this way is that the interpreter is going through a life crisis. He explains, in the sent and unsent letters and postcards to his son (11–17; 19–25; 96–120; 176–200, 218–223, 340–347; 13–21, 24–30, 109–138, 201–229, 249–255, 387–398), how he broke up with the boy's mother Isolde, because he feared he was only a bad replacement for Isolde's former husband Tristan, who died in a car accident. According to the Tristan and Isolde story, Isolde has a place in her heart only for Tristan. Since the interpreter's Isolde already has a Tristan, he can never be the only one for her and leaves her out of jealousy.

Interestingly, the story of Tristan and Isolde is also in line with the novel's theme of breaking down the borders between people and places since, as Bakhtin puts it, heroes of chivalric romances like *Tristan and Isolde* "belong to a *common storehouse* of images, although this is an international storehouse and not, as in the epic, one that is merely national" (153). Bakhtin's argument reduces the role of authors of the Tristan and Isolde stories to that of an *animator* in Erving Goffman's sense: Authors animate versions of *Tristan and Isolde* – they are not the creators of the story. And although *Venerin volos* does not tell only the story of Tristan and Isolde and the author Shishkin does not only animate a part of an "already existing common storehouse of images," the book does present individuals as products, so to say, of common cultural storehouses. "Человек есть хамелеон: живущий с мусульманами – мусульманин, с волками – волк" (560). ["Man is a chameleon: if he lives with Muslims, he's a Muslim; with wolves, a wolf" (493)], as formulated in the book.

In the mind of a person who lives in between cultures and times, as the interpreter does, being such a chameleon becomes rather confusing when it comes to the question of identity and differentiation between oneself and others: the interpreter hears in his head voices from the interviews we read in *Venerin volos*, because he has heard them in reality. His mind is an *animator* of his experiences – and as such also a portrait of the world he lives in – as is arguably the mind of the author Shishkin, whose experiences the interpreter-narrator is built upon. If it is "plausible to say that the culture is speaking through the actor, using the actor to reproduce itself" (40), as the social psychologists Kenneth and Mary Gergen put it, it is also fair to say that *Venerin volos* is a portrait of a culture and a time – or rather cultures and times in plural – of contemporary Europe and the continent's historical connections with Russia and Central Asia.

By partially erasing the differences between subjects – between the interviewer, the asylum seekers, the translator, and the other contemporary or historical characters in the book – Shishkin reduces the value of those differences on which identity markers like culture, roles, gender, age, nationality, race, and so on, are dependent and instead emphasizes what people have in common: life. This emphasis is also made in the book's title: In the novel, we are told that the plant maidenhair grows wildly in Rome but only indoors in Russia. Conditions and cultures are different, but life is life, no matter where one comes from or where one resides. Yet, it is underlined in the novel that the value, voice, and agency the individuals achieve depend to a large extent on the coincidental fact of where they were born and on the status of their country of birth in a global hierarchy of nation states. As one Russian asylum seeker says: "Я, может, тоже хотел честно жить и работать, а меня за честность и мордой в говно! […] Что, швейцарцы, что ли, лучше русских? Предки мои, что ли, были хуже ваших? Может, они не хуже, а лучше" (427). ["Maybe I wanted to live and work honestly, too, but all they gave me for my honesty was shit! […] What, are the Swiss better than the Russians? Were my ancestors any worse than yours? Maybe not, maybe they were better" (377).] Similarly to Langvad's protagonist, the asylum seeker is angry at the fact that he is trapped in a global hierarchy of power and powerlessness.

Since everything in *Venerin volos* is said to be happening simultaneously, the very foundation for concepts of cultural and national identity is undermined. For such collective identities are entirely dependent not only on the excluding and exclusive *cultural memories* that support a group's identity but also on what Ernest Renan called the "obligatory forgetting" of elements that do not support this identity. Heljarskinn is an example of such an "obligatorily forgotten" element in the Icelandic national identity. The identity problems with which Langvad's protagonist struggles are partly caused by the incoherence in Her life trajectory: She feels She does not belong in the Danish culture She knows and wishes to belong in a Korean culture that She does not know, because She was adopted. The book's lack of structure and plot reflects Her lack of control over Her story and a critical stance towards transnational adoption. But the formal incoherence indicates also that a major problem in Her life is that She has been robbed of the opportunity to get to know intimately the culture and language Her biological body signals to everyone She should or could have known had She not been adopted and grown up in Denmark.

Venerin volos is arguably not merely a critique of the practical administration of immigration legislation, as the asylum interviews in the novel alone could indicate. In fact, the novel repudiates the very concept of identity, since it is because of the phenomenon of identity that the conflicts between ethnic groups produce refugees – to which Langvad would surely add transnational adoptees. It is because of borders that separate nations and because of national immigration legislations that some people may be refused the life Westerners enjoy. The case of Langvad's protagonist is an example of how being transported into the West does not guarantee a person of non-Western appearance the feeling of belonging in the life of a white Westerner.

Interestingly, while Shishkin's novel is not monologic like Langvad's book, it is not polyphonic in Bakhtin's sense, either. For whereas authors of polyphonic novels portray their characters as separate beings from themselves with their own voices, Shishkin, so to speak, erases the borders between the different characters as well as between the characters and the narrator. And he includes enough autobiographical facts from his own life to make the borders between the interpreter-narrator and himself as the book's historical author blurred too. It remains unclear whom the voices in the book belong to, and the book thus also modulates a view of all the people in the world as equally worthy of being remembered and included. In depicting the past as a reservoir out of which knowledge can be drawn to tackle the present, Shishkin's novel is not that different from Birgisson's *Den svarte vikingen*. But although Shishkin's book describes how even the smallest details from the past may be significant enough to be remembered, his personal life story illustrates that sometimes it is impossible to return to who one once was: publishing *Venerin volos* meant that Shishkin could no longer work for the Swiss Immigration Office.

The Viability of the Idea of Individual and National Identity

To conclude, I will return to the three answers I offered and argue that the idea of individual and national identity *is* still relevant today. First, as Shishkin's novel underlines, citizens of different nation states are discriminated against due to their country's standing in the global hegemonies of power. Secondly, Langvad's and Birgisson's books thematise the fact that individuals of darker complexion are not recognised as equals to white individuals within national contexts like that of Denmark or Iceland, nor do they, in Langvad's book, feel as if they are recognised as such. Thirdly, Birgisson's book shows how the official national narrative of Iceland does not include the story of the nation's heterogeneous past, exemplified by Geirmund Heljarskinn's story.

The three books give insights into what has been left out of the national narratives of three European countries. They question the ideas of individual and national identity and show the difficulties these ideas lead to or have caused in the lives of individuals. But by doing so, they stress that the idea of individual and national identity is still viable; today, this idea is able "to maintain itself or recover its potentialities" to a great extent. And this is, of course, problematic in many ways for those individuals who do not manage to create a sense of belonging or to obtain the legal right to belong in safe and prosperous countries in the West. It is also problematic in the sense that the national histories we learn in schools are unreliable and do not really tell the whole truth about a nation's past. The works I have analysed challenge the concept of the national narrative through their form, genre, and content. Birgisson introduces Geirmund Heljarskinn into Icelandic history, Langvad gives a textual shape to the sense of displacement experienced by the book's adopted protagonist, and Shishkin points to similarities and differences between people who disrupt the borders of national space and time.

Works Cited

Anderson, Benedict. "Memory and Forgetting." *Imagined Communities: Reflections on the Origin and Spread of Nationalism*. London: Verso, 1991. 187–207.

Assmann, Jan. *Cultural Memory and Early Civilization: Writing, Remembrance, and Political Imagination*. Trans. David H. Wilson. Cambridge: Cambridge University Press. 2011 [1992].

Assmann, Jan. *Das kulturelle Gedächtnis: Schrift, Erinnerung und politische Identität in frühen Hochkulturen*. Munich: C. H. Beck, 1992.

Assmann, Aleida. *Cultural Memory and Western Civilization*. Cambridge: Cambridge University Press, 2011.

Assmann, Aleida. *Erinnerungsräume: Formen und Wandlungen des kulturellen Gedächtnisses*. Munich: Beck, 1999.

Bakhtin, Mikhail. "The Problem of Speech Genres." *Speech Genres and Other Late Essays*. Trans. Vern W. McGee. Ed. Michael Holquist and Caryl Emerson. Austin, TX: University of Texas Press, 1986. 60–102.

Bhabha, Homi K. *The Location of Culture*. London: Routledge, 2004 [1994].

Birgisson, Bergsveinn. *Den svarte vikingen*. Oslo: Spartacus, 2013.

Birgisson, Bergsveinn. *Geirmundar saga Heljarskinns*. Reykjavík: Bjartur & Veröld, 2015.

Birgisson, Bergsveinn. *Mannen fra middelalderen*. Oslo: Vigmostad Bjørke, 2020.

Birgisson, Bergsveinn. Personal conversation. 2014.

Birgisson, Bergsveinn. *Reisen til livsvannet*. Oslo: Vigmostad Bjørke, 2020.

Birgisson, Bergsveinn. *Soga om Geirmund Heljarskinn*. Trans. Jan Ragnar Hagland. Oslo: Pelikanen, 2016.

Brooks, Peter. *Reading for the Plot*. New York: Knopf, 1994.

Gergen, Kenneth and Mary Gergen. "Narrative and the Self as Relationship." *Advances in Experimental Social Psychology*. Ed. Leonard Berkowitz. San Diego: Academic Press, 1988. 17–56.

Goffman, Erving. "Footing." *Forms of Talk*. Philadelphia: University of Pennsylvania Press, 1981. 124–159.

Høgh, Søren Laganger. "Gul humor: Maja Lee Langvad *Find Holger Danske*." *Litteraturnu.dk*. 2 July 2006. https://litteraturnu.dk/gul-humor-maja-lee-langvad-find-holger-danske/.

"Identity." *Merriam-Webster Dictionary*. *Merriam-Webster Dictionary*. https://www.merriam-webster.com/dictionary/identity. Accessed 6 May 2020.

"Interviewtræt Maja Lee Langvad: 'I journalister giver ikke op så let'." *Politiken.dk*. 12 February 2014. http://politiken.dk/kultur/boger/litteraturpris/ECE2541383/interviewtraet-maja-lee-langvad-i-journalister-giver-ikke-op-saa-let/. Accessed 6 May 2020.

Kochetkova, Natal'ia. "Pisatel' Mikhail Shishkin: 'U Boga na Strashnom sude ne budet vremeni chitat' vse knigi'." *Izvestia*. 22 June 2005. http://izvestia.ru/news/303564. Accessed 13 March 2020.

Langvad, Maja Lee. *Dage med galopperende hjertebanken*. Copenhagen: Gyldendal Trade 140, 2017.

Langvad, Maja Lee. *Find Holger Danske*. Valby: Borgen, 2006.

Langvad, Maja Lee. *Find Holger Danske: Appendix*. Copenhagen: Gladiator, 2014.

Langvad, Maja Lee. *Hun er vred: Et vidnesbyrd om transnational adoption*. Copenhagen: Gladiator, 2014.

Langvad, Maja Lee. "Interviewtræt Maja Lee Langvad: 'I journalister giver ikke op så let'." 12 February 2014. http://politiken.dk/kultur/boger/litteraturpris/ECE2541383/interviewtraet-maja-lee-langvad-i-journalister-giver-ikke-op-saa-let/. Accessed 13 March 2020.

Langvad, Maja Lee. "Læserne spørger: Maja Lee Langvad." *Information.no*. 8 March 2014. http://www.information.dk/490483. Accessed 6 May 2020.

Renan, Ernest. "What is a Nation." In *Nation and Narration*. Ed. Homi K. Bhabha. Trans. Martin Thom. London: Routledge, 1990. 9–22.

Schmidt, Malin. "Jeg så mig selv som hvid." *Information.no*. 10 December 2013. https://www.information.dk/udland/2013/12/saa-hvid.

Shishkin, Mikhail. *Maidenhair*. Trans. Marian Schwartz. Rochester, NY: Open Letter, 2012.

Shishkin, Mikhail. *Venerin volos*. Moskva: Vagrius, 2005.

"Testimony." Wikipedia. http://en.wikipedia.org/wiki/Testimony. Accessed 6 May 2020.

Tetzlaff, Marie. "Lesbiske forfattere: Man taler altid ud fra sine kropslige erfaringer." *Politiken.* *no.* 16 March 2014. https://politiken.dk/kultur/boger/interview_boger/art5506801/Lesbiske -forfattere-Man-taler-altid-ud-fra-sine-kropslige-erfaringer. Accessed 6 May 2020.

Verne, Jules. *The Mysterious Island.* Trans. Jordan Stump. New York: Modern Library, 2001 [1874].

Verne, Jules. *Twenty Thousand Leagues under the Sea.* Trans. and critical material by Walter J. Miller and Frederick P. Walter. Annapolis, MD.: US Naval Institute Press, 1993 [1870].

"Viability." Wikipedia. http://en.wikipedia.org/wiki/Viability. Accessed 6 May 2020.

Xenophon. *The Anabasis of Cyrus.* Trans. Wayne Ambler. Trans. and annot. Wayne Ambler, with an introduction by Eric Buzzetti. 2008. Ithaca, New York: Cornell University Press, 2008 [orig. ca. 370 BC].

2. Creating (Im)migrant Literature in Sweden since the 1970s

Satu Gröndahl

Historical Background: Some Remarks

The occurrence of (im)migrant literature in Sweden is often understood as a cultural phenomenon commencing during the 1970s, in a period of increasing globalization, labour migration and emancipatory civil movements such as women's liberation, ethnic movements and the rise of indigenous people.[1] Generally, there is a notable tendency to explain the emergence of (im)migrant literature against the backdrop of the modern conception of a 'multicultural nation,' with a starting point in sociological and political changes during the second half of the 20th century. Wiebke Sievers has compared the development of (im)migrant literature in fourteen countries, mainly in Europe, and according to her, the occurrence of this literature is strongly connected to national policies and practices in relation to human rights. Full recognition of this writing should have occurred earlier in countries where equal rights for all people "have become inscribed into the legal framework and the national imaginary" (501). The literary production of (im)migrant and ethnic minority writers has often been understood in a framework of the progressive affirmative ethos, and the authors have been described as "a vanguard of cultural change in their respective countries" (Sievers 500). (Im)migrant literature has contributed to the renewal of national literary canons and is today mostly understood as part of modernization processes. However, the naturalisation of this literature took a long time and met a great deal of resistance within the scholarly world, with its monolingual and monocultural understanding of national literature prevailing far into the 20th century. Nevertheless, we can also talk about much earlier migrant or exile authors in Sweden and mention, for example, Frans Michael Franzén (1772–1847). Franzén was a Finnish poet and clergyman who fled to Sweden after Finland was ceded to Russia after the Finnish War (1808–1809). He was born in Northern Ostrobothnia in Finland at a time when the country was an integral part of Sweden. Franzén belonged to the

---

[1] Concepts like '(im)migrant literature' are highly problematic in literary theory, and new terms are constantly being proposed. Terms such as 'migration literature,' 'multicultural literature,' 'hybridity,' 'cosmopolitanism,' 'transculturalism,' 'transnationalism,' and 'migratory aesthetics' are being disputed, and the abundance of these terms demonstrates that concepts of immigration and immigrants are both controversial and politically charged (cf. Heith, Rantonen & Gröndahl 16). I use the term '(im)migrant literature' in order to focus on the literary text, rather than on the author's background or biography. At the same time, I am aware of the negative connotations of most of the terminology in the field.

Swedish-speaking minority, and the Russian invasion of the country caused him an emotional crisis which made him choose Sweden as his place of residence. As many exile or migrant authors, he never fully came to peace with the leaving of his mother-country, and after becoming a member of the Swedish Academy, he insisted that exile results in a painful state of mind since one's body lives in one nation, but one's "soul belongs to another" (Laitinen 139).

There were also authors who started their literary production in Sweden after World War II, when Sweden received asylum seekers and refugees from war-torn Europe and the Baltic States. This post-war literature, written by refugees from countries such as Germany, Estonia, and Poland, exhibits literature of a different character to what later was labelled as 'multicultural,' 'ethnic,' '(im)migrant' or 'translingual' writing, since many of these migrants or refugees were intellectuals or already recognized authors acquainted with the European and Scandinavian literary tradition.

The authorship of Nelly Sachs (1891–1970), a refugee of Jewish origin who came to Sweden from Germany in 1940, illustrates in a clear fashion how disparate the field of (im)migrant literature is in Sweden. Her career as a poet started after her emigration to Sweden, and she received the Nobel Prize in Literature in 1966. When arriving in Sweden, Sachs was familiar with Swedish literature and acquainted with Selma Lagerlöf (1858–1940), a seminal Swedish author and a cultural celebrity, who helped when Sachs fled to Sweden with her family.[2] The preconditions for authors like Franzén and Sachs differed in many ways from the prospects of those who arrived in Sweden without any affiliation to the country; yet the physical and psychological alienation seems to be a common denominator for many (im)migrant authorships.

When studying Swedish exile or (im)migrant literature, the early authorships could offer an interesting comparative material to the future studies of the field. The feelings of dislocation, fragmented history, and the state of being barred from one's native country are by no means phenomena that belong primarily to the second half of 20th century. Instead, what distinguishes contemporary Swedish (im)migrant literature, created since the 1970s, from the former exile or migrant literatures is the development of a parallel literary institution that functions in other languages than Swedish. Publishing houses for non-Swedish literature, magazines, criticism, infrastructure, and the cluster of writers and authors using 'other languages' in their production form a literary field that is still largely unexplored.

The Development of (Im)migrant Literature in Sweden

The framework of modern Swedish society was created during the period between the 1930s and 1970s, with its proud social engineering project *folkhem* ('the people's home'), a vision of the Swedish welfare state. During the 1970s, the expanding labour market, the upward economic situation and the reformistic social welfare politics formed a basis and possibility for the development of (im)migrant literature in Sweden on a large

---

[2]   https://www.nobelprize.org/prizes/literature/1966/sachs/facts/ Accessed 24 March 2020.

scale. A progressive reform of policies on migration was passed in the Swedish parliament in 1975, with the motto of "equality, freedom of choice and partnership" (Schierup & Ålund 193). The idea of nation was rapidly changing, and civil rights movements increased all over the world.

According to Carl-Erik Schierup and Aleksandra Ålund, the reform was based on a liberal universalist perception of citizenship and "an inclusive multicultural conception of the nation" (ibid.). New structures and organizations were founded, and the existing administrative units were commissioned to carry out the reformistic policies. For example, The National Council for Cultural Affairs (Statens Kulturråd), a government authority, formed specific subsidies for the needs of literature published in other languages than Swedish. Migrant and minority associations were given an important role as actors in civil society, and publishing houses with focus on literature in immigrant languages received various forms of support. During certain periods, The National Council for Cultural Affairs even provided operational subsidies for these publishing houses, not only grants for printing individual works.

What is exceptional for Sweden and has distinguished the Swedish welfare policy from other European countries until the turn of the millennium is that the cultural and language rights of ethnic minorities were initially formulated from the perspective of immigrants' needs, based on the conception of a 'multicultural' society. Sweden ratified the European Charter for Regional or Minority Languages and the Framework Convention for the Protection of National Minorities in 1999. After the conventions came into force in 2000, there has been an official separation between integration policy and minority policy, the latter being directed to national minorities and national minority languages.[3] Due to this political development, comparative studies on literature of autochthonous or indigenous minorities and (im)migrant literature have been a self-evident starting point for ethnic literary studies in Sweden. This circumstance also mirrors the influence of sociology of literature and sociology of language on the field, but this point of departure does not necessarily fit in other national contexts. In general, it is important not to neglect the national particularities when studying the development of (im)migrant literatures in different countries.

Early Studies on (Im)migrant Literature in Sweden

At first, scholarly studies of immigrant and ethnic minority writing appeared mostly within the area of philological studies such as German studies, as the first generation of exile and migrant authors mostly wrote in their native language. Studies also emerged when multidisciplinary centres and institutions were initiated or founded during the 1970s, with the aim of studying immigration and multiculturalism in general. While questions about labour market, integration and ethnic relations were understood as prioritized subjects for these centres from the very start, other themes related to migration,

---

[3] The national minorities and minority languages in Sweden are Jews/Yiddish, Roma and Travellers/Romani Chib, Sámi/Sámi languages, Sweden-Finns/Finnish and Tornedalians/Meänkieli.

such as bilingualism and immigrant literature, were pursued as broader subjects later on, mainly during the 1990s and the 2000s. For exemple, the Centre for Multiethnic Research at Uppsala University was founded in 1984 and given the specific task of primarily focusing on the cultural dimensions of ethnicity.

The Immigrant Institute, a non-governmental organization founded in 1973 and located in Borås, has since then documented the works of immigrant writers as well as biographical data on the authors.[4] During the 1970s the Immigrant Institute began publishing bibliographies of immigrant and exile authors in Sweden. While the first volume *Lexikon över invandrarförfattare i Sverige* ['Lexicon of Immigrant Authors in Sweden,' Diehl & Strömberg 1977] dealt with authors of different ethnic backgrounds, the following volumes were based on group presentation. These lexicons, published from the 70s to mid-90s, dealt with Estonian, Finnish, Latin American, and Polish immigrant authors in Sweden.[5] Moreover, other private non-profit organizations, such as the Society for Judaic Studies (Sällskapet för judaistisk forskning), published bibliographies within their field of interest (cf. Rohlén-Wohlgemuth, *Svensk judisk bibliografi*).

Among the earliest academic studies published in Sweden, one can mention Helmut Müssener's *Exil in Schweden. Politische und kulturelle Emigration nach 1933* (1974). Müssener's work deals with German immigration to Sweden from Germany, Austria, and German-speaking areas in former Yugoslavia. Besides Müssener's exhaustive work on German political and cultural emigration, some other studies on exile literature were published in Sweden prior to the 1980s, such as Sven Hugo Persson's *Från grymhetens till motståndets estetik: Peter Weiss tidiga författarskap och dramat Marat/Sade* [From Cruel Aesthetics to the Aesthetics of Resistance: Peter Weiss' Early Authorship and the Drama Marat/Sade, 1979] and Helmer Lång's *Svenska europeer. Essäer om invandrarförfattarna Martin Allwood, Karl H. Bolay, Jörgen Nash, Alexander Weiss* [Swedish Europeans: Essays on Immigrant Authors Martin Allwood, Karl H. Bolay, Jörgen Nash, Alexander Weiss, 1976]. Helmer Lång raises the question, as has been done by many critics ever since, of why scholarly studies of, and public interest in, immigrant and exile literature have taken so long to get off the ground; even professional authors of foreign origin have suffered a reception of silence (12–13). Nevertheless, the interest in (im)migrant literature seemed to grow substantially around the turn of the millennium, when so-called 'second generation' (im)migrant authors entered the literary scene with their perceptive narratives of adolescents from the segregated suburbs of big cities.

However, some larger works on Swedish emigrant literature appeared in the USA before more systematic studies on immigrant and ethnic writing in Sweden. For example, during the 1990s, books such as Lars Wendelius' *Kulturliv i ett svenskamerikanskt lokalsamhälle. Rockford, Illinois* [Cultural Life in a Swedish-American Local Community: Rockford, Illinois, 1990] and Anna Williams *Skribent i Svensk-Amerika. Jakob Bonggren, journalist och poet* [A Writer in Swedish America: Jakob Bonggren, Journalist and Poet, 1991] were published. It could also be said that the interest in the immigrant life of one's own group in other countries helped when one attempted to recognize the cultural 'other,' and this interest acted as a bridge to studies of immigrant literature

---

4   http://www.immi.se/ Accessed 24 March 2020.
5   See Järvengren, Mäntykangas, Nowakowski, and Soutkari.

in Sweden. Even though (im)migrant literature in Sweden received support from The National Council for Cultural Affairs and was understood as an important contribution to the forming of Swedish culture, within literary studies it was merely seen as a documentary form of art rather than belles-lettres in its own right.

Situating (Im)migrant Literature

As we have seen, the earliest studies of (im)migrant literature published in Sweden before the 1980s consisted of general mappings and overviews of works and authors, and as such, they represent the empirically oriented and positivist tradition, with their compilations of authorships and themes. Today, these studies form an important source for contemporary studies of (im)migrant literature. After the 1980s, the mapping of the various immigrant literatures and authorships continued, and the scope of ethnic groups expanded. Bibliographies and shorter overviews were published continuously, such as Anneli Eriksson's *Grekisk invandrarlitteratur i Sverige* [Greek Immigrant Literature in Sweden, 1982], Leonardo Rossiello's "Latinamerikanska författare i Sverige" [Latin American Authors in Sweden, 1995] and Mana Aghaee's *Lexikon över iranska författare i Sverige* [Lexicon of Iranian Authors in Sweden, 2002].

These surveys were often written by cultural workers or scholars with roots in immigrant communities and with knowledge of the specific group's history. Ethnic literatures were more often than not described as autonomous literary fields, mostly written in native languages. These descriptions were often written against the backdrop of the political and cultural development in the country of origin rather than the politics of identity in the new country. From this point of view, these '(im)migrant' literatures can hardly be seen as expressions of a 'multicultural' Swedish literature, even though they were subsidised by the Swedish support system for immigrant literature. For instance, the works of several Sweden-Estonian authors, such as Helga Nõu (1934), are still mainly seen as a vital part of Estonian literature, even though the majority of her works were published in Sweden. Some second-generation Estonian authors who chose Swedish as their literary language, such as Enel Melberg (1943) and Mare Kandre (1962–2005), have nevertheless been characterized as important contemporary authors of contemporary Swedish literature (Warfwinge 270-271).

Also Mana Aghaee's perceptive study of Persian writing in Sweden locates this particular (im)migrant or exile literature in a historicizing, Iranian context rather than a Swedish one (315).[6] The article begins with a review of the long history of the Persian, or Farsi, language that has been used as a lingua franca since the 10th century A.D., and the exile production in Sweden is perceived as a continuation of Persian literature. The exile production in Sweden is nevertheless praised for dealing with gender-related issues and new genres – like feminist magazines and gender-related themes – and it has been pointed out that publishing in Sweden offers opportunities for freedom of speech on a larger scale than in Iran.

---

[6] For situating (im)migrant literature in Sweden, see also Heith, Gröndahl & Rantonen 214.

Sweden-Finnish literature, on the other hand, has from its very start during the 1970s and until the 2010s first and foremost been connected to working-class literature. Sweden-Finnish writing is also described as an autonomous literary field, mainly deriving from the genre of social realistic literature, a tradition with deep roots in Finnish literary history. This cultural-sociological point of departure connects to earlier German-inspired sociology of literature about *Gastarbeiterliteratur*, which is also referenced in Finnish studies on Sweden-Finnish literature.[7] Maijaliisa Jokinen's article from 1996, like many other overviews, illustrates the problematic definition of immigrant or ethnic literatures. As they are initially seen as expressions for minority life, in the case of Sweden-Finns first and foremost as cultural expression of the working class, the choice of works and authors focused on tends to confirm certain stylistic features and themes as more typical than others. As Jokinen states, her article focuses on such areas of Sweden-Finnish cultural life that are an expression of "consciousness of group identity, minority belonging, or Finnish roots" (381). There is an essentializing pre-understanding that describes Sweden-Finnish literature as working-class, even though it encompasses other genres too. This essentializing, or 'classifying,' mechanism can be compared to ethnifying discourses on what is termed 'multicultural' literature. Olli Löytty has raised the question of why Sweden-Finnish literature has not been included in studies of Nordic (im)migrant or multicultural literature (64). He ponders why, for instance, Ingeborg Kongslien does not mention any Sweden-Finnish authorships in her comprehensive overviews; not even Antti Jalava, who writes in Swedish and whose *Asfaltblomman* (1980) "sparked a heated debate in Sweden" regarding an immigrant's double identity and the loss of his or her mother tongue (ibid.). The fact that Sweden-Finnish literature is not understood as an axiomatic part of Swedish (im)migrant literature might be connected to a perception of cultural closeness between Sweden-Finns and 'ethnic' Swedes, as well as the tendency to reduce this literature exclusively to the category of 'class' literature.

These early studies situate the (im)migrant literatures spatially and temporally in a different context than the Swedish one. Generally, the starting point is to scrutinize how these literatures relate to the canonized literary history of the home country, often resulting in descriptions of uncompleted and fragmentary literary fields, doomed to diminish and vanish in the long run. One interesting exception is literature written in Northern Kurdish, Kurmanji, which attracted much attention in Sweden around the turn of the millennium. As Kurmanji has been a forbidden language in Turkey, and it has been criminalized to write in this language, Sweden with its freedom of the press and generous subsidy system for literature in foreign languages became a sort of international residence for authors from North Kurdistan.[8] In general, the Kurdish diaspora has played an important role in developing Kurdish culture and language, and countries like Sweden have "contributed tremendously" to the development of Kurdish literature (Ahmadzadeh 90).

---

[7] See, e.g., Pynnönen, *Siirtolaisuuden vanavedessä. Tutkimus ruotsinsuomalaisen kirjallisuuden kentästä vuosina 1956-1988* [In the Wake of Migration. A Study of the Sweden-Finnish Literary Field during 1956–1988 (1991)].

[8] M. Tayfun claims in his sociological survey *Kurdiskt författarskap och kurdisk bokutgivning. Bakgrund, villkor, betydelse* [Kurdish Authorship and Kurdish Publishing: Background, Conditions, Meaning, 1998] that the number of Kurdish writers and authors in Sweden was bigger than in their home country in the last decades of the 20th century (Tayfun 10). See also Heith, Gröndahl & Rantonen 24.

Most Swedish literary histories published during the late 20th century and the 2000s in Sweden include at least some (im)migrant and ethnic literature authors. The most decisive criterion for the selection of authorships in canonized literary history has been language. In the second edition of *Den Svenska Litteraturen* ('Swedish literature,' 2000), several (im)migrant and ethnic authors are presented, but all of them are mentioned on illustrative pages and in fact boxes, not in the main body of the text, and as such, the presentation mirrors a marginalized position in this context. Nevertheless, a whole page is devoted to German-born Peter Weiss (1916–1982), including an illustration, and it is obvious that the work tries to do justice to his multifaceted contribution as an author, playwright, and social commentator. On the other hand, it can be mentioned that several authors with immigrant backgrounds, such as Theodor Kallifatides (1938), Rita Tornborg (1926), Mare Kandre (1962–2005), and Susanna Alakoski (1962) have been frequently presented in less prestigious works with a focus on contemporary Swedish literature.

The change in the language-political situation since the ratification of the Council of Europe's minority conventions in 1999 seems to have resulted in practices that are more inclusive when concerning representation of literature written in minority languages. The monolingual paradigm is modified in one of the latest Swedish literary histories, *Nordens litteratur* (2017), where Ulf Teleman and Margareta Peterson underline the importance of describing literatures written in the historical languages of Sweden (Teleman 23, Peterson 13). As policies have historically influenced practices concerning minority languages versus immigrant languages in Sweden, this can be an indication that the 'new' (immigrant) languages of Sweden may also be included in canonized literary histories in the future.[9] The ideological vantage point of equal treatment of linguistic rights, regardless of the legal status of the speech community, is still a powerful concept in Sweden.

Postcolonial and Post-Structuralist Attempts

At the turn of the millennium, postcolonial theory building also gained a foothold in literary studies in Sweden and soon proved in a Nordic and Swedish context to apply to domestic circumstances. There are nevertheless few literary studies on (im)migrant literature that apply the theoretical postulates of postcolonial studies in a thorough way, although for many scholars this direction has served as a general framework and a source of inspiration, first and foremost illuminating the (dis)locations and identity-building processes as well as dismantling canons and epistemologies and, of course, aspects of power-critical perspectives.

Eila Rantonen's and Matti Savolainen's article "Postcolonial and Ethnic Studies in the Context of Nordic Minority Literatures" in the anthology *Litteraturens gränsland. Invandrar- och minoritetslitteratur i nordiskt perspektiv* [Borderland of Literature:

---

[9] The interaction between legislation of minority rights and immigrant languages rights is treated, for example, in Gröndahl, "Multicultural or Multilingual Literature? A Swedish Dilemma?"

Immigrant and Minority Literature from a Nordic Perspective, 2002] can be seen as the first theoretical attempt to give an overview of literature and postcolonial studies in relation to the history of Nordic countries. The general umbrella for the anthology can, on the one hand, be found in the framework of postcolonial and ethnic studies; on the other, in the sociology of language, as it examines the role of language in immigrant writing and also the interplay of languages of different statuses. Alongside the theoretical framework, international anthologies with focus on literature in different languages, such as Werner Sollors's *Multilingual America: Transnationalism, Ethnicity, and the Languages of American Literature* (1998), have served as sources of inspiration for this work. As Sollors underlines, the multitudes of texts written in languages other than English had "slipped from view" in the wake of 'English-only' policies, based on myths of a monolingual past, monolingual civil harmony and "the supposedly better language skills of monolingual people" (3,5). The anthology can be seen as an example of the re-examination of American literature in the light of multilingualism. Also, in Sweden, the existence of non-Swedish literature has barely been mentioned in canonized literary histories during the twentieth century, but on the other hand, civil organizations, cultural workers, and scholars have been collecting data and working in this field since the 1970s. As a matter of fact, one could say that writing in foreign languages has been officially supported to a considerable extent in Sweden, especially during the period between the 1970s and 1980s, but also after.

The postcolonial approach has also been, more specifically, later applied to the concept of (im)migrant literature with a focus on, among other things, racialized and sexualized stereotypes and the understanding of this literature as a spatially and temporally non-coherent cultural form (cf. Gröndahl, "Politik, litteratur och makt" 25–44). Pirjo Ahokas' study on Astrid Trotzig's authorship illustrates stereotyping and racializing mechanisms and can be seen as an illustrative example of studies inspired by post-colonial approaches. Ahokas refers to international studies on literature written by international adoptees from Asia and considers that also in Trotzig's production, dislocation, hybridized identity, racialization, and the idealized whiteness constitute basic elements. Nevertheless, she underlines that not only does a sense of displacement pervade the writing of Korean-born adoptees in Sweden, but the works also describe markedly different identity processes, characterized by "early separation from their birth mothers and birth nations, as well as their subsequent integration into white adoptive families and a white-dominated nation" (167).

Lars Wendelius' reflective *Den dubbla identiteten. Immigrant och minoritets litteratur på svenska 1970-2000* [The Double Identity: Immigrant and Minority Literature in Swedish 1970-2000, 2002] is based on the sociology of Pierre Bourdieu and on postcolonial debate, and the main focus is placed on the position of immigrant and minority writers in the Swedish literary scene. Wendelius also discusses the authors' treatment of identity and language-related questions and refers to Gayatri Spivak, Stuart Hall, and Homi Bhabha. He refers to John Edwards' study *Language, Society, and Identity* that deals with the question of language and group identity, language shift, and 'linguistic ethnicity' among minorities. Wendelius' materials deal with the first generation of immigrant authors who have learned Swedish as their second language, after arriving in Sweden. In his analysis of the works of immigrant and minority authors, respectively, Wendelius also focuses on differences between these groups. Wendelius' attempt to compare texts by immigrant and minority authors mirrors the changed minority-political situation in Sweden at the turn of the millennium. After the recognition of national minorities in 1999, it became a topical issue to scrutinize the positioning of different 'ethnic' literatures in relation to one another. As previously mentioned, until the turn of the millennium very little distinction was made between immigrant and historical minorities and their languages in Sweden (cf. Gröndahl, "Multicultural or Multilingual Literature").

The anthology *Litteraturens gränsland. Invandrar- och minoritetslitteratur i nordiskt perspektiv* ['Borderland of Literature: Immigrant and Minority Literature from a Nordic Perspective,' Gröndahl 2002] can be understood as a companion volume to Wendelius' work as it deals with immigrant and minority literature mainly written in minority of Nordic countries. These works were produced within the project 'De nya litteraturerna i Sverige' [The New Literatures in Sweden] and carried out at The Centre for Multiethnic Research, Uppsala University, in 2000-2002.[10] Most of the articles in the anthology focus on literature written by authors with roots in Swedish immigrant groups. Sweden stands out among the Nordic countries as having the broadest immigrant population and the most extensive production of literature in the field. Estonian, Greek, Kurdish, Persian, Polish, and Sweden-Finnish literatures are discussed in the anthology, besides the Sámi, Tornedalian, Romani, and Greenlandic literature. These articles also illustrate the heterogeneity of the anachronous category of '(im)migrant literature,' defined in-between nations and languages and associated with different spatial and temporal locations.

Deconstructing (Im)migrant Literature

It seems that deconstructionist attempts gained strength at the turn of the millennium. Since the 1990s, there has been massive criticism among ethnologists and media scientists concerning the image and construction of 'the others' in Swedish society.[11] Also, the critique centring on the concept of 'multiculturalism' became more widespread, as it was increasingly understood as an ethnifying and racializing concept that had lost its explanatory content. One angle of this discussion was the desire for more assimilatory policies and culturally homogeneous national states, which, at an ideological level, was formulated as the desire to attain 'common values' for all members of any given society. As Schierup and Ålund underline, during the 1990s, 'multiculturalism' went out of fashion as a common denominator of the nation, and the question of ethnic and cultural identity was regarded as a question for each individual (195).

---

[10] The project was founded by The Bank of Sweden Tercentenary Foundation.

[11] Ylva Brune analyses in *Nyheter från Gränsen. Tre studier i journalistik om 'invandrare', flyktingar och rasistiskt våld* [News from the Border: Three Studies in Journalism on 'Immigrants,' Refugees, and Racist Violence, 2004] how the symbolic identities of 'immigrants' are formed in the news media, creating discursive borders between 'Swedes' and 'immigrants,' and at the same time, confirming an antiquated notion of the Swedish nation and Swedish people.

Several young authors with roots in immigrant communities made their literary debut during the 2000s; these writers questioned the concepts of 'multiculturalism' and 'the immigrant.' Consequently, the time had come to evaluate the recent debate in the field of scholarship. Interestingly enough, the works of these authors, namely Johannes Anyuru (1979), Marjaneh Bakhtiari (1980), Jonas Hassen Khemiri (1978), and Alejandro Leiva Wenger (1976), were often reviewed in joint articles, even though they used different genres in their writing. One can say that there still was a tendency to lump together works and authors under the common denominator of 'multicultural.' These authors' reflective way of writing about the experiences of the 'second generation' bears witness to a conscious commentary on an ongoing scholarly debate about multiculturalism and even about actual theory building within ethnic studies in general. In a way, there was a carnivalistic approach of deconstruction of text and meaning since literary critics had tended to reduce these texts to authentic representations of 'migrancy' or 'ethnicity.' As Wolfgang Behschnitt mentions, these new immigrant novels often appropriate, reflect, repeat, distort, or subvert the same political and theoretical discourses with which critics try to "conceptualize them as literary phenomena" (80). The utterances of these young authors could also be seen as a late manifestation of the central ideas of New Criticism, underlining the concept of literature as a self-referential aesthetic object and individual work, while denying the relevance of the authors' biographical details.

Further, the problematic concept of '(im)migrant' and 'minority' literature was criticized during the 2000s. Magnus Nilsson, for example, underlined that there has been "overwhelming attention paid to Swedish 'immigrant and minority literature' in recent years"; in his opinion, this had contributed to the ethnification of Khemiri's and Bakhtyari's production and contributed towards equating the authors' life experiences and their works (Nilsson, "Swedish 'Immigrant Literature' and the Construction of Ethnicity" 200). So, immigrant literature was, according to Nilsson, understood as an authentic presentation of multicultural experiences and as an expression of immigrant identity, a reader position that Nilsson terms 'identity political.' On the other hand, Behschnitt links the term 'immigrant literature' to the relationship between texts and categorization, and he emphasizes that the text should reflect categorization. As he mentions, the authors take part in public debate and "inscribe themselves into the discourse on literature, migration, and cultural diversity" ("The Voice of the 'Real Migrant'" 81). As the term is used by Behschnitt at a metalevel, to signify a category within Swedish literary discourse and literary practice, it is also possible to diminish the ethnifying label of the authors.

The scholarly discussion of authenticity was indeed in many respects inspired by Behschnitt who discusses the literary and societal context and expectations on Khemiri's, Leiva Wenger's, Anyuru's, and Bakhtiari's works and arguments, indicating that they distance themselves from the expectations placed on 'immigrant literature.' Demands are placed on the authenticity of works as evaluation criteria for 'immigrant literature,' a literature that is expected to be realistic and based on an author's own life experiences (Behschnitt & Mohnike).

The language of 'second-generation migrant authors' also attracted the attention of linguists within Scandinavian Studies. These linguists added to the conclusions and analyses of the deconstructionist attempts mentioned above, which focused on authenticity as a keyword. As Roger Källström mentions in his linguistic study, linguistic and grammatical deviation, the use of urban youth slang, and elements of a multilingual speech environment are used by Alejandro Leiva Wenger and Jonas Hassen Khemiri extremely consciously, as stylistic features that correspond to the focalizer's modes and intentions (157). Therefore, the 'immigrant Swedish' or 'Rinkeby Swedish,' as used by Leiva Wenger and Khemiri, have to be seen as stylistic devices, not as an expression of any kind of 'authentic' language spoken in the suburbs, as many critics had supposed. Nevertheless, focusing on language as notional and fundamental element in the works of authors whose names connote migratory history and the role of 'the other' in Swedish society, signals an increasing interest in language as a theoretical vantage point in studies on (im)migrant literature. Hereafter, more attention was paid to linguistic features, especially literary multilingualism. Studies deriving from theorizing literary multilingualism nevertheless include many aspects of previous multicultural or ethnic studies. Multilingual features can be analysed, for instance, as narratological tools when expressing hybridization, resistance, new challenges, and positions, and also alienation, otherness, and racialization.

Working Class Literature after the Turn of the Millennium

The critical view of the concept of multiculturalism can also be seen in class-related studies on (im)migrant literature after the turn of the millennium. During the liberal market period of the 1980s, working class literature was not given much attention from the critics and the genre became marginalized within literary studies. The upswing came with a new generation of authors in the 1990s, who began to write about their childhood conditions during the downhill slide of the 'folkhem' in the Swedish welfare state beginning in the 1970s. Among these were authors with roots in migrant groups (Gröndahl, "Sweden-Finnish Literature" 37, 40–50). There has been a reborn interest in working-class literature in Sweden since the middle of the 1990s, and the studies in this field expanded during the same period, when the criticism of 'multicultural society' as a concept accelerated. However, the term 'working-class literature' is still discussed in the Swedish debate, and 'class literature' seems to have replaced the previous concept (cf. Johansson Rissén 10–11). Among these 'class authors' we can find two significant women authors with roots in the Sweden-Finnish group, namely Susanna Alakoski (1962) and Eija Hetekivi Olsson (1973) whose novels deal with stark descriptions of the dark sides of the welfare state, the ill-conceived social security system, child poverty, and alcohol abuse.

Magnus Nilsson's *Den föreställda mångkulturen. Klass och etnicitet i svensk samtidsprosa* [The Imagined Multiculturalism: Class and Ethnicity in Contemporary Swedish Novels, 2010] deals with the debate about class literature on a broad basis and he discusses what he calls the ethnifying of contemporary Swedish literature. The pervading thesis in Nilsson's work is based on studies such as Nancy Fraser's essays on welfare states' distribution policy and identity policy, respectively, and the general framework of Marxist-inspired analysis. According to Nilsson, contributing to a debate based on

37

ethnifying multiculturalism, "class is removed as a category, or the phenomenon is understood as a category of cultural identification that is analogous to the category of ethnicity" (*Den föreställda mångkulturen* 74-78).[12]Nilsson's argumentation is based on a reading of six authors' production, among them Susanna Alakoski, Marjaneh Bakhtiari, and Hassan Loo Sattarvandi – all of them described by critics who used connotations of their immigrant background. Nilsson emphasizes that their works are given "incorrect interpretations" when they are read with a starting point in the identity-political strategy. Nilsson presents an alternative model of reading, with an extensive deconstructive attempt, suggesting that ethnicity should be disapproved of as an analytical category because it is understood incorrectly and in an affirmative way (*Den föreställda mångkulturen* 221). Nilsson's approach underlines the significance of class as the most fundamental category when interpreting contemporary Swedish literature. Yet it is quite common that class-related studies also relate to intersectional approaches, and that the relation between categories such as sex/gender and race/ethnicity are included as a part of the analysis.

The unwillingness or reluctance to consider 'race/ethnicity' as an explanatory, socially constructed category in migrancy-related studies nevertheless catches the attention as a particular tendency in Nilsson's studies. This feature can perhaps also be understood against the backdrop of a common feature in Swedish society and Swedish scholarly studies, namely avoidance of the term 'race.' It has been pointed out that, since Sweden was the leading nation for racial biological research for a long period, 'race' as a subject is in general connected to feelings of unpleasantness and shame. According to Jenny Nilsson and Erika Jönsson, 'race' is for the most part an unmentionable subject for people from the Swedish middle class and it has been scrubbed from legal texts and official documents, as well as from "many scholarly contexts" (26).[13] Within literary studies it has been pointed out that the denial of 'race' as a significant sociological category does not necessarily relate to actual practices in the country. Pirjo Ahokas has in her study on autobiographical literature by Korean adoptee Astrid Trotzig underlined that the existing racism and racialization in Sweden undermines the image of Sweden "as a country that supports colour-blind multiculturalism as the official discourse bolstering ethnic diversity" (168).

From Dismantling Canons to Language as a Nodal Point

Nevertheless, there are today several different ways to understand (im)migrant literature in Sweden. First, the description of the literary canon is changing. On the one hand, the national literary canons in the Nordic countries are being dismantled and fragmentised; on the other hand, new literary areas claim to be recognized. This development goes

---

12 Fraser, Nancy 1997: *Justice Interruptus: Critical Reflections on the "Postsocialist" Condition.* Routledge. New York & London.
13 Jenny Nilsson and Erika Jönsson used 'race' as a topic of conversation with Swedish informants in a sociolinguistic study on how a controversial and taboo subject is handled within a speech situation, and how the informants express shame (26).

hand in hand with a renewal of literary history where the chronological exposition of literature has in many respects been replaced with the presentation of particular divisions into genres, themes, sociological baselines, etc. As Ann-Sofie Lönngren, Heidi Grönstrand, Dag Heede, and Anne Heith mention in the anthology *Rethinking National Literatures and the Literary Canon in Scandinavia* (2015),

> there has been an increasing appearance of "new" literatures constructed around language, ethnicity, sexuality, gender and social class. These "alternative" literatures, often categorized as, for example, migratory, minority, and queer literatures, have an ongoing impact on that which usually counts for Nordic literature [...] (xiii)

The idea of the dismantling of canons is not new, and many scholars within the field of ethnic or postcolonial studies have for decades been pointing out that the concept of 'national' literature is changing. The cartographies of 'centre' and 'periphery' are being reframed, and binarism is no longer a core principal when understanding a national literary canon. Even the volume *Migrants and Literature in Finland and Sweden* (2018) points out the complexity of grouping literatures according to nation, but it is also underlined that new subcategories such as (im)migrant literature can be questioned, not least because these categories are heterogeneous (Heith, Gröndahl & Rantonen 13–14). The volume has its backdrop in the understanding of (im)migrant literature as a historical phenomenon rather than exclusively consisting of contemporary literature; and earlier authorships, like the Latvian essayist and researcher Zenta Mauriņa's (1897–1978), are included in the anthology. As mentioned above, one interesting topic for future studies on (im)migrant literature could be chronological and comparative studies.

In addition, studies in language and language-related topics have increased during the last years. One of the newest research areas is sociologically oriented studies on literature and language revitalization. Language revitalization is a relatively recent subfield of linguistics, focusing on reversing the extinction of languages; during the past years, studies on minority and migrant literature in Sweden have been connected to this field. Joshua Fishman's seminal work in the field, *Reversing Language Shift: Theoretical and Empirical Foundations of Assistance to Threatened Languages* (1991) proceeds from factors on the individual and societal level, while the group level used to be largely missing. The point of departure in Sweden is connected to the sociology of literature, focusing on the interplay between national language policies and practices, and the role of minority organizations and individual authorships. For example, literature written in Finnish in Sweden does not characterise itself as a typical cultural expression recurring in the situation of language revitalization in the same way as the Tornedalian literature written in Meänkieli. While literature in Finnish focuses mainly on identity-related issues, directed at an adult readership, literature in Meänkieli is more concentrated on genres that support language revitalization, such as children's literature and drama, as well as supporting the corpus-planning of the language (Gröndahl, "Minority Literature as an Emancipatory Force").

Also the ideas of the role of language(s) when constituting literary history have changed dramatically during the latest decades. One work often quoted when discussing literary multilingualism has been Yasemin Yildiz' *Beyond the Mother Tongue: The*

Postmonolingual Condition (2012). As Yildiz points out, literary scholarship has been dominated by a monolingual paradigm, resulting in literary history based on national languages. While German Romantics during the late eighteenth century promoted a language philosophy that focused on mother tongue as the authentic means of expression, literature as an institution became connected to the national state and national language (Yildiz 6–7). The concept of literary multilingualism proceeds strongly in contemporary literary studies as a paradigmatic research area. The potency of multilingual literature studies encompasses a wide scope, with a starting point in contextualizing and deconstructionist literary studies. Literature is seen as a construction between nationalities, languages, and cultures, while literary multilingualism is able to challenge or undermine monolingual and monocultural literary canons. In other words, studies in literary multilingualism seem to respond to many of the questions raised when the concept of 'multiculturalism' and 'multicultural society' was demounted, and when multicultural or ethnic studies more or less resulted in a dead end, producing racializing and ethnifying discourses. For example, Heidi Grönstrand's analysis of Eija Hetekivi Olsson's novel *Miira* (2016) deals with language-ideological analysis concerning Swedish school milieu and shows how inequality is ultimately generated by monolingual practices that produce structural discrimination (40). Grönstrand manages to analyse language ideologies and 'othering' of certain languages (and ethnic groups) without ethnifying or essentializing the minority in question. Yet it remains to be seen if 'language' and 'multilingualism' will in the long run function as more neutral analytical tools than 'ethnicity,' as they obviously belong to the categories through which power relations manifest. As we know, such categories quickly become politicized, and different groups of interest claim an interpretative prerogative of their definition.

As studies in multilingual literature avoid traditional categorizations and definitions that derive from nations, national borders, and linguistic boundaries, these entities become irrelevant when applied to migrant or translingual literature (Sorvari 158–160).[14] When it comes to the corpus of studies, literary multilingualism generally seems to have been studied in connection to three research objects: a) text and aesthetics, b) individual authors and authorship, and c) literary institutions in a global, national, or regional context. In other words, descriptions of what is included in literary multilingualism consist of wide focus areas. Monika Schmitz-Emans has divided the concept of 'literature' and 'multilingualism' into five contiguous and interrelated domains. She also mentions intermediality (relations between different media, such as writing and music) and multilingualism in one language (different varieties of one language) as focus areas (11–16). In one of the latest contributions in the field of literary multilingualism in the Nordic countries, the comprehensive volume *The Aesthetics and Politics of Linguistic Borders: Multilingualism in Northern European Literature* (2019), Rolf Kauranen, Markus Huss, and Heidi Grönstrand also underline the wide extent of the area:

> On one level, literary multilingualism has been regarded as a textual phenomenon. On another level, it has been studied vis-à-vis the author as an intertextual phenomenon manifest in an oeuvre. Third, previous studies of literary multilingualism have proposed views that focus on the literary field or literary world, on local as well as on national and global levels (6).

---

[14] See also Behschnitt & Nilsson.

It remains to be seen how studies in literary multilingualism will change the understanding of (im)migrant literature. So far, it seems that the framework of literary multilingualism is used as an umbrella for multiple kinds of studies even though the only common denominator is actually the interplay between more than one language (or more than one language variety) in literature. This does not mean that this point of departure is in any way questionable or undertheorized; on the contrary, studies on literary multilingualism seem to have great potential for future literary studies. Nevertheless, we have to bear in mind that the linguistic, structural and political preconditions cause literature and literary criticism to develop in different ways in different contexts, language areas, and nation states. It is necessary to underline the importance of a contextualizing as well as comparative approach to 'multicultural,' 'multilingual,' and '(im)migrant literatures.'

Works Cited

Aghaee, Mana. "Den persiska litteraturen i Sverige." *Litteraturens gränsland. Invandrar- och minoritetslitteratur i nordiskt perspektiv.* Ed. Satu Gröndahl. Uppsala: Centrum för multietnisk forskning, 2002. 315–332.

Aghaee, Mana. *Lexikon över iranska författare i Sverige.* Uppsala: M. Aghaee, 2002.

Ahmadzadeh, Hashem. "Classical and modern Kurdish literature." *Routledge Handbook on the Kurds.* Ed. Michael M. Gunter. New York: Taylor & Francis, 2018. 90–103.

Ahokas, Pirjo. "Is Love Thicker Than Blood? A Bi-cultural Identity Process in Astrid Trotzig's *Blod är tjockare än vatten.*" *Migrants and Literature in Finland and* Sweden. Eds. Satu Gröndahl & Eila Rantonen. Helsinki: Finnish Literature Society, 2018. 166–186.

Behschnitt, Wolfgang. "'The Voice of the 'Real Migrant': Contemporary Migration Literature in Sweden." *Migration and Literature in Contemporary Europe.* Eds. Mirjam Gebauer & Pia Schwarz Lausten. München: Martin Meidenbauer, 2010. 77–92.

Behschnitt, Wolfgang & Mohnike, Thomas. "Interkulturelle Authentizität? Überlegungen zur 'anderen' Ästhetik der schwedischen 'invandrarlitteratur.'" *Über Grenzen, grenzgänge der Skandinavistik. Festschrift zum 65. Geburtstag von Heinrich Anz.* Eds. Wofang Behschnitt & Elisabeth Herrman. Würzburg: Ergon Verlag, 2007. 27–58.

Behschnitt, Wolfgang & Nilsson, Magnus. "'Multicultural Literatures' in a Comparative Perspective." *Literature, Language, and Multiculturalism in Scandinavia and the Low Countries.* Eds. Wolfgang Behschnitt, Sarah De Mul & Liesbeth Minnaard. Rodopi: Amsterdam – New York: Textxet, 2013. 1–16.

Brune, Ylva. *Nyheter från gränsen. Tre studier i journalistik om 'invandrare,' flyktingar och rasistiskt våld.* Institutionen för journalistik och masskommunikation. Göteborg: Göteborgs universitet, 2004.

Diehl, Barbro & Strömberg, Gabriella. *Lexikon över invandrarförfattare i Sverige.* Borås: Immigrant-institutet, 1977.

Edwards, John. *Language, Society and Identity.* London & New York: B. Blackwell, 1985.

Eriksson, Anneli. *Grekisk invandrarlitteratur i Sverige.* Borås: Invandrarförlaget, 1982.

Fishman, Joshua. *Reversing Language Shift. Theoretical and Empirical Foundations of Assistance to Threatened Languages.* Clevedon: Multilingual Matters, 1991.

Grönstrand, Heidi. "'Var kommer du ifrån... ursprungligen?' Eija Hetekivi Olssonin Miira kieli-ideologioiden taistelutantereena." *Avain* 3 (2018): 26–31.

Gröndahl, Satu. *Litteraturens gränsland. Invandrar- och minoritetslitteratur i nordiskt perspektiv.* Ed. Satu Gröndahl. Uppsala: Centrum för multietnisk forskning, 2002.

Gröndahl, Satu. "Politik, litteratur och makt. Hur görs 'invandrar'- och 'minoritetslitteratur'?" *Framtidens feminismer. Intersektionella interventioner i den feministiska debatten.* Eds. Paulina de los Reyes & Satu Gröndahl. Stockholm: Tankekraft förlag, 2007. 25–44.

Gröndahl, Satu. "Multicultural or Multilingual Literature: A Swedish Dilemma?" *Literature for Europe?* Eds. Theo D'haen & Iannis Goerlandt. Amsterdam – New York: Rodopi, 2009. 173–195.

Gröndahl, Satu. "Sweden-Finnish Literature: Generational and Cultural Changes." *Migrants and Literature in Finland and Sweden.* Eds. Satu Gröndahl & Eila Rantonen. Studia Fennica Litteraria 11. Helsinki: Finnish Literature Society, 2018. 37–56.

Gröndahl, Satu. "Minority Literature as an Emancipatory Force: The Development of Tornedalian and Sweden-Finnish Literature." *Ways of Being in the World: Studies on European Minority Literatures.* Ed. Johanna Laakso. Central European Uralic Studies 1. Wien: Praesens Verlag. Forthcoming.

Heith, Anne, Gröndahl, Satu & Rantonen, Eila. "Introduction: 'The Minoritarian Condition.' Studies in Finnish and Swedish Literatures after World War II." *Migrants and Literature in Finland and Sweden.* Eds. Satu Gröndahl & Eila Rantonen. Studia Fennica Litteraria 11. Helsinki: Finnish Literature Society, 2018. 11–36.

Johansson Rissén, Ann-Christine. *Arbetarlitteraturens återkomst. En diskursinriktad analys kring föreställningar om den samtida arbetarlitteraturen i Sverige 1999-2007.* Magisteruppsats i Biblioteks- och informationsvetenskap vid Institutionen biblioteks- och informationsvetenskap / Bibliotekshögskolan 2008:86. Borås: Högskolan i Borås, 2008.

Jokinen, Maijaliisa. "Sverigefinska kultursträvanden." *Finnarnas historia i Sverige* 3. Ed. Jarmo Lainio. Stockholm & Helsingfors: Nordiska museet & Finska historiska samfundet, 1996. 379–424.

Järvengren, Eva. *Lexikon över latinamerikanska författare i Sverige.* 2nd, rev. ed. Borås: Immigrant-institutet, 1992.

Kauranen, Ralf, Huss, Markus and Grönstrand, Heidi. "Introduction. The Processes and Practices of Multilingualism in Literature." *The Aesthetics and Politics of Linguistic Borders. Multilingualism in Northern European Literature.* Eds. Heidi Grönstrand, Markus Huss and Ralf Kauranen. New York: Routledge, 2019. 27–47.

Källström, Roger. "Litterärt språk på tvärs. Lite om språket hos Leiva Wenger och Hassen Khemiri." *Språk på tvärs. Rapport från ASLAs höstsymposium Södertörn, 11-12 november 2004.* Eds. Boel De Geer & Anna Malmbjer. Uppsala: ASLA, 2005. 147–158.

Laitinen, Kai. *Suomen kirjallisuuden historia.* Helsinki: Otava, 1991.

Lång, Helmer. *Fyra svenska européer. Essäer om invandrarförfattarna Martin Allwood, Karl H. Bolay, Jörgen Nash, Alexander Weiss.* Borås: Immigrant-institutet, 1976.

Lönngren, Ann-Sofie, Heidi Grönstrand, Dag Heede & Anne Heith. "Editors' Introduction." *Rethinking National Literatures and the Literary Canon in Scandinavia.* Eds. Ann-Sofie Lönngren, Heidi Grönstrand, Dag Heede & Anne Heith. Cambridge: Cambridge Scholars Publishing, 2015. ix–xiii.

Löytty, Olli. "Immigrant Literature in Finland: The Uses of a Literary Category." *Rethinking National Literatures and the Literary Canon in Scandinavia.* Eds. Lönngren, Ann-Sofie, Heidi Grönstrand, Dag Heede & Anne Heith. Cambridge: Cambridge Scholars Publishing, 2015. 52–75.

Migrants and Literature in Finland and Sweden. Eds. Satu Gröndahl & Eila Rantonen. Studia Fennica Litteraria 11. Helsinki: Finnish Literature Society, 2018. 37–56.

Müssener, Helmut. *Exil in Schweden. Politische und kulturelle Emigration nach 1933.* Stockholmer germanistische Forschungen 14. Stockholm: Hanser, 1974.

Mäntykangas, Arja. *Lexikon över finska författare i Sverige*. Borås: Immigrant-institutet, 1992.

Nilsson, Magnus. "Swedish 'Immigrant Literature' and the Construction of Ethnicity." *TijdSchrift voor Skandinavistiek* 31.1 (2010): 119–216.

Nilsson, Magnus. *Den föreställda mångkulturen. Klass och etnicitet i svensk samtidsprosa.* Hedemora: Gidlunds förlag, 2010.

Nilsson, Jenny & Jönsson, Erika. "Varning för känsligt innehåll!" *Språktidningen* 7 (2018): 25–29.

Nowakowski, Tadeusz. *Lexikon över polska författare i Sverige*. Borås: Immigrant-institutet, 1996.

Persson, Sven Hugo. *Från grymhetens till motståndets estetik. Peter Weiss tidiga författarskap och Marat/Sade.* Litteraturvetenskapliga institutionen. Göteborg: Göteborgs universitet, 1997.

Peterson, Margareta. "Nordisk litteratur i ett svenskt perspektiv." Eds. Margareta Peterson & Rikard Schönström. *Nordens litteratur*. Lund: Studentlitteratur, 2017. 11–18.

Pynnönen, Marja-Liisa. *Siirtolaisuuden vanavedessä. Tutkimus ruotsinsuomalaisen kirjallisuuden kentästä vuosina 1956-1988.* Helsinki: Finnish Literature Society, 1991.

Rantonen, Eila & Savolainen, Matti. "Postcolonial and Ethnic Studies in the Context of Nordic Minority Literatures." In: *Litteraturens gränsland. Invandrar- och minoritetslitteratur i nordiskt perspektiv.* Ed. Satu Gröndahl. Uppsala: Centrum för multietnisk forskning, 2002. 71–94.

Rohlén-Wohlgemuth, Hilde. *Svensk judisk bibliografi.* Stockholm: Skrifter utgivna av Sällskapet för judaistisk forskning, 1977–1999.

Rossiello, Leonardo. "Latinamerikanska författare i Sverige." In: *Hårdrock, hundar och humanister.* Göteborg: Göteborgs universitet, 1995. 253–260.

Schierup, Carl-Ulrik & Ålund, Aleksandra. "The End of Swedish Exceptionalism? Citizenship, Neo-liberalism and the Politics of Exclusion." *Citizens at Heart? Perspectives on Integration of Refugees in the EU after the Yugoslav Wars of Succession.* Eds. Li Bennich-Björkman, Roland Kostić, Branka Likić-Brborić. Uppsala: Hugo Valentin Centre, 2016. 193–215.

Schmitz-Emans, Monika. "Literatur und Vielsprachigkeit. Aspekte, Themen, Voraussetzungen." *Literatur und Vielsprachigkeit.* Ed. Schmitz-Emans, Monika. Hermeia Grenzüberschreitende Studien zur Literatur- und Kulturwissenschaft 7. Heidelberg: Synchron, 2004. 11–26.

Sievers, Wiebke. "How Immigrant and Ethnic-Minority Writers Have Become a Vanguard of Cultural Change: Comparing Historical Developments, Political Changes and Literary Debates in Fifteen National Contexts." *Immigrant and Ethnic-Minority Writers since 1945: Fourteen Contexts in Europe and Beyond.* Eds. Wiebke Sievers & Sandra Vlasta. Leiden and Boston: Brill Rodopi, 2018. 498–518.

Sollors, Werner. "Introduction: After the Culture Wars; or, From 'English Only' to 'English Plus'." *Multilingual America. Transnationalism, Ethnicity, and the Languages of American Literature.* Ed. Werner Sollors. New York & London: New York University Press, 1998. 1–16.

Sorvari, Marja. "Altering Language, Transforming Literature: Translingualism and Literary Self-translation in Zinaida Lindén's Fiction." Special issue: Translingualism and Transculturality in Russian Contexts of Translation. Guest editor: Julie Hansen. *Translation Studies* 11.2 (2018): 158–171.

Soutkari, Anni. *Lexikon över estniska författare i Sverige*. Borås: Immigrant-institutet, 1992.

Tayfun, Mehmet. *Kurdiskt författarskap och kurdisk bokutgivning. Bakgrund, villkor, betydelse.* Spånga: Apec, 1998.

Teleman, Ulf. "Nordens språk." *Nordens litteratur.* Eds. Margareta Peterson & Rikard Schönström. Lund: Studentlitteratur, 2017. 23–34.

43

Warfvinge, Katarina. "Från flyktingslitteratur till sverigeestnisk litteratur. En immigrantlitteratur under femtio år." *Litteraturens gränsland. Invandrar- och minoritetslitteratur i nordiskt perspektiv.* Ed. Satu Gröndahl. Uppsala: Centrum för multietnisk forskning, 2002. 257–272.

Wendelius, Lars. *Kulturliv i ett svenskamerikanskt lokalsamhälle. Rockford, Illinois.* Uppsala: Centrum för multietnisk forskning, 1990.

Wendelius, Lars. *Den dubbla identiteten. Immigrant och minoritetslitteratur på svenska 1970-2000.* Uppsala: Centrum för multietnisk forskning, 2002.

Williams, Anna. *Skribent i Svensk-Amerika. Jakob Bonggren, journalist och poet.* Avd. för litteratursociologi vid Litteraturvetenskapliga institutionen. Uppsala: Uppsala universitet, 1991.

Yildiz, Yasemin. *Beyond the Mother Tongue: The Postmonolingual Condition.* New York: Fordham University Press, 2012.

PART II
Migration, Identity, and Literature

3. Andersen, Ibsen, and Strindberg as Migrant Writers

Helena Březinová

Introduction

It is fair to say that nineteenth-century Scandinavia experienced a literary renaissance of sorts, when international audiences became aware of Scandinavian authors like Hans Christian Andersen (1805–1875), Henrik Ibsen (1828–1906), and August Strindberg (1849–1912). Importantly, these authors did not merely export their works in translation but, first, also physically relocated themselves abroad. Ever since Andersen achieved success abroad, the strategy Scandinavian authors needed to succeed seemed evident to them: to achieve an international breakthrough, one had to pay visits to the right addresses, initiate the process of translation, and then spread the news at home of one's success abroad. It is reasonable even to speak of a new paradigm for the marketing of literature. Ever since Andersen penetrated the German market, the strategy had two tracks: first, to ensure the works achieved recognition abroad, predominantly in Germany, and, second, to balance out any negative criticism in Copenhagen, Christiania, or Stockholm.

Although Ibsen, Strindberg, and even Andersen spent decades abroad, they have rarely been treated as migrant or exile authors. This paradox should, however, be considered since discussions in which our age is called the age of migrants and migration often fail to mention the fact that long-term migration has had an impact on literature and writers since time immemorial and the authors of the eighteenth and nineteenth centuries were not necessarily migrating less than their colleagues today. In this essay, I shall therefore first focus on the similarities in the motivation of the three aforementioned authors for leaving their homelands. Afterwards, I shall examine their writings through the prism of Edward Said's reflections on literary exiles and Mikhail Bakhtin's conception of dialogue in order to identify possible influences that their migratory experience may have had on their works.

Transnational Authors

In her book *Writing Outside the Nation* (2001), Azade Seyhan states: "Description such as exilic, ethnic, migrant, or diasporic cannot do justice to the nuances of writing between histories, geographies, and cultural practices" (9). One will also run into problems of definition when speaking of Hans Christian Andersen, Henrik Ibsen, and August Strindberg. They all lived abroad for at least several years, sometimes even decades, and some of their most famous works were written outside their nations. Inevitably, the question therefore arises whether these authors – who are unreservedly embedded in the national canons – ought to be considered migrant authors and, if so, in what respect. To a certain degree, the transnational biographies of these Scandinavian authors challenge the normally national character of the literary canons. Clearly, the nation state turned out in many respects not to be identical with their spiritual homeland. "The exile," writes Edward Said (1935–2003), "knows that in a secular and contingent world, homes are always provisional. Borders and barriers, which enclose us within the safety of familiar territory, can also become prisons and are often defended beyond reason and necessity. Exiles cross borders, break barriers of thought and experience" (147). Said considers exile to be an incomparable experience and a precondition for critical thought. Migratory aspects of a writer's biography can, doubtless, partly reposition and reframe his or her writing. Here, I will try to show how this is so by looking at Andersen, Ibsen, and Strindberg since all three writers were searching for their spiritual homeland outside their native lands. I shall first present their own assessments of their migratory working lives as documented in their correspondence, and then I shall apply Bakhtin's theory of polyphony and dialogue to some of their works. Concerning Bakhtin who, like Said, also experienced exile, John Neubauer has astutely remarked: "Bakhtin, though he could settle in Moscow, was a 'permanent exile.' For him, homelessness was a condition of an intellectual freedom and the dialogical novel. As a modern prodigal son, he refused to resubmit to the patriarchal power, preferring the *Geworfenheit* of exile to the *Geborgenheit* of unitary society" (278). In several respects, Andersen, Ibsen, and Strindberg, like Bakhtin, also refused the security of a unitary society.

Before considering this further, however, it is important to find the proper term for the status of Andersen, Ibsen, and Strindberg when living abroad.

Exiles, Expatriates, and Travellers

Andersen was more traveller than migrant. He travelled for a total of nine years of his life. When abroad, he mainly collected impressions, which he used in his writing back in Denmark. No wonder, then, that so many an Andersen fairy tale, play, or novel deals with migratory topics and describes the feeling of homelessness or estrangement from home. Ibsen spent a total of 27 years of his productive life outside his native Norway, in Germany and Italy, and he wrote his best-known plays abroad – *Brand*, *Peer Gynt*, *Et dukkehjem* (*A Doll's House*), and *En folkefiende* (*An Enemy of the People*), just to name a few. Strindberg resided outside his native Sweden from 1883 until 1899 and even decided to write some of his works in French. For each of the three authors, the sojourns or residences abroad began as a *Bildungsreise* (educational journey), which was considered obligatory for a man of letters in the nineteenth century.

Søren Frank aptly points out that migration literature as a topic of scholarly interest was introduced and colonized by the field of post-colonial studies and was originally reserved for authors connected with the British Commonwealth or embedded in other post-colonial settings ("Hvad er migrationslitteratur" 4). Frank's reflections on migration and literature become problematic, however, when he calls the twentieth century the century of migration.[1] After all, the preceding centuries were by no means demographically stationary. Indeed, with the great Atlantic migrations, nineteenth-century Europe was much more on the move than it is today. Compared to this wave of migration, when millions of Swedes and Norwegians left for the Americas, the situation on the Scandinavian Peninsula in the twentieth century appears almost static. What is even more important, however, is that migration has been part of a writer's life since time immemorial and the nineteenth century in particular was a time of expatriate artists' colonies.

Surprisingly, the self-imposed exiles of writers living in artists' colonies in nineteenth-century Europe is usually not considered to be part of migrant or migration literature. What type of migrants were the three Scandinavian literary superstars, Andersen, Ibsen, and Strindberg?

It is important to note that both Ibsen and Strindberg used the term *exile* when describing their own status. Strictly speaking, it is a misnomer since neither man was officially persecuted in a way that would justify its use. Strindberg was apparently aware of the grandiloquence of the word since he toned it down with adjectives. In his French introduction to *Le Plaidoyer d'un fou* (*A Madman's Defense*), he used the attribute "demi-volontaire" (269). In his letter to Émile Zola he described himself as *l'exile volontaire*.

Ibsen, by contrast, in Norwegian referred to his status as one of *landflygtighed* (genuine exile or banishment). In a letter from 1866 to his friend Michael Birkeland, he called himself a "landflygtig poet" ["exiled author"].[2] He used the word again when he recalled the Norwegian reception of his play *Kjærlighedens Komedie* (1862, *Love's Comedy*): "Så lystes jeg da i ban; alle var imod mig […]. Så gik jeg i landflygtighed!" ("Letter to Peter Friedrich Siebold") ["Then I was banished; everybody was against me […]. I went to exile."]

Since "voluntary exile" can easily seem like a contradiction in terms, it would probably be more suitable to call these writers emigrants or expatriates. In his essay "Reflections on Exile," Said stresses that unlike the word refugee, which is a political category, exile "carries with it, I think, a touch of solitude and spirituality" (144). He refers to Hemingway and Fitzgerald as expatriates who lived voluntarily in an alien country, usually for personal or social reasons. "Hemingway and Fitzgerald," Said remarks, "were not forced to live in France. Expatriates may share in the solitude and estrangement of exile, but they do not suffer under its rigid proscription." On the other hand, Said considers James Joyce an exile author, not an expatriate. His criterion for doing so is that Joyce was in fierce opposition to his country of origin: "James Joyce *chose* to be in exile: to give force to his artistic vocation. In an uncannily effective way – as Richard Ellmann

---

[1] "It seems pointless to dispute the fact," Frank writes, "that the twentieth century was an age of migration" (*Migration and Literature* 1).

[2] All translations from Danish, Norwegian, and Swedish are mine, with the exception of the quotation from Hans Christian Andersen's fairy tale "Ole Lukøie."

has shown in his biography – Joyce picked a quarrel with Ireland and kept it alive so as to sustain the strict opposition to what was familiar" (145).

Said is here implying that without leaving Ireland Joyce would not have been able to write the way he did. An essential motivation for Ibsen's and Strindberg's leaving home was their occupation. They therefore repeatedly stressed the feeling of being allied with exiled authors; they present writing outside the nation as an essential precondition for being able to do their work. The same applies for Andersen's continuous travelling. Hence, when categorizing Ibsen's and Strindberg's status as migrants, we can choose between the terms expatriate and exile, yet in Said's understanding the term exile appears more apt. Though Ibsen and Strindberg were expatriates (since their migration was not forced), they seem to have styled themselves as exiles who had been banished from their spiritual homelands.[3]

Ibsen mentions staying abroad as an essential condition for writing in an informative letter to the Norwegian Ministry of Church Affairs and Education. In his opinion, no other author so far had so extensively "anvendt sit eget Erhverv till Udviklingsrejser i Udlandet. Jeg har nu med min Familje været fraværende i fem Aar" ("Letter to Kirke- og Undervisningsdepartementet") ["used his own profession for educational journeys abroad. Together with my family, I have now been absent for five years"]. Clearly, Ibsen blends the concept of an *udviklingsrejse*, as he himself calls it, and more or less permanent emigration, when we consider the five-year duration of his "travels."

In fact, Ibsen's ambiguous description of his own status corresponds perfectly with the description of Strindberg's sojourns abroad, which appears on the official homepage of Strindbergsmuseet. Significantly, in the section "Strindbergs liv" [Strindberg's Life], the writer's sixteen years in France, Switzerland, Germany, and Denmark are entitled "Strindberg på resa" ["Strindberg travelling"].

The *Bildungsreise*: The First Step into Emigration

Ibsen's term *udviklingsrejse* is identical to the concept of *Bildungsreise*, a journey taken to get educated or to mature. Most famously, it entered the field of literature in Goethe's emblematic *Bildungsroman, Wilhelm Meisters Lehrjahre* (1795–96). When Ibsen stayed in Copenhagen during his first long trip in 1852, where he was getting acquainted with the theatres, he wrote to Det norske Theater in Bergen that he had met Hans Christian Andersen. By then internationally acknowledged, Andersen is presented by Ibsen as something like a guru who could guarantee a successful *Bildungsreise*:

---

[3] With reference to the exile status of Erich Auerbach (1892–1957), the authors of the volume *Spiritual Homelands* describe the experience of exile as not necessarily tragic but rather as a choice essential to the modern condition as such: "Choosing a homeland is an act of election that simultaneously implies a process of un-election and conscious dissociation. If the modern condition, as Erich Auerbach wrote from his own place of exile, involved 'the task of making oneself at home in existence without fixed points of support,' then the election of place is both an act of self-orientation and one of defiant rootedness in a 'boundless and incomprehensible' world" (Biemann et al. 2).

Med H. C. Andersen er jeg bleven bekjendt; han raader mig meget til, fra Dresden af at gjøre en Tour til Wien for at see Burg-Theatret; maaskee kommer han paa samme Tid til at opholde sig der, og vil da veilede mig, hvis ikke, saa vil forhaabentlig Professor Dahls Assistence kunne udrette det Samme.

[I have made the acquaintance of H. C. Andersen; he strongly advises me to travel from Dresden to Vienna to see the Burgtheater; maybe he will be there at the same time, and he would gladly advise me; if not, then probably the assistance of Professor Dahl will do.]

Travel stipends were an integral part of the art world at that time. Consequently, in his letters to the Norwegian institutions, reporting on his travels, Ibsen paints a picture of himself as an industrious student of foreign culture and manners, and he clearly styles himself as an artist walking in the footsteps of Wilhelm Meister:

Og foruden denne bestemte Kundskabsmasse formener jeg ogsaa at have vundet frem till den indre Forædling i Syn, i Betragtning og i Dom, som vel tillsidst bør sættes som Rejsens højeste Formaal.
("Letter to Kirke- og Undervisningsdepartementet")

[And besides acquiring a certain body of knowledge, I also presume that I have attained to the inner refinement of vision, of reflection and of judgement, which should in the end be set as the highest purpose of the journey.]

One side effect of the *Bildungsreise* for Andersen, however, was his need to leave home over and over again, for Ibsen and Strindberg to extend their stays abroad far beyond what can reasonably be considered a trip. Apparently, the Goethean concept of *Bildungsreise*, according to which travelling for education is supposed to result in the homecoming of a mature person, is significantly reformulated in the lives of the three writers: the possibility of coming home is absent or radically challenged. In his letter to a close friend Henriette Hanck, Andersen described the feeling of profound estrangement from home. The letter dates from August 1841, shortly after he had returned to Copenhagen from what he called his "Oriental" journey, which lasted from October 1840 to July 1841 (described in his *En Digters Bazar*, 1842). He writes:

Hvorledes jeg nu finder det her hjemme spørger De? Jeg synes aldeles ikke om at være her! jeg finder Kjøbenhavn smaalig, trist og haard; der er en evig Lyst til at grine af Alt; ja jeg kunde og maatte sige meget ondt, skulde jeg ret udtale mig om de første indtryk, men det vilde maaskee fremstille mig selv, som en ægte Kjøbenhavner. Mueligt er det ikke bedre i fremmede Byer, men paa Reisen mærker man ikke dette Smaae, dette Kritikkoglerі, og det er noget af det Lykkelige ved at reise. Gud veed naar jeg nu kommer afsted igjen.

[How do I find it at home, you ask? I utterly dislike being here! I find Copenhagen narrow, dull, and crude; there is an eternal urge to mock everybody; indeed, I could and should say a lot of wicked things were I honest about my first impressions, yet that would perhaps show me to be a real Copenhagener. Maybe things are no better in foreign cities, but when travelling you don't feel the pettiness, the hocus-pocus of the critics; this is the most fortunate thing about travelling. Lord knows when I will get the chance to leave again.]

Clearly, Andersen's intense travelling changed his views of his homeland.

Ibsen, too, repeatedly expressed similar feelings in his correspondence. In a letter from 1867 to his Danish mother-in-law, who was also a writer, he presented travel as a necessary condition for writing: "Italien bør og maa Du se, ikke paa en flygtig Gjennemrejse, men under et længere Opphold. Faa Rejsestipendium, ikke søg, men kræv, forlang" ("Letter to Magdalene Thoresen"). ["You must see Italy, not only pass through it; you must spend more time there. Get a travel stipend; don't apply for it, demand it."] This advice follows a passage in which Ibsen recalls his life *deroppe*, which means "up there." *Deroppe* is an adverbial of place that Ibsen used in his letters as a standard reference to Norway. In this context, it is reasonable to see it as meaning "provincialism." In this passage, Ibsen implicitly refers to the psychological change he underwent after embarking on his journey:

> Jeg begriber mangegange ikke hvorledes Du holder ud deroppe! Livet deroppe, saaledes som det nu staar for mig har noget ubeskrivelig kjedende ved sig; det kjeder Aanden ud af ens Væsen, kjeder Dygtigheden ud af ens Vilje; det er det forbandede ved de smaa Forholde, at de gjør Sjælene smaa.
> ("Letter to Magdalene Thoresen")

> [I don't understand how you can stand the life up there! Life *deroppe*, the way it seems to me now, has something unspeakably tiresome about it; it beats the spirit out of you, beats the capability out of your will. This is the curse of being in a narrow environment: it narrows the soul.]

The essence of the message is in the words *saaledes som det nu staar for mig* ["the way it seems to me now"], which demarcate a chasm between Ibsen prior to his journey and then at the time of this letter from Sorrento in 1867. He expresses an identical feeling in a letter to Georg Brandes, the Danish critic and scholar, from 1872. He describes the change of his worldview "et svælgende dyb mellem igår og idag" ["a gulf between yesterday and today"], explaining: "Da jeg havde været i Italien forstod jeg ikke hvorledes jeg havde kunnet føre en tilværelse forinden jeg havde været der." ["After having been to Italy, I could not understand how I could have ever lived before then."]

A *Bildungsreise* without a Finale

It is useful to recall at this point Jürgen Habermas's criticism of the concept of *Bildung* and of the genre of the *Bildungsroman*. He considers the motivation for establishing the genre as reactionary and argues that it was an *Öffentlichkeitsersatz* (surrogate for the public) because the *Bildungsroman* protagonist typically withdraws from society and concentrates instead on cultivating himself. According to Habermas, the *Bildungsroman* replaced the *Gesellschaftsroman*, which deals with political processes (17). From this standpoint, the Scandinavian migrant writers Ibsen and Strindberg gave up involvement in the public affairs of their homelands in order to concentrate on their personal literary projects. That is why Ibsen renounced the state when mentioning the Jews, who were able to develop their art thanks to their statelessness. In a letter to Brandes, he writes about the Jewish people:

> Hvorved har det bevaret sig i isolation, i poesi, trods al råhed udenfra? Derved at det ikke har havt nogen stat at trækkes med. Var det forblevet i Palæstina, vilde det for længe siden være gået under i sin konstruktion, ligesom alle andre folk. Staten må væk!

> [How did they remain in isolation, in poetry, despite all the cruelty from outside? The reason is that they never have had a state to drag along with them. If they had stayed in Palestine, they would have perished in their own state long ago. Like all other peoples. Down with the state!]

In this letter to Brandes, Ibsen excludes the possibility that he himself could ever become a publicly engaged member of a community; inner life, for Ibsen, becomes a surrogate for society. The same standpoint appears in another Ibsen's letter to Brandes from more than ten years later, this time from Rome:

> Når jeg tænker på, hvor træg og tung og sløv forståelsen er derhjemme, når jeg lægger mærke til, hvor lavtliggende den hele betragtningsmåde viser sig at være, så overkommer der mig et dybt mismod og jeg synes mangen gang, at jeg ligeså gerne straks kunde afslutte min literære virksomhed. Hjemme behøver man egentlig ingen digterværker; man hjælper sig så godt med "Storthingstidenden" og "Luthersk ugeskrift." Og så har man jo partibladene. Jeg har ikke noget talent til at være statsborger og heller ikke til at være orthodox, og hvad jeg ikke føler talent for, det afholder jeg mig fra.
> ("Letter to Georg Brandes")

> [When I think of how stiff, ponderous, and slow understanding is in Norway, when I notice how shallow and narrow the whole perspective there is, I fall into deep despair and I often think of immediately terminating all my literary activity. At home, no belles-lettres is needed; people make do with the "Storthingstidenden" (Parliamentary journal) and the "Luthersk ugeskrift" (Lutheran weekly). Together with the party press. I have talent neither for being a citizen nor for being orthodox, and what I don't feel I have talent for, I abstain from.]

All three authors considered their long-term stays abroad to be a precondition of their writing and felt that coming home again was impossible or at least extremely difficult. They prioritized an integrity that was possible only when they were writing outside the nation state, which was, in fact, growing stronger in that period.

Pragmatic Reasons for Not Coming Home: Fighting Domestic Criticism

In addition to the emotional aspects of these writers' having left their homelands, one can also identify some strictly pragmatic reasons. Andersen and, after him, Ibsen and Strindberg made sure that notices about their books being published and becoming successful abroad appeared in periodicals at home. International versus domestic reception is a recurring topic in the letters of Andersen, Ibsen, and Strindberg.[4] In a letter to his mother-in-law from 1865, Ibsen, tellingly, goes straight from describing his reasons for leaving Norway to giving instructions that his new piece, *Brand*, must be reviewed not by a Norwegian critic but by a Danish one:

[Men jeg maatte ud af Svinskheden deroppe for at blive nogenlunde tvættet. Deroppe kunde jeg aldrig føre noget sammenhængende indre Liv; derfor var jeg et i min Produktion og et andet udenom; – men derfor blev Produktionen heller ikke hel. Jeg ved jo nok at jeg vist ikke endnu har andet end et Gjennemgangspunkt inde, men jeg kjender dog fast Grund under Fødderne. Jeg har skrevet et stort dramatisk Digt isommer […]. I indlagte Brev beder jeg Clemens Petersen kritisere det og at gjøre det snart; Kritiken i Norge duer ikke.]
("Letter to Magdalene Thoresen")

[But I had to leave the wickedness of up there in order to make myself clean. I could never live a coherent inner life up there; that's why I was one person in my work and someone else outside it; but, consequently, my work was not coherent either. I know that I have only reached a temporary inner state so far, but I feel I am on firm ground. I wrote a long verse drama in the summer […]. In the enclosed letter I ask Clemens Petersen to review it and to do so soon. Criticism in Norway is not good.]

Strindberg's departure from Sweden was clearly inspired by Ibsen's having left,[5] and his loathing of the criticism at home also played a key role in this. In a letter to his Norwegian colleague and friend, Alexander Kielland, from October 1881, Strindberg summed up the reception of his *Svenska folket* [The Swedish People, 1881–82], a four-part cultural history:

Skrif mig några rader till oppmuntran och bed Brandes läse mitt *Svenska Folket!* Jag står så helvetes ensam i denna eldsvåda jag lagat till; Det fins inte en som icke vill bränna mig i brasan! Jag tror att jag missräknat mig på min nation – de äro så stock-dumma och konservativa att det icke fins några som gå med mig och de som skulle vara med mig äro afundsjuka så att de lemna mig i sticket! Nästa höst går jeg också i landsflykt!
("Letter to Alexander Kielland")

[Write me some encouraging lines and ask Brandes to read my *Svenska Folket!* I am so damn alone in this fire that I have stoked up. There is no one who would not like to burn me in the blaze! I must have been mistaken about my nation – they are so witless and conservative that not

---

4 Foreign in contrast to domestic reception is mentioned in a letter by Andersen's friend and the heir to all his property, Edvard Collin, after Andersen's death. According to Collin, Andersen was convinced that the Danish critics, unlike their German counterparts, were treating him with bias: "Men den bratteste Overgang i hans Væsen viste sig efter Opholdet i Weimar, hvor han var blevet feteret paa en Maade, der vel kunde forvirre Hovedet paa ham. Efter denne Jagen fra Fest til Fest og omgivet af Smiger, befandt han sig pludselig i det gamle borgerlige ædruelige Hjem; hans Phantasi havde foregjøglet ham en Modtagelse i den tydske Stiil." (Collin, "Letter to Jonna Stampe") [Yet the most abrupt personality change was after his Weimar sojourn, where he was feted in a way that may have confused him. After racing from one party to another and being surrounded by flattery, he was suddenly back in his sober old bourgeois home. His imagination made him daydream about being received in the German style.]

5 It is noteworthy that Strindberg's reception abroad was strongly influenced by the reception of Ibsen's plays. An example might be a Slovak review from 1919 which presents Strindberg's play *Kamraterna* as a parody of Ibsen's *Et dukkehjem* (Gáborová 65).

53

a single person stands by me, and those who should are so envious that they let me down instead! Next autumn I too shall go into exile!]

At the time when he received this letter, Kielland lived in Copenhagen where he stayed from 1881 till 1883. This is why Strindberg used the adverb "too" in connection with "exile." When Strindberg again mentions his Swedish critics in a letter written in Berlin in January 1893, his remarks are typically tinged with sarcasm:

I London har jag anbud att få "Fadren" spelad och en agent tar mina pjeser för England och Kolonierna. I Rom öfversättas mina bästa pjeser till Italienska och är jeg Ibsen i hälarne. Jag har icke läst en Svensk tidning sedan före jul. Antager att man smickrar sig med att jag lidit nederlag och förtiger. Hur har man betett sig? Är landet sig likt?
("Letter to Birger Mörner")

[In London, I was offered that "Fadren" [The Father, 1887] could be staged, and an agent would see to my plays in England and the colonies. In Rome, my best plays are being translated into Italian and I am on Ibsen's heels. I haven't read a Swedish newspaper since before Christmas. I assume they flatter themselves that I have suffered defeat and keep silent. How did they act? Is the country as it has always been?]

From this letter, it is obvious that besides his aversion to criticism at home, Strindberg's motivation for leaving his native land was to promote his writings abroad as Ibsen did.

Transgressing National Literature: From Scandinavia to *Weltliteratur*

In a letter from July 1872 to Brandes, Ibsen declared Germany the pragmatic starting point of an international career of any Scandinavian writer. After the scandal that arose when Brandes had lectured on modern literature in Copenhagen the year before, Ibsen encouraged him to leave Denmark for Germany:

Det glæder mig at Deres forelæsninger udkommer på tysk. Nogle uddrag, som allerede skal have været oversatte i "Ueber Land und Meer" har vakt megen opmærksomhed og interesse; jeg hørte dem omtale i den literære forening i Dresden. Kom her ned! Det er i udlandet vi nordboer skal vinde vore feltslag; en sejr i Tyskland, og De vil være ovenpå hjemme.
("Letter to Georg Brandes")

[I am glad that your lectures have come out in German. Some extracts, those which were translated for "Ueber Land und Meer," got plenty of attention and interest; I heard them being discussed in the literary society in Dresden. Come here to the South! We Northerners should win our battles abroad; a victory in Germany and you'll have the upper hand.]

Ibsen was right in his conviction. Jens-Morten Hanssen confirms it in his quantitative study of the staging of Ibsen's plays in Germany and their subsequent spread and migration around the globe: "The German introduction of Ibsen paved the way for him being introduced into other language areas and cultural markets" (14).[6] Although Hanssen partly disputes the German stage reception of Ibsen's plays as being the key factor for their global spread, he is convinced that it was the German version of the plays that greatly contributed to Ibsen becoming world famous as a dramatist. In fact, Hanssen's findings about Germany's cultural hegemony comport with something that Ibsen himself felt intensely. This is clear from a letter Ibsen wrote in Rome in 1879:

[Men i begyndelsen af Oktober indtræffer vi ialfald igen i München, såfremt ingen uforudset hindring skulde komme ivejen. Jeg har rigtignok oftere tænkt på at sende Sigurd alene derop for at fortsætte studeringerne; men det er mig dog i mange henseender ønskeligt at komme mere ind i det germanske literære liv igen; hernede står man dog i de fleste henseender altfor meget udenfor tidens bevægelser.
("Letter to Marcus Grønvold")

[But at the beginning of October, I will definitely be in Munich again, unless something untoward bars my plans. Admittedly, I have often thought of sending Sigurd [1859–1930, Ibsen's only child] alone up there (*derop*) to continue his studies, yet in many respects, it is desirable for me to come back to Germanic literary life; here, one is in most regards too much outside the current movements.]

Clearly, it was useful to prolong the *Bildungsreise* or even make it a permanent state of affairs. Among the chief reasons, perhaps even the strongest, was that it helped to keep a writer from ending up "too much outside the current movements."

Domestic or, rather, Scandinavian audiences[7] alone could by no means satisfy the ambitions of these authors. In their letters, they express the urge to make it internationally. This is evident from Ibsen's hurt reaction when the pharmacist and literary enthusiast H. C. Thaulow expressed a wish to publish Peter Friedrich Siebold's German translation of *Brand* in Christiania. In a letter, Ibsen writes:

Indgaar De paa hans Forslag, saa vil hele Deres Arbejde være spildt; thi der findes ingen norsk Boghandler, der har saa udbredte Forbindelser, at han skulde kunne skaffe Bogen Indgang i Tydskland. Hernede maa den udkomme; herfra maa den sendes till Anmeldelse i Aviser og Tidsskrifter; kort sagt, der maa tages en hel Del Foranstaltninger, som kun en tydsk Forlægger vil kunne være i Stand till.
("Letter to Peter Friedrich Siebold")

---

[6] Hanssen elucidates his point when commenting on Ibsen's international breakthrough with the play *Pillars of Society* (1877), "which was soon published in three different German translations and staged by more than sixty theatre companies in the German-speaking areas of Central Europe in the late 1870s (…). The very first Hungarian, Serbian, Czech, and Dutch performances of *Pillars of Society* used translations based on German translations, thereby constituting specific side effects of Ibsen's German success" (15).

[7] The extraordinary connectedness of the authors in Scandinavia in the second half of the nineteenth century is documented by Tor Ivar Hansen: "Helt sentralt stod Gyldendal Forlag og forlagssjef Frederik V. Hegel, men bak ham stod en skandinavisk leserskare som etterspurte den norske litteraturen og en bokbransje som hadde rettet blikket mot sine skandinaviske naboland" (Hansen 182). [Absolutely central was the Gyldendal publishing house and the publisher Frederik V. Hegel, but there was also a Scandinavian readership that demanded Norwegian literature and a book trade that kept an eye on the neighboring Scandinavian countries.]

[If you accept his suggestion, all your work will be in vain; no Norwegian bookseller has connections so far-reaching that he can promote the book in Germany. It has to be published here in Germany, and from here it must be sent for review in newspapers and magazines; in short, a lot needs to be done and only a German publisher can do it.]

The letter provides evidence of Ibsen's ambition to make it onto the literary scene in Germany and, indeed, all Europe. In order to justify to his compatriots his long absence from Norway, Ibsen wrote a letter to Prime Minister Emil Stang, offering this explanation and asking for help in clearing the way for his son's diplomatic career in Norway. The letter was written in Munich in 1889, a quarter of a century after Ibsen had left his homeland:

Derved vilde nemlig hele min litterære livsbane være bleven forrykket og bragt ud af sporet. Deroppe fra vilde jeg aldrig have kunnet erobre mig den stilling i verdenslitteraturen, som jeg nu er indehaver af. Deroppe fra vilde det aldrig være faldet i min lykkelige lod, således som nu, at bære det norske navn videre ud omkring i verden end nogen anden nordmand hidtil har formået på digtningens område, – og vel ikke på noget andet område heller.
("Letter to Emil Stang")

[Doing this would have derailed my whole literary career. From up there [deroppe], I would never have been able to gain the position in world literature that I have now. Up there, I would never have had the good fortune, which I have now, to carry the name of Norway further than any other Norwegian in the field of literature – indeed, perhaps in any field.]

In the essay "Ibsen og hans tyske Skole" [Ibsen and his German School], Georg Brandes confirms Ibsen's statement: according to him, Ibsen provided a shot in the arm to the languishing state of German literature (423–24). Brandes here has clearly adopted Goethe's conception of *Weltliteratur* as the mutual enrichment of national literatures, which prevents literary stagnation. In short, Brandes sees Ibsen as an author of world literature. But, returning to my argument, it must be said that all three authors – Andersen, Ibsen, and Strindberg – had to reside abroad in order to be integral to Weltliteratur. It is clear from their letters that each of them left his homeland for a foreign environment that felt less oppressive to them. Strindberg even appeared to be indifferent to the language he usually wrote in, choosing instead to write some of his books in French.

Writing Outside Home – Home in Writing

In his book *Migration and Literature*, Frank asks the apposite question: "Does literature written by a migrant automatically qualify as migration literature?" (15) Frank's answer is no. Instead, he argues, that what should count most is the formal and thematic qualities of a work, not the writer's origin. Frank, then, is trying to avoid the traditional biographical approach. Instead, he claims, what constitutes migration literature is, for example, the migratory content of a book, its *heteroglossia*, how the writing reflects being between two or more cultures, foreignness of voice, and inconclusiveness.

As already mentionned, the writings of Andersen, Ibsen, and Strindberg are not usu-ally categorized as migrant or migration literature, despite the long-lasting migrancy of the authors. This suggests a general assumption that their long-term sojourns abroad did not inform their writing in any fundamental way – at most, only at the level of motifs and topoi. It is, of course, always largely a matter of speculation to apply biographical information mechanically in one's interpretation of a work of fiction. I am, however, inclined to agree with Said when in his "Introduction: Criticism and Exile" he challeng-es the formalism worshipped by so many scholars of literature for long periods in the twentieth century. "Looking back from the present, one can," he writes, "discern a trend in much of the great Western criticism of the twentieth century that draws readers away from experience and pushes them instead toward form and formalism" (xvii). Instead, he suggests taking into account "historical experience" since:

> the study of literature is not abstract but is set irrecusably and unarguably within a culture whose historical situation influences, if it does not determine, a great deal of what we say and do. I have been using the phrase "historical experience" throughout because the words are neither technical nor esoteric but suggest an opening away from the formal and technical toward the lived, the contested, and the immediate. (xxxi)

In what follows, I suggest some interpretative tools that allow one to take an author's exile experience into consideration when interpreting his or her work, trying not to slip into "esoteric" (biographical) readings as mentioned by Said.

An author's long-term absence from home, together with the unease at the thought of returning, can be better understood using Bakhtin's dialogization since, as he observed, dialogical prose radically challenges the dominating culture by incorporating voices from outside and these voices renounce the unitariness of a nation, society, or home. Hence, Bakhtin's category of dialogue offers a fruitful fusion between the lived and the technical perspective when interpreting a work of literature.

Andersen: Domestic Fowl versus Migratory Birds

In many of Andersen's novels and fairy tales, the reader is confronted with a dichotomy between home and the world outside. Strikingly often, strangers and strangeness rep-resent a chance to change one's life for the better. A good example of this is the fairy tale "Tommelise" (1835, Thumbelina) in which the female protagonist has to escape her Nordic home by moving to the South, which is depicted as an idyllic refuge. In Anders-en's fairy tales, if the protagonists are deprived of the possibility of escaping or leaving home, the implied reader is guided by the narrator to view their destiny with unease or anxiety; this is the case in "Hyrdinden and Skorsteensfeieren" (1845, The Shepherdess and the Chimney Sweep) and in "Ole Lukøie" (1842). In the latter fairy tale, the little boy Hjalmar and his guide Ole Lukøie witness a highly informative dispute over travelling versus staying home, which I quote here unabridged:

"Skal vi nu ligge paa Landet, eller reise udenlands?" spurgte Brudgommen, og saa blev Svalen, som havde reist meget og den gamle Gaard-Høne, der fem Gange havde ruget Kyllinger ud, taget paa Raad; og Svalen fortalte om de deilige, varme Lande, hvor Viindruerne hang saa store og tunge, hvor Luften var saa mild, og Bjergene havde Farver, som man her slet ikke kjender dem!

"De har dog ikke vor Grønkaal!" sagde Hønen. "Jeg laae en Sommer med alle mine Kyllinger paa Landet; der var en Gruusgrav, som vi kunde gaae og skrabe i, og saa havde vi Adgang til en Have med Grønkaal! O, hvor den var grøn! jeg kan ikke tænke mig noget kjønnere."

"Men den ene Kaalstok seer ud ligesom den anden," sagde Svalen, "og saa er her tidt saa daarligt Veir!"

"Ja det er man vant til!" sagde Hønen.

"Men her er koldt, det fryser!"

"Det har Kaalen godt af!" sagde Hønen. "Desuden kunne vi ogsaa have det varmt! havde vi ikke for fire Aar siden en Sommer, der varede i fem Uger, her var saa hedt, man kunde ikke trække Veiret! og saa have vi ikke alle de giftige Dyr, de have ude! og vi er fri for Røvere! Det er et Skarn, som ikke finder at vort Land er det kjønneste! han fortiente rigtig ikke at være her!" og saa græd Hønen. "Jeg har ogsaa reist! jeg har kjørt i en Bøtte over tolv Mile! der er slet ingen Fornøielse ved at reise!"

"Ja Hønen er en fornuftig Kone!" sagde Dukken Bertha, "jeg holder heller ikke af at reise paa Bjerge, for det er kun op og saa er det ned! nei, vi ville flytte ud ved Gruusgraven og spadsere i Kaalhaven!"

Og derved blev det.

["Shall we go to a summer resort, or take a voyage?" the bridegroom asked. They consulted the swallow, who was such a traveler, and the old setting hen who had raised five broods of chicks. The swallow told them about the lovely warm countries where grapes hang in great ripe bunches, where the air is soft, and where the mountains have wonderful colors that they don't have here.

"But they haven't got our green cabbage," the hen said. "I was in the country with all my chickens one summer and there was a sand pit in which we could scratch all day. We also had access to a garden where cabbages grew. Oh, how green they were! I can't imagine anything lovelier."

"But one cabbage looks just like another," said the swallow, "and then we so often have bad weather. It is cold here – it freezes."

"That's good for the cabbage," said the hen. "Besides, it's quite warm at times. Didn't we have a hot summer four years ago? For five whole weeks it was so hot that one could scarcely breathe. Then too, we don't have all those poisonous creatures that infest the warm countries, and we don't have robbers. Anyone who doesn't think ours is the most beautiful country is a rascal. Why, he doesn't deserve to live here!" The hen burst into tears. "I have done my share of traveling. I once made a twelve-mile trip in a coop, and there's no pleasure at all in traveling."

"Isn't the hen a sensible woman!" said Bertha, the doll. "I don't fancy traveling in the mountains because first you go up and then you go down. No, we will move out by the sand pit and take our walks in the cabbage patch."

That settled the matter.][8]

8 The English wording is from Jean Hersholt's translation, which is accessible online (unpaginated) at https://andersen.sdu.dk/vaerk/hersholt/OleLukoie_e.html

Undeniably, the fictional world here is radically dialogical. The point of view of the narrator is somewhere in between, his position is inconclusive. The dialogue is an example of the Bakhtinian hidden polemic, which is an indirect attack or criticism of another person: "One word acutely senses alongside it someone else's word speaking about the same object, and this awareness determines its structure" (196). The polemic seems to be openly directed at the interlocutor, but the whole dialogue is, in fact, a sideward glance at the hen and her domestic way of living. The little boy Hjalmar, who is the explicit witness to the dialogue, may possibly understand it as a warning against marriage since this would greatly reduce the possibility of traveling or migrating. But this interpretation is insufficient since the dialogue is a true polyphony of voices presenting conflicting ways of life. The narrator does not interfere in the dispute; his or her comment is restricted to the information that the hen has burst into tears and to the laconic conclusion: "That settled the matter." Yet in the argument between domestic fowl and migratory birds one particular *modus vivendi* seems to be given preference. This *modus vivendi* is not tantamount to leaving for good or emigrating. As opposed to being domesticated, travel like that of migratory birds would suffice – provided, of course, that it is permitted by the bride. The parallel between the story and the constantly traveling Andersen is obvious. At any rate, the dialogue can usefully be interpreted as a polyphony of voices or dialogical prose as described by Bakhtin. No single objective world has been established by the author's authoritative voice; rather, the author presents a plurality of each of the world views that appears to each character.

Dialogical and Monological Marital Dramas

Regarding Ibsen's self-imposed exile, it is revealing to juxtapose his dramas *Et Dukkehjem* (1879, *A Doll's House*) and *Fruen fra Havet* (1888, *The Lady from the Sea*) and to look at them in terms of Bakhtinian polyphony. True, Bakhtin restricted this term to the novel and he explicitly renounced the possibility of drama being polyphonic. Yet, as we have seen, his terms "polyphony" and "dialogization" can also be fittingly applied to theatre (see Keyssar).

If we employ Bakhtin's categories of dialogue and monologue when interpreting the finale of the two dramas, then the female protagonist, Nora Helmer, in the finale of *Et Dukkehjem* has to leave the unitary monological world; to retain her integrity, she has no choice. Hence, the voices in the play never merge into one, and it is fair to call what happens a radical dialogization or *heteroglossia* of communication.

The finale of *Fruen fra Havet*, by contrast, can instructively be interpreted as two conflicting voices merging, because of empathy, into one. The female protagonist, Ellida Wangel, who longs for the mystical stranger, eventually decides to stay with her husband and thus excludes the possibility of opening up a new world. The polyphony of voices in *Et Dukkehjem* becomes a monologue in *Fruen fra Havet*. The radical duality of the world views in *Et Dukkehjem* is something that was observed by one of Ibsen's contemporaries, the critic John Paulsen (1851–1924):

Stykket strider rigtignok mod Dramaets hele Theori og Praxis, thi i Stedet for at ende med et stedse raskere Tempo i Handlingen, og en ovenpaa Spændingen tilfredsstillende Løsning, slutter Stykket med en bred, psykologisk Deduktion. Skuespillets Problem forbliver uløst.[9]

[The play defies the whole theory and practice of drama because instead of ending in the plot's increasingly swifter tempo and a satisfying resolution following the suspense, it ends in a broad, psychological deduction. The problem of the play remains unsolved.]

The drama ends in a radical polyphony, each consciousness in a world of its own. Nora seizes her own voice and verbalizes her needs in a monologue world – not even the author can monopolize the right and power to speak on her behalf. The ending opens up a dialogical world.

The finale of both Ibsen's marital pieces, I would argue, may fruitfully be juxtaposed with the stages of Ibsen's life in exile. Ibsen wrote *Et Dukkehjem* in Rome and Amalfi from 1878 to 1879, after years of self-imposed exile and more than a decade before returning to Norway. *Fruen fra Havet*, on the other hand, was written in 1888 and it is his penultimate drama before returning to Norway for good in 1891. The exile life corresponds well with the double-voicedness in *Et Dukkehjem*; by contrast, in *Fruen fra Havet* Ellida and her husband Wangel's voices ultimately merge and Ellida thereby renounces her need to seek a new world that might exist somewhere else. Hence, this drama is in tune with Ibsen's looming return home and the double-voicedness becomes a monologue. This reading fits well with Said's description of the exile's experience:

> The exile's new world, logically enough, is unnatural and its unreality resembles fiction. Georg Lukács, in *Theory of the Novel*, argued with compelling force that the novel, a literary form created out of the unreality of ambition and fantasy, is *the* form of "transcendental homelessness." Classical epics, Lukács wrote, emanate from settled cultures in which values are clear, identities stable, life unchanging. The European novel is grounded in precisely the opposite experience, that of a changing society in which an itinerant and disinherited middle-class hero or heroine seeks to construct a new world that somewhat resembles an old one left behind forever. In the epic there is no *other* world, only the finality of *this* one. Odysseus returns to Ithaca after years of wandering; Achilles will die because he cannot escape his fate. The novel, however, exists because other worlds *may* exist, alternatives for bourgeois speculators, wanderers, exiles. ("Reflections on Exile" 144)

For Nora in *Et Dukkehjem*, undoubtedly, there is a possibility that another world exists. Moreover, as Said stresses, there is the infiniteness of this world and the necessity of constructing a new one. The process of constructing a new world implies the instability of the system, its unfinishedness and unresolvedness.

---

[9] Vigdis Ystad quotes Paulsen in her introduction to the play on the *Henrik Ibsens skrifter* website.

The Only Home Is … Writing

In her *Writing Outside the Nation*, Seyhan identifies the feeling of not belonging that the exiled, migrant or refugee authors have. Strikingly often, they

> express the sentiment that neither a return to the homeland left behind nor being at home in the host country is an option. They need an alternative space, a third geography. This is the space of memory, of language, of translation. In fact, this alternative geography can now be figured as a terrain (of) writing, as the Greek roots of its two syllables suggest (15).

Andersen's, Ibsen's, and Strindberg's writings can, indeed, be advantageously interpreted as a third geography or alternative space. In an 1897 letter to Brandes, Ibsen described his feelings about home when his viewpoint changed from *deroppe* to *heroppe*, that is, after he moved back to Norway:

> Kan De gætte hvad jeg går og drømmer om og planlægger og udmaler mig som så dejligt? Det er: at slå mig ned ved Øresund, mellem København og Helsingør, på et frit åbent sted, hvor jeg kan sé alle havsejlerne komme langvejs fra og gå langvejs. Det kan jeg ikke her. Her er alle sunde lukkede i enhver ordets betydning, – og alle forståelsens kanaler tilstoppede. Å, kære Brandes, man lever ikke virkningsløst 27 år ude i de store fri og frigørende kulturforhold. Her inde eller, rettere sagt, her oppe ved fjordene har jeg jo mit fødeland. Men-men-men: hvor finder jeg mit hjemland? Havet er det, som drager mig mest. Forresten går jeg her i ensomheden og planlægger noget nyt dramatisk noget.

> [Can you guess what I dream of and fancy as something beautiful? To settle at Øresund, between Copenhagen and Helsingør, at a free and open place where I can see all the vessels sailing far out to sea and coming in from far away. From here, I can't see it. Here, all straits are closed, in all the meanings of the word – and all the channels of understanding clogged. Oh, dear Brandes, one doesn't live idly out there in the great free and liberating cultural environment for 27 years. Here, inside, or rather up here next to the fjords, is my country of birth. But, but, but: where do I find my homeland? The sea draws me the most. By the way, I am here in my solitude, and am planning a new dramatic something.]

In the letter, Ibsen first grieves over his homecoming, and immediately after that, he mentions his intention to write a new play indicating that the only home imaginable is writing. According to Said, writing as the only possible home is the core message of the exile autobiography of the philosopher Theodor Adorno (1903–1969): "Adorno's reflections are informed," Said concludes, "by the belief that the only home truly available now, though fragile and vulnerable, is in writing." Hence, Said remarks, the mission of any exile is to oppose the strictly managed world where life is pressed into ready-made forms, prefabricated homes (147).

According to Ibsen, the loss of his Norwegian home is counterweighed by 27 years of writing in the freedom of exile. Bearing this in mind, one may be somewhat surprised, for example, by the Norwegian Wikipedia entry on Ibsen. Despite the allegedly open intention of this online encyclopedia, which is created and edited by volunteers, the entry still attests to the popular image of Ibsen. It is therefore conspicuous that the

61

paragraph "Fotturen i 1862" [Hiking in 1862], a description of Ibsen's walking trip in Norway, amounts to 500 words, and the one called "Tilbake i Norge" [Back to Norway] to nearly 500 words also, while Ibsen's "Utlendighet" [Life Abroad] amounts to a mere 200 words. Actually, rather than surprising, it is symptomatic that the entry stresses the Norwegianness of this national icon.

Migration literature should not, as Frank has rightly pointed out, be defined solely by the biography of the author. Yet, I would argue, an outspokenly transnational biography of a writer should not be ignored. In their own lives as migrants and as writers, Ibsen, Strindberg, and Andersen before them, challenged the nation state and the unitary community – both in the ways they employ the stranger in their writings and in their emphasis on the dialogical nature of their historical experience.[10]

Works Cited

Andersen, Hans Christian. "Ole Lukøie." *H. C. Andersens eventyr*, vol. 1. Ed. Erik Dal. Copenhagen: Hans Reitzels, 1963.

Andersen, Hans Christian. Letter to Henriette Hanck, 22 August 1841. Available online: https://andersen.sdu.dk/brevbase/brev.html?bid=2172. Accessed 11 March 2020.

Bakhtin, Mikhail. *Problems of Dostoevsky's Poetics*. Minneapolis: University of Minnesota Press, 1984.

Biemann, Asher D. et. al. "Introduction." *Spiritual Homelands: The Cultural Experience of Exile, Place and Displacement among Jews and Others*. Eds. Asher D. Biemann et al. Berlin and Boston: Walter de Gruyter, 2019. 1–10.

Brandes, Georg. "Henrik Ibsen og hans Skole i Tyskland." *Tilskueren* 7 (1890): 423–450.

Collin, Edvard. Letter to Jonna Stampe, 8 March 1878. Available online: https://andersen.sdu.dk/brevbase/brev.html?bid=21540. Accessed 11 March 2020.

Frank, Søren. "Hvad er migrationslitteratur." *Kritik* 45.203 (2012): 2–10.

Frank, Søren. *Migration and Literature: Günter Grass, Milan Kundera, Salman Rushdie, and Jan Kjærstad*. New York: Palgrave Macmillan, 2008.

Gáborová, Margita. "Strindbergs Dramatik in Bratislava (Pressburg) auf Deutsch." *Acta Universitatis Carolinae – Philologica* 3 (2019): 63–69.

Habermas, Jürgen. *Strukturwandel der Öffentlichkeit: Untersuchungen zu einer Kategorie der bürgerlichen Gesellschaft*. Berlin: Luchterhand, 1969.

Hansen, Tor Ivar. "Et forsøk til en bokhistorisk tilnærming til skandinavismen." *Skandinavismen: Vision og virkning*. Odense: Syddansk Universitetsforlag, 2018.

Hanssen, Jens-Morten. *Ibsen on the German Stage 1876–1918: A Quantitative Study*. Tübingen: Narr Francke Attempo, 2018.

"Henrik Ibsen." *Wikipedia*. Availabe online: https://no.wikipedia.org/wiki/Henrik_Ibsen. Accessed 11 March 2020.

Ibsen, Henrik. Letter to Det norske Theater, 16 May 1852. Available online: https://www.ibsen.uio.no/BREV_1844-1871ht|B18520516NTB.xhtml. Accessed 11 March 2020.

Ibsen, Henrik. Letter to Emil Stang, 11 December 1889. Available online http://www.edd.uio.no/cocoon/ibsen/BREV_1880-1889ht%7CB18891211ESta.xhtml. Accessed 11 March 2020.

---

[10] This work was supported by the European Regional Development Fund project "Creativity and Adaptability as Conditions of the Success of Europe in an Interrelated World" (reg. no.: CZ.02.1.01/0.0/0.0/16_019/0000734).

Ibsen, Henrik. Letter to Georg Brandes, 17 February 1871. https://www.ibsen.uio.no/BREV_1844 -1871ht|B18710217GB.xhtml. Accessed 11 March 2020.

Ibsen, Henrik. Letter to Georg Brandes, 23 July 1872 b. Available online: https://www.ibsen.uio .no/BREV_1871-1879ht|B18720723GB.xhtml. Accessed 11 March 2020.

Ibsen, Henrik. Letter to Georg Brandes, 3 January 1882. Available online: https://www.ibsen.uio .no/BREV_1880-1889ht|B18820103GB.xhtml. Accessed 8 April 2020.

Ibsen, Henrik. Letter to Georg Brandes, 3 June 1897. Available online: https://www.ibsen.uio.no /BREV_1890-1905ht|B18970603GB.xhtml. Accessed 11 March 2020.

Ibsen, Henrik. Letter to Georg Brandes, 4 April 1872 a. Available online: https://www.ibsen.uio .no/BREV_1871-1879ht%7CB18720404GB.xhtml. Accessed 5 March 2020.

Ibsen, Henrik. Letter to Kirke- og Undervisningsdepartementet, 16 February 1869. Available online: http://www.edd.uio.no/cocoon/ibsen01_01/BREV_1844-1871ht|B18690216Kdep .xhtml. Accessed 11 March 2020.

Ibsen, Henrik. Letter to Magdalene Thoresen, 15 October 1867. Available online: https://www .ibsen.uio.no/BREV_1844-1871ht%7CB18671015MT.xhtml. Accessed 5 March 2020.

Ibsen, Henrik. Letter to Magdalene Thoresen, 3 December 1865. Available online: https://www .ibsen.uio.no/BREV_1844-1871ht%7CB18651203MT.xhtml. Accessed 11 March 2020.

Ibsen, Henrik. Letter to Marcus Grønvald, 9 March 1879. Available online: https://www.ibsen.uio .no/BREV_1871-1879ht%7CB18790309MG.xhtml. Accessed 11 March 2020.

Ibsen, Henrik. Letter to Michael Birkeland, 5 October 1866. Available online: https://www.ibsen .uio.no/BREV_1844-1871ht|B18661005MB.xhtml. Accessed 11 March 2020.

Ibsen, Henrik. Letter to Peter Friedrich Siebold, 3 February 1870 b. Available online: https://www .ibsen.uio.no/BREV_1844-1871ht%7CB18700203PFS.xhtml. Accessed 11 March 2020.

Ibsen, Henrik. Letter to Peter Hansen, 28 October 1870 a. Available online: https://www.ibsen.uio .no/BREV_1844-1871ht|B18701028PHa.xhtml. Accessed 11 March 2020.

Keyssar, Helene. "Drama and the Dialogic Imagination: *The Heidi Chronicles* and *Fefu and Her Friends*." *Modern Drama* 34.1 (1991): 88–106.

Neubauer, John. "Bakhtin versus Lukács: Inscriptions of Homelessness in Theories of the Novel." *Exile and Creativity: Signposts, Travelers, Outsiders, Backward Glances*. Edited by Susan Rubin Suleiman. Durham and London: Duke University Press, 1998. 263–280.

Said, Edward. "Introduction: Criticism and Exile." *Reflections on Exile and Other Essays*. Cambridge, MA, and London: Harvard University Press, 2000. xi–xxxv.

Said, Edward. "Reflections on Exile." *Reflections on Exile and Other Essays*. Cambridge, Mass, and London: Harvard University Press, 2000. 137–149.

Seyhan, Azade. *Writing Outside the Nation*. Princeton and Oxford: Princeton University Press, 2001.

Strindberg, August. "Le Plaidoyer d'un fou." *August Strindbergs Samlade Verk*. Vol. 25. Stockholm: Norstedts, 1999. 264–517.

Strindberg, August. Letter to Alexander Kielland, 3 October 1881. Available online: https:// litteraturbanken.se/f%C3%B6rfattare/StrindbergA/titlar/StrindbergsBrev2/sida/283/faksimil . Accessed 11 March 2020.

Strindberg, August. Letter to Birger Mörner, 26 January 1893. Available online: https://litteratur banken.se/f%C3%B6rfattare/StrindbergA/titlar/StrindbergsBrev9/sida/123/faksimil. Accessed 11 March 2020.

Strindberg, August. Letter to Émile Zola, 26 August 1887. Available online: https://litteraturbanken.se /f%C3%B6rfattare/StrindbergA/titlar/StrindbergsBrev6/sida/262/faksimil. Accessed 11 March 2020.

Ystad, Vigdis. "Innledning til Et dukkehjem." Available online: https://www.ibsen.uio.no/DRINNL _Du|intro_background.xhtml. Accessed 17 March 2020.

63

4. Emigration and the Image of the USA in Henrik Ibsen's *Samfundets støtter* (*Pillars of Society*)

Martin Humpál

Henrik Ibsen's 1877 play *Samfundets støtter* (or *Pillars of Society*, as it is usually trans-lated into English)[1] is the first in a series of the author's last twelve dramas that many critics consider to be a coherent whole. In Norwegian they are called 'samfunnsdramaer' and in English they are known as 'dramas of contemporary life.' To what extent it makes sense to speak of these twelve plays as of a coherent whole, is a matter of dispute. None-theless, it is obvious that, beginning with *Pillars of Society*, Ibsen began to employ his new-found method of realist representation and, at the same time, to focus on current social problems. The play is thus clearly influenced by the Danish critic Georg Brandes's famous call for a literature that would critically examine the problems of contemporary society, or, as he worded it in his famous precept, "at sette problemer under debatt" ("to set up problems for debate").[2] The first Norwegian writer who took up this challenge was Bjørnstjerne Bjørnson whose two plays from 1875, *Redaktøren* (*The Editor*) and *En Fallit* (*The Bankrupt*), represent the beginning of realist drama in Norway. With *Pillars of Society* Ibsen evidently wanted to follow suit.

The play was an international breakthrough for Ibsen. It was enthusiastically received in Germany and was thus the first step on the author's journey to world fame.[3] It was frequently staged until the end of the 19th and well into the 20th century. However, by degrees it became one of the less performed Ibsen plays.[4] In hindsight it is one of the weaker pieces of Ibsen's *oeuvre*, especially because of its psychologically implausible ending: the main character, an utterly corrupt politician, not only confesses his sins but also fully understands what he has done wrong and what the right things to do are. Because of this entire about-face in the protagonist's behavior, most theatergoers nowa-days have difficulty in accepting the drama as being true to life. The ending is, in a way, typically Bjørnsonian, in the sense that the idealistic closure is incongruous with the rest of the play.

Nonetheless, *Pillars of Society* was part of world drama for several decades, and it has several ingredients that are characteristic of Ibsen's plays of contemporary life, e.g., criticism of corruption, false morals, social hypocrisy, women's inequality, as well as

---

[1] Another common way of translating the title is *The Pillars of the Community*.
[2] It should be pointed out that Georg Brandes liked *Pillars of Society*. See, e.g., Fulsås and Rem 79.
[3] See, e.g., Ferguson 238-239 and Fulsås and Rem 73.
[4] See, e.g., Cardullo 43.

emphasis on the necessity of truth and freedom. In this chapter, I will point out that such topics in *Pillars of Society* are interconnected with one aspect which, when considered within the entire body of Ibsen's last twelve plays, is quite unusual: the theme of emigration to the USA. In none of the remaining eleven dramas does it play such an important role as in *Pillars of Society*.

The story takes place in a small Norwegian coastal town, and it is relatively obvious that Ibsen uses this town as a microcosm of Norway as a whole. The majority of characters that appear in the play are members of bourgeois families, and the main feature of their behavior is an all-pervasive hypocrisy: no matter how immoral their lives may be behind the facade, the ultimate imperative of their community is to keep up appearances at all costs and to follow conventional moral codes. In this regard, *Pillars of Society* is a truly scathing satire: almost none of the local characters escapes Ibsen's mocking perspective. The play also portrays the community as extremely closed-minded and xenophobic. The townspeople are convinced that only their own community, or Norwegian society, is the best and morally purest and it is therefore necessary to protect it from different ways of life and thinking that occasionally intrude upon it from elsewhere. It is in this context that the United States of America and migration to the USA play an important role.

The first disdainful remarks about Americans appear almost immediately after the play begins. There is an American ship called *Indian Girl* in the local shipyard, and the local workers are supposed to repair it. The sailors from *Indian Girl* are repeatedly described with crude words: "udskud af menneskeheden" (14) ["scum of the earth" (17)], "dette ryggesløse pak" (68) ["depraved" – "that pack of animals" (44)], and even "udyr" (122, 166) ["wild animals" (72)].[5] Yet the townspeople's contempt is not limited to American sailors, they extend it to include all Americans:

ADJUNKT RØRLUND. Nå, slige udskud af menneskeheden vil jeg sletikke tale om. Men selv i de højere kredse, – hvorledes står det til *der*? Tvivl og gærende uro på alle kanter; ufred i sindene og usikkerhed i alle forholde. Hvorledes er ikke familjelivet undergravet derude? Hvorledes ytrer sig ikke frække omstyrtningslyster lige over for de alvorligste sandheder? (14–15)

[RØRLUND: Such scum of the earth [i.e., the sailors] I wouldn't even waste my breath on. But even in higher circles—what do you find *there*? Doubt and distraction on every side; troubled minds and unstable relationships. How family life's been undermined out there! How arrogantly they delight in perverting the most sacred truths! (17)]

Sometimes such remarks concern not only the United States but other big countries, or the so-called great world, in general: "ADJUNKT RØRLUND: Denne forgyldte og sminkede yderside, som de store samfund bærer tilskue, – hvad dølger den egentlig? Hulhed og rådenskab, om jeg så må sige. Ingen moralsk grundvold under fødderne" (14) ["RØRLUND: Those gilded, glittering facades that the great societies hold up—what

---

5   All quotes from the original come from the critical edition of *Henrik Ibsens skrifter*. For the English versions of the quotes, I have used Rolf Fjelde's translation of *Pillars of Society*, included in Ibsen's *Complete Major Prose Plays*. Here I should mention that Fjelde's rendering of the expression "dette ryggesløse pak" unfortunately does not include the translation of the adjective "ryggesløs," which means "depraved," "dissolute."

do they actually hide? Emptiness and corruption—if you ask me. No moral foundation underfoot" (17).] None of the big countries is mentioned concretely, yet the context often makes the reader or spectator think mostly of the USA.

The main character, Karsten Bernick, is a corrupt shipowner and politician who makes various shady deals, but almost no one seems to know about them, because on the surface he is morally impeccable. In fact, he is praised by everyone as the main guardian of morality in town and, at the same time, as someone who works tirelessly for the town's well-being: he is known to have invested in big projects that have improved the inhabitants' standard of living in several respects. He also regularly gives money to charity and other good causes. He even presents himself as someone who sacrifices himself for higher goals, that is, "til samfundets beste" (137) ["for the good of the community" (80)]. However, all of this is nothing but duplicity. In reality, he is an unscrupulous businessman who is only interested in what benefits him. He often behaves in an unethical way, and it becomes obvious that he is capable of crimes. As it turns out in the course of the play, he is determined to send his brother-in-law to certain death.

Ibsen incorporated into *Pillars of Society* one of the issues that were widely discussed in the 1870s: the so-called "floating coffins." Zucker has described it as follows:

> Several cases came to light at this time of ruthlessly greedy owners of dockyards who repaired ships in a very slipshod fashion, insured them heavily, and then sent them out to sea, causing the death of the crew in the first storm that came along. The subject of the "floating coffins" caused a great deal of discussing in the British Parliament, in the Norwegian press, and even in mass meetings in Christiania. (147)

Although the U.S. shipowners were not the only perpetrators in this regard, in Ibsen's drama it is mainly Americans who are guilty of such horrible crimes:

Fuldmægtig Krap kommer med breve og aviser fra højre.

FULDMÆGTIG KRAP
Udenrigsposten, herr konsul; – og et telegram fra New-York.
KONSUL BERNICK *tager det*
Ah, fra rederiet for «Indian Girl.» […]
KONSUL BERNICK *der har læst telegrammet*
Nej, dette er virkelig ægte amerikansk! Rentud oprørende –
FRU BERNICK
Gud, Karsten, hvad er det?
KONSUL BERNICK
Se der, herr Krap; læs!
FULDMÆGTIG KRAP *læser*
«Gør mindst muligt af reparationen; send «Indian Girl» over så snart flydefærdig; god årstid; svømmer i nødsfald på lasten.» Nå, det må jeg sige –
KONSUL BERNICK
Svømmer på lasten! De herrer ved godt at med den last går skibet tilbunds som en sten, dersom der tilstøder noget.
ADJUNKT RØRLUND
Ja, der ser man hvorledes det står til i disse lovpriste store samfund.

KONSUL BERNICK

Det har De ret i; ingen agt for menneskeliv engang, så snart fordelen kommer med i spillet.
[...]

KONSUL BERNICK *ser igen i telegrammet*

Atten menneskeliv tager de herrer ikke i betænkning at sætte på spil – [...] Ja, jeg gad se den reder hos os, som kunde bekvemme sig til sligt! Ikke *en*, ikke en eneste *en* – (46–49)

[(KRAP *enters from the right, carrying letters and newspapers.*)

KRAP. The foreign mail, Mr. Bernick—and a telegram from New York.
BERNICK *(taking it)*. Ah, from the owners of the *Indian Girl.*
[...]
BERNICK *(who has read the telegram)*. Well, how typically American! Absolutely disgusting!
MRS. BERNICK. Goodness, Karsten, what is it?
BERNICK. Look at that, Mr. Krap. Read it!
KRAP *(reading)*. "Do least possible repairs. Send *Indian Girl* over soon as seaworthy. Profitable season. Cargo will float her in emergency." Well, I must say—
BERNICK. "Cargo will float her!" Those men know very well, with that cargo she'd go down like a stone if anything happened.
RØRLUND. Yes, there we see what goes on in these celebrated great societies.
BERNICK. You're right. No concern for human life the moment there's profit involved.
[...]
BERNICK *(glancing again at the telegram)*. Those gentlemen don't hesitate a moment to risk eighteen human lives – [...] I'd like to see the shipowner among us who could stoop to anything like this! Not *one,* not a single *one* –] (33–34)

Despite of what Bernick says here, he himself makes sure that the ship *Indian Girl* receives only minimum repairs and is sent out to sea. What is worse, the reason for this is that he wants his brother-in-law Johan to die. Johan could potentially reveal a secret from the past that could destroy Bernick's career, and Bernick knows that Johan has decided to return to the USA on *Indian Girl.*

This is the most terrible example of how Bernick fails to practice what he preaches. Another example of his duplicity is that now and then he actually *does* want to behave like an American, if it suits his purpose. In the following passage, this relates, once again, to his plan to have his brother-in-law killed. Bernick tries to convince himself that letting Johan die is justifiable, and therefore he discusses his plan in a veiled manner with Rørlund, speaking of a hypothetical case of building a railroad and sacrificing one of the workers:

KONSUL BERNICK

Ja, men nu sætter jeg et særligt tilfælde. Jeg sætter, der fandtes et borehul, som skulde sprænges på et farligt sted; men uden at dette borehul sprænges, vil ikke jernbanen kunne komme istand. Jeg sætter, ingeniøren ved, det vil koste livet for den arbejder, som skal tænde minen; men tændes må den, og det er ingeniørens pligt at sende en arbejder hen for at gøre det.

ADJUNKT RØRLUND

Hm –

KONSUL BERNICK

Jeg ved, hvad De vil sige. Det vilde være stort, om ingeniøren selv tog lunten og gik hen og tændte borehullet. Men sligt gør man ikke. Han må altså ofre en arbejder.

ADJUNKT RØRLUND

Det vilde aldrig nogen ingeniør gøre hos os.

KONSUL BERNICK

Ingen ingeniør i de store lande vilde betænke sig på at gøre det.

ADJUNKT RØRLUND

I de store lande? Nej, det tror jeg nok. I hine fordærvede og samvittighedsløse samfund –

KONSUL BERNICK

Å, der er adskilligt godt ved *de* samfund.

ADJUNKT RØRLUND

Og det kan De sige, De, som selv –?

KONSUL BERNICK

I de store samfund har man dog plads til at fremme et gavnligt foretagende; der har man mod til at ofre noget for en stor sag; men her snevres man ind af alskens smålige hensyn og betænkeligheder.

ADJUNKT RØRLUND

Er et menneskeliv et småligt hensyn?

KONSUL BERNICK

Når dette menneskeliv står som en trusel imod tusenders velfærd.

ADJUNKT RØRLUND

Men De opstiller jo rent utænkelige tilfælder, herr konsul! Jeg forstår Dem slet ikke idag. Og så viser De hen til de store samfund. Ja, derude, – hvad gælder et menneskeliv der? Der regner man med menneskeliv som med kapitaler. Men *vi* står dog på et ganske andet moralsk standpunkt, skulde jeg mene. Se til vor hæderlige skibsrederstand! Nævn en eneste reder her hos os, som for ussel vinding vilde ofre et menneskeliv! Og tænk så på hine skurke i de store samfund, som for fordelens skyld bortfragter det ene usødygtige skib efter det andet –

KONSUL BERNICK

Jeg taler ikke om usødygtige skibe!

ADJUNKT RØRLUND

Men jeg taler om dem, herr konsul (152–154).

[BERNICK. But now, take a specific example. Suppose there's a charge of explosives that has to be set off at a particularly dangerous spot; but unless it's detonated, the railroad can never be built. Suppose the engineer knows it will cost the life of the man that lights the fuse; but it has to be done, and it's the engineer's duty to send a workman out to do it.

RØRLUND. Hm—

BERNICK. I know what you'll say. The great thing would be for the engineer himself to take the match and go and light the fuse. But people don't do such things. So he has to sacrifice a workman.

RØRLUND. No engineer here would ever do that.

BERNICK. No engineer in one of the larger countries would give it a second thought.

RØRLUND. In the larger countries? No, I don't doubt it. In those decadent, unscrupulous societies—

BERNICK. Oh, there's a lot that's good in those societies.

RØRLUND. And you can say that? You, who yourself—?

BERNICK. In large societies you at least have room to evolve a project on a generous scale. They have the courage to sacrifice for a great cause; but here, one's hobbled by all kinds of trivial issues and restrictions.

RØRLUND. Is human life a trivial issue?

BERNICK. When that human life is an obstacle to the welfare of thousands.

RØRLUND. But you're posing quite hypothetical situations, Mr. Bernick! I don't understand you at all today. And then harping on these big societies. Yes, out there—what's a human life worth to them? They rate human life as so much capital. But to my mind, we take a different moral position completely. Look at our foremost shipping magnates. You can't name a single one of them who'd sacrifice a human life for some paltry profit! And then think of those scoundrels in the larger countries who, for the sake of their dividends, send out one unseaworthy ship after another—

BERNICK. I'm not talking about unseaworthy ships!

RØRLUND. But I'm talking about them, Mr. Bernick. (87–88)]

The conviction of the locals that their community is the best and morally superior to communities in other countries creates an extremely oppressive milieu in *Pillars of Society*, one for which Aksel Sandemose's term "Janteloven" is perfectly appropriate. Therefore it is not surprising that some individuals in the play dream of escaping to the USA. In fact, two characters have already escaped: Lona Hessel, whom Bernick once loved, but he eventually married her younger half-sister Betty for money (105 [63]), and Johan Tønnesen, Betty's younger brother. Several years ago, Lona and Johan went to the USA, each at a different point in time, and Lona took care of Johan throughout their years in the USA, as if he were her own son.

In the first act, Lona and Johan pay an unexpected visit to the town, and their presence there and in Bernick's house contributes substantially to the plot's development.[6] However, these two characters also play another, symbolic, role. It is obvious that Ibsen has made Lona and Johan the most positive characters of the entire drama. I could enumerate many of their good qualities, but I will mention only two, because they co-create the final message of the play. Lona and Johan love truth and freedom, and Lona utters the final sentence of *Pillars of Society*: "sandhedens og frihedens ånd, – *det* er samfundets støtter" (208) ["the spirit of truth and the spirit of freedom—*those* are the pillars of society" (118)].

The merciless pressure of conventions in Norway does not allow individuals to be themselves. Instead, they are forced to adjust to the unwritten rules of behavior. This affects women even more strongly than men. Lona is a feminist, so it is no wonder that she eventually emigrated to the USA where she found more freedom as a woman; however, Johan also has learned some lessons about women's equality to men in America. When Bernick tells him that his sister Marta as a single woman has almost no money, the conversation continues as follows:

---

[6] At the time when Ibsen wrote the play, the Norwegian-American who has returned to Norway from the USA was a common character-type in Norwegian literature; see Mannsåker 236.

JOHAN TØNNESEN
Den stakkers Marta!
KONSUL BERNICK
Stakkers? Hvorfor det? Du tror da vel ikke at jeg lader hende savne noget? Å nej, det tør jeg dog sige, at jeg er en god broder. Hun bor naturligvis sammen med os og spiser ved vort bord; lærerinde-gagen kan hun rundeligt klæde sig for, og et enligt fruentimmer, – hvad skal hun med mere?
JOHAN TØNNESEN
Hm; på den vis tænker vi ikke i Amerika.
KONSUL BERNICK
Nej, det tror jeg nok; i et opagiteret samfund, som det amerikanske. Men her i vor lille kreds, hvor, Gud ske lov, fordærvelsen til dato ialfald ikke har fåt indpas, her nøjes kvinderne med at indtage en sømmelig om end beskeden stilling (93).

[JOHAN. Poor Martha!
BERNICK. Poor? Why? You don't think I'd let her want for anything? Oh no, I dare say I've been a good brother to her. She lives with us here, of course, and eats at our table. Her teacher's salary keeps her nicely in clothes; and as a single woman—what more does she need?
JOHAN. Hm. That isn't the way we think in America.
BERNICK. No, I suppose not—in a high-pressure society like that. But here in our little community, where up to now, thank God, corruption hasn't made any inroads, women are content to assume a decent, modest role in life. (57)]

To sum up, one can say that Ibsen uses the USA as a counter-image to what Norwegian society represents. In fact, the play is quite simplistic in this concrete regard: almost everything Norwegian is negative, and almost everything American is positive,[7] no matter how cliché-ridden it is.[8] Likewise, Norwegian emigrants to America are shown as more noble people than most of those who stay in Norway and adjust to the pressure of the local conventions and hypocrisy.

To conclude, I would like to emphasize what Ibsen implies about identity in relation to emigration. While many people assume that emigrants must end up with a split identity, Ibsen shows something else in *Pillars of Society*. He indicates that in a country (in this case in the USA) where one does not need to conform to conventions and false morals as strongly as in Norway, people can be, or can become, or can remain, true to themselves. In contrast, in Norway, as Ibsen portrays it in this play, everyone has to lead a life of duplicity and hypocrisy, and this gives him or her a split personality. This is confirmed toward the end of the drama. After Bernick confesses what he has done wrong,

---

[7] Guldal offers a very subtle reading of *Pillars of Society* and argues that, despite its overall positive image of America, the play still reveals Ibsen's prejudices against the U.S.A. While Guldal may be right on a few points, some of his statements are, in my opinion, exaggerated, such as this one: "Ibsen *is going out of his way to* represent them [the American sailors] negatively" (301; my emphasis).

[8] Here are some examples of the clichéd images of the U.S.A.: "FRØKEN BERNICK Derude må det være skønt; en større himmel; skyerne går højere end her, en friere luft svaler over menneskenes hoveder" (173) ["MARTHA BERNICK. It must be beautiful there—the sky wider, the clouds higher than here, and the air more free overhead—" (98)]; "FRØKEN BERNICK Der havde han færdedes ude i det blanke dirrende solskin og suget ungdom og sundhed af hvert luftdrag;" (176) ["MARTHA BERNICK. Over there he'd been thriving in the bright, vibrant sunlight, drinking in youth and health with every breath" (100)].

he feels enormously relieved, because he no longer needs to lead a double life, and Lona comments on it with a sentence concerning his identity:

KONSUL BERNICK
[…] Har jeg end ikke altid efterstræbt pengefordel, så er jeg mig ialfald dog nu bevidst, at et begær og en higen efter magt, indflydelse, anseelse, har været drivkraften i de fleste af mine handlinger.
[…]
Mine medborgere, jeg vil ud af usandheden; den har været nær ved at forgifte hver eneste trævl i mig. De skal vide alt. *Jeg* var for femten år siden den skyldige.
[…]
FRØKEN HESSEL
Der vandt du endelig dig selv! (198–202)

[BERNICK. […] Even if I haven't always gone after profit, nonetheless I'm aware now that a hunger and a craving after power, status and influence has been the driving force behind most of my actions.
[…]
My friends and neighbors, I'm through with lies; they've come close to poisoning every fiber of my being. I'll tell you everything. Fifteen years ago, *I* was the guilty one.
[…]
LONA. At last, you've found yourself!] (112–114)

The same message concerning identity follows in what Bernick at this point says to his thirteen-year-old son Olaf who originally wanted to escape to the USA, because he did not like it at home:

KONSUL BERNICK
[…] Herefter skal du få lov til at vokse op, ikke som arvetager til *min* livsgerning, men som den, der selv har en livsgerning ivente.
OLAF
Og får jeg også lov til at blive, hvad jeg vil?
KONSUL BERNICK
Ja, det får du.
OLAF
Tak. Så vil jeg ikke blive samfundets støtte.
KONSUL BERNICK
Så? Hvorfor ikke det?
OLAF
Nej, for jeg tror, det må være så kedeligt.
KONSUL BERNICK
Du skal blive dig selv, Olaf; så får resten gå, som det kan. (205–206)

[BERNICK: From now on you'll have leave to grow up, not as the executor of *my* lifework, but for the lifework that will be your own.
OLAF. And will I also have leave to be what I want?

71

BERNICK. Yes.
OLAF. Thank you. Then I don't want to be a pillar of society.
BERNICK. Oh, why not?
OLAF. Because I think it must be so boring.
BERNICK. You just be yourself, Olaf. It'll all follow from that – (116)]

As I have indicated at the beginning, it is hard to believe that someone like Bernick would make such a total about-face and begin to give wise advice to others, as the main character does at the end of the play. One thing seems rather clear, though: Ibsen's dislike of contemporary Norwegian society was so strong that he would use any instrument available in order to criticize it. Thus, despite the fact that he knew very little about the USA and was little interested in it, in *Pillars of Society* he confronted his compatriots with the following message: it is not emigration that will destroy your soul, it is succumbing to the pressure of conventions and false morals in Norway.[9]

Works Cited

Cardullo, Robert J. "The Pillar of Ibsenian Drama: Henrik Ibsen and *Pillars of Society*, Reconsidered." *Moderna språk* 105.1 (2011): 43–57.

Ferguson, Robert. *Henrik Ibsen. Mellom evne og higen*. Trans. Bjørn Alex Herrman. Oslo: Cappelen, 1996.

Fulsås, Narve and Rem, Tore. *Ibsen, Scandinavia and the Making of a World Drama*. Cambridge: Cambridge University Press, 2018.

Gulddal, Jesper. "Contrasting Visions: Perceptions of America in Henrik Ibsen's *Pillars of Society*." *Nineteenth-Century Contexts* 34 (2012): 289–304.

Ibsen, Henrik. *Pillars of Society*. In *The Complete Major Prose Plays*. Trans. and introduced by Rolf Fjelde. New York: Plume, 1978. 9–118.

Ibsen, Henrik. *Samfundets støtter. Et dukkehjem. Gengangere. En folkefiende*. Ed. Vigdis Ystad et al. *Henrik Ibsens skrifter*, vol. 7. Oslo: Aschehoug, 2008.

Mannsåker, Jørund. *Emigrasjon og dikting: Utvandringa til Nord-Amerika i norsk skjønnlitteratur*. Oslo: Det Norske Samlaget, 1971.

Zucker, A. E. *Ibsen the Master Builder*. New York: Henry Holt, 1929.

9   This work was supported by the European Regional Development Fund-project "Creativity and Adaptability as Conditions of the Success of Europe in an Interrelated World" (No. CZ.02.1.01/0.0/0.0/16_019/000 0734).

5. Christer Kihlman's Autobiography *Alla mina söner* (*All My Sons*) in the Perspective of *Orientalism* by Edward W. Said

Jan Dlask

Christer Kihlman and the Argentina Books

The Finland-Swedish author Christer Kihlman (1930–2021) became famous after his socially committed books were published during the 1960s and 1970s.[1] They criticised the Finland-Swedish upper-class, of which Kihlman himself was a member. Nevertheless, at the beginning of the 1980s Kihlman wrote two quite different texts, called the Argentina or South America books: *Alla mina söner* (1980, henceforth referred to as *AMS*; translated as *All My Sons*, 1984) and *Livsdrömmen rena* (1982, Life's Pure Dream). Both are first-person autobiographies, based on the author's own experience from the end of the 1970s and the beginning of the 1980s when he stayed in South America on several occasions, especially in Buenos Aires and other parts of Argentina.

For more than one reason, the reception of these books was not very positive (for more see Carlson, "Poikarakkauden houkutus" 16; Carlson, *Paikantuneita haluja* 97–98, 112–114; Westö – Kihlman 237–238, 249). Consequently, for a few decades even literary scholars more or less avoided analysing them. In Alhoniemi's monograph on Christer Kihlman and his father Bertel (1989), not even one of the writer's four prose books published after *Dyre prins* (1975; translated as *Sweet Prince*) are included.[2] On the other hand, in his essay collection on Kihlman's works Toiviainen mentions the South America books but critically, as had some of their former reviewers (6, 77–84, 88, 98, 99).

Only ten years later, Kuhalampi ("Muiden kapina") analysed the problem of power and otherness in the Argentina books. Their renaissance in literary research followed. In the new millennium Carlson ("Poikarakkauden houkutus") examined how various spaces and places configure the representations of sexual identity in Kihlman's *AMS*. Also two chapters of his doctoral thesis (*Paikantuneita haluja*) which are devoted to six of Kihlman's books are only based on the two Argentina books, continuing Carlson's interest in the relation between sexuality and space in Kihlman's *oeuvre*. The author of

---

[1] *Se upp Salige!* (1960; Look Out, You Blessed!); *Den blå modern* (1963; trans. *The Blue Mother*); *Madeleine* (1965); *Människan som skalv: En bok om det oväsentliga* (1971; The Human Who Trembled: A Book about the Inessential).

[2] The others are *På drift i förlustens landskap* (1986; Drifting amidst the Scenery of Loss) and *Gerdt Bladhs undergång* (1987; trans. *The Downfall of Gerdt Bladh*).

this study dealt with the question of socially committed genre in the case of Kihlman's *AMS* (see Dlask).

Nevertheless, an interpretation of Kihlman's 1980 book in the sense that the Finnish literary scholar Pekka Tarkka proposed already in 1990 has never been done. Tarkka writes:

[Kihlman vill] visa fram mötet mellan två olika världar och två olika värdesystem. Han beskriver sitt eget möte, som medelålders europeisk och 'rik' intellektuell, med en ung, fattig, argentinsk homosexuell prostituerad. (11)

[Kihlman wants to show the meeting between two different worlds and two different systems of values. He describes his own meeting, as a middle-aged European and 'rich' intellectual, with a young and poor Argentinian homosexual prostitute.]

Europe (or the European North, Finland, and sometimes also Sweden) is thus represented by the well-educated author himself, aged between forty and fifty. Argentina (or the whole of Latin America) is represented by the barely educated boy named Juan, aged twenty. He is a former artist, a musician, singer, and guitar player, with whom the author falls in love.

In this way, the text could be seen as Kihlman's thorough analysis of dissimilarities between the two persons, their backgrounds, and the two countries, Argentina and Finland, or even broader entities. It seems that the only common ground for the two countries is the blue and white colour in their national flags: Finland as a part of Europe is an industrial land – Argentina is a developing one, and its economic situation is described in many ways in *AMS* as catastrophic. The society is cruel, the social gaps between the classes are enormous, people (inclusive of Juan) are without homes, jobs, money, and education. The dissimilarities are far from only geographical (e.g., climatic), national, economic, and social. They are also cultural, political, religious, linguistic, and temperamental. The differences manifest themselves on many levels: the Argentinian partiality for folk music, song and Tango, football, eating meals together and closer physical contact on the one hand, and the specificity of nakedness in Finnish saunas on the other hand; the Argentinian talkativeness, spontaneity, happiness, and wastefulness and the Finnish loneliness, melancholy, and spleen; the Argentinian Catholicism and Finnish Protestantism (sometimes atheism), characterised by the Catholic shyness and the Protestant mental speculation, both including some kind of dual morality; differences in language use (kinds of answers expected in Finland/Argentina, ways of swearing, ways to talk about feelings), and different approaches to suicide, mental disorders, and to life in general.

It must be stressed that the analysis in *AMS* is the author's, the intellectual Kihlman's – and although Juan tends to represent the whole country of Argentina for him (*AMS* 39), a scholar can hardly interpret him on so general a level. Therefore, both the author and Juan will be discussed first of all as individuals having their own individual experience, whatever background or entity they may represent.

Edward W. Said's *Orientalism*

This broad spectrum of identities, mentalities and values, often perceived in opposition to each other, can be seen in the theoretical-methodological frame of the 1978 book *Orientalism* by Edward W. Said. In it, the author developed the idea of "orientalism" to define how the West, especially Great Britain, France, and the USA historically patronized representations of "the East," "the Orient," that is claimed to be an imaginative projection of the West. Said described a gradual constitution of the discourse concerning the Orient as a complex structure in a historical relation to the economic and political expansion of Europeans to the East. The key element in it is, according to Said, the artificially created and maintained opposing characters of both worlds – the primitive and exotic East vs. the rational and civilized West. The book played a key role in forming and developing post-colonial studies, and was re-published several times as well as translated into more than thirty languages. In this article, the focus is on the ways the *Oriental* people and peoples were viewed by the West, the *Orientalists*, as described by Said. They were stamped with an otherness that was constitutive and of an essentialist character; they were seen as thinking and behaving in a manner opposite to Europeans – not quite as human as Europeans – strange, different, eccentric, suspect, primitive, backward, and passive (Said, passim; see also below). These and other Oriental characteristics were viewed as lower in the West, and if not directly lower, then too exotic.

As mentioned, for Said "the East" means the societies and peoples who inhabit the "Orient," the places of Asia, North Africa and the Middle East. The question is thus whether this concept is also suitable for South America. "The Orient" consists of nations having most often their own original languages and religion (typically, Arabic and Islam). The origin of South American inhabitants is mostly European – although Juan is Creole, since his grandmother was Indian and his grandfather came to Argentina from Sicily at the end of the 19th century (*AMS* 80–81). Furthermore, Argentina's official language – Spanish – and major religion – Catholicism – both originate from Europe. The South American countries also gained their independence much earlier than the "Oriental" countries, during the first decades of the 19th century (Argentina in 1816).

Regardless of these dissimilarities, the colonial past is common both for the Orient and South America. A colonial perspective is proposed also by Carlson (see above):

Alla mina söneria voisi pitää niiden kokemusten representaatioina, joiden varassa toisen kohtaamisen vaikeudet ja kolonialistisen alistuksen kysymykset nousevat esiin suomalaisessa kirjallisuudessa muutamia vuosia ennen jälkikoloniaalisen ajattelun läpimurtoa. (*Paikantuneita haluja* 117–118)

[*AMS* could be considered as representations of that experience, on which basis the difficulties of the other's meeting and the questions of the colonial subordination arise in Finnish literature several years before the breakthrough of postcolonial thinking.]

According to Carlson, the problem is thus relevant also for Finland, which has no historical background as a colonizer of overseas countries, and its literature. Nevertheless, Said's book (the first edition) and *AMS* were only published in an interval of two years, 1978 and 1980. When writing *AMS*, Kihlman was most probably not familiar with Said's concept; *Orientalism* was translated into the languages of Kihlman's fatherland later, to Swedish in 1993 and to Finnish in 2011, and neither Said nor *Orientalism* are mentioned in Mårten Westö's interview book with Kihlman, mapping his life and career as writer and intellectual (see Westö – Kihlman).

On the other hand, as Kihlman points out in *AMS*, Argentina was not the first developing country that he visited – during the 1970s he stayed in several of them. Very near the beginning of the text, the author pledges to himself that this time in Argentina he is not going to act in the same way as he had in the past, like a sentimental upper-class Chekhov character, promising help to poor people in the Third World and forgetting about them when having to return home (53–54).

The main question is this: Are there any parallels between Kihlman's approach to Latin America and Said's theories in *Orientalism*?

Many Prejudices...

As mentioned, the text of *AMS* tells the author's autobiographical story. According to Carlson, the Lejeunian autobiographical pact is hard to question in the case of *AMS*: firstly, Kihlman has several times referred to this work as clearly autobiographical, both in newspaper interviews and in Mårten Westö's book; secondly, many stylistic and structural devices emphasize the autobiographical character of the work (*Paikantuneita haluja* 103). In my interpretation the book is read as autobiographical as well: it is assumed that the narrator is Christer Kihlman, the author. I have chosen this strategy since it enables us to interpret *AMS* not only as pure *belles-lettres*, but also in the broader context of the author's entire thought world; this does not imply that the reading of *AMS* as a fictive work would be impossible.[3]

Kihlman's love story concerns the young Juan: the two men's relationship is referred to not only as a liaison but also as a friendship or a father-son relationship (in both directions) (cf. the title; *AMS* 34). In addition, both persons also have their own wives who are characters in the book.[4] Although *AMS* as such is officially written by Kihlman and although the narrative voice is also always his, it is pointed out several times that the book is to be considered as a joint project of the author and Juan, who thus becomes co-author of the book (see 70, 134, 195, 196). As a result of this strategy, the presentation of Juan's perspective plays a key role in some parts of the text;[5] this concerns, firstly, its

---

[3] The fact that the author acknowledges Juan's proper name as being Aldo (cf. the importance of names for Lejeunian autobiographical theory) and that he has omitted the sexual dimension of his and Juan/Aldo's relationship at Juan/Aldo's request (see Westö – Kihlman 227–254) can suggest that the autobiographical pact in the case of *AMS* is perhaps not completely unquestionable.

[4] Kihlman had already written about his own bisexuality (rather than homosexuality) in his 1971 book.

[5] The fact that the former main character ("master"; in this case the author of *AMS*) changes to a subordinate one in this way, can be seen as a hallmark of the postcolonial novel (Carlson, *Paikantuneita haluja* 103).

important *leitmotif*, Juan's experience as a homosexual prostitute (called a "taxi boy"), which he had been since he was fourteen years old after escaping to Buenos Aires from his small hometown of Chivilcoy. Secondly, it is the chapter about Juan's stay in Europe, where his view of the European North, Sweden, and Finland is described. The author and Juan meet altogether four times: besides Juan's visit to Europe, the author stays in Argentina three times as a tourist, getting to know the city of Buenos Aires, as well as the countryside.

At first sight, many of the characteristics that Said found from a Western point of view as typically Oriental correspond to the way in which Kihlman in some cases views the Argentinians. As a young Argentinian artist, Juan is already sufficiently exotic. One of the first commentaries concerning him is: "En snäll pojke, följsam som alla sydlänningar. Icke kantig som vi nordbor" (18) ["A nice boy, flexible like all southerners. Not awkward as us northerners" (14)]. Although it is a positive view, the colonial stereotype is unquestionable.

Said mentions "unkindness to animals" as a typical characteristic of Orientals (38); the author feels sick when his Argentinian companions run a dog over during a car journey and are not at all upset by this accident (25). Orientals are considered to be lazy, according to Said (345). Kihlman's characters also may act in a similar way: Juan claims that his hands are those of an artist, not created for hard work. He prefers to work as a taxi boy rather than in a factory, as a factory job is so badly paid that it can never cover one's basic expenses (cf. 28, 123, 132). The Argentinians do not watch films in a sophisticated intellectual way like the author does, but naively (215), which corresponds to Said's observation that according to Orientalists Orientals are childlike (40). The Oriental exoticism (Said 290) and fatalism (Said 345) can be seen in the mystical and magic way in which things in Argentina sometimes happen: ghosts have been seen and everybody is convinced of their existence (89–91, 262).

Stressing conformity and not having any individuality (Said 48, 287) can be seen in the way an Argentinian football match is described (206). The flood of people in the streets of Buenos Aires is endless (54, 114, 164–5), and the masses of human beings in the event lead to a certain collectivism in thinking that is described by Kihlman as the opposite of the solitude preferred by himself and people in Finland.

Han [Juan] kunde inte leva om han inte kände att han var en av hundra, som kände som han och talade samma språk som han [...] En bland tiotusen, en liten prick bland miljonerna [...] han måste få känna massans tryck och massans trygghet. (165)

[He [Juan] could not live if he did not feel himself one of hundreds, who felt as he did and spoke the same language as he did [...] One among tens of thousands, a minute dot among millions [...] he had to feel the pressure and security of the masses.] (117)

In this sense, it can seem symptomatic how many times the author points out that both Juan and his Argentinian friends are not exceptional or unique; they are even representatives of a certain "type" (97, 133, 134, 135, 136, 148). On the other hand, the last statement in the book concerning this matter is the opposite: "Han är inte typisk" (256) ["He is not typical" (183)]. In the same way, Said mentions a typical notion of the

77

Orientalists, that the Arab is little impressed by scenery when travelling (237). Also the author of *AMS* was convinced in the beginning that Juan did not have any sense of the beauty of nature – but, after two years, he realised that it had been his own prejudice, after having seen Juan enjoying a scene of a red massif over the sea (38–39).

Does this perhaps mean that Kihlman goes through a certain development during the text, at least in relation to some of his prejudices?

Argentinian Barbarism and Despotism

According to Said, Europeans ascribe to the Orientals a tendency towards barbarism and despotism (4, 86, 203, 205, 290). The frame for Kihlman's story is situated in the late 1970s, the period after the bloody and brutal military coup that brought Jorge Rafael Videla Remondo to power. In fact, there is a state of war in Argentina, and several people are shot every day. In such conditions of unrest, people have to be patient and meek when they are in contact with authorities. It is not recommended to speak of some formerly well-known cultural personalities such as Victor Jara or Gabriel García Márquez. The land has become a police state and the presence of the feared secret police can often be felt. The atmosphere is even worse in Montevideo in neighbouring Uruguay (11, 14–15, 21, 58–60, 63–65, 67, 114).

The author witnesses an arrest of a person in a nightclub, made by armed policemen in civilian clothes. His reaction is based on this opposition: "Plötsligt befann jag mig mitt i repressionens Latinamerika […] ty den skandinaviska upplevelsen av mänskliga rättigheter hade jag i blodet" (58) ["Suddenly, I found myself in the Latin America of repression […], for I had the Scandinavian notion of human rights in my blood" (43–44)]. In this way, Latin America means repression (despotism, as expressed by Said), while Scandinavia means human rights, its opposite.

In the beginning, the author tends to see repressive politics in every single thing he comes across in Argentina (14–15). Gradually he recognizes, nevertheless, that this is not the subject matter he wants to write about (21).

Kihlman, a 1960s radical, thus does not see writing about Argentinian despotism as productive anymore. The explanation he mentions is that economic and political crisis is the normal situation for the whole continent of South America and that hundreds of journalists can analyse it in a better way than he can (75).

Argentinian Masculinity

One of the text's main *leitmotifs* is Argentinian masculinity; the word *maskuliniteten* is mentioned as early as the first page where the author begins his stay in this land, in a sentence connecting it with the Argentinian dictatorship. Argentina is thus critically presented as an extremely masculine land: "i detta land där maskuliniteten är en myt och rättesnöre" (10) ["in this country where masculinity is a myth and the norm" (9)].

The first men the author meets are connoisseurs of women; they talk about them as if discussing horses or objects of pleasure. An Argentinian man's role is to care for his wife and children – but at the same time, it is only men who decide and who choose to do what they themselves want to do. Men in Argentina cannot be seen as weak or sensitive, not even in the most tragic moments of life (11, 61, 132, 142, 260).

Kihlman's analysis of homosexuality and Argentinian men concerns focusing on both the aggressive (masculine) and the tender (feminine) component. Nevertheless, the latter is not possible to show, since desire for tenderness does not suit the Argentinian picture of masculinity – even for homosexuals (141–142). Regardless of the homosexual topics and themes in which Juan is represented, he is also described as an extremely masculine Argentinian, whose Latin view of women is hard to accept for the author's wife Selinda (157). "Han var argentinare, han var 'porteño', en maskulin produkt av Buenos Aires" (135). ["He was Argentinian, the prototype for a certain type and not an especially unusual type at that" (96)]. Symptomatic of this is the dual morality in which Juan views his women prostitute colleagues. While the author blames economic or social deprivation for their fate, according to Juan – also a prostitute – they belong to the "risk group" since they are women. They are unrealistic, they dream of a life of luxury and becoming rich easily; their inclination to the profession is also based on their overpowering sexual needs (103, 104, 107). But, on the other hand, Juan does not see any moral problem in the case when a loving Argentinian wife prostitutes herself to get money for her husband in order to make his life easier (192).

In the text of *AMS*, the status of Argentinian women is seen as subordinate to men. A woman who loves her husband – or a mother who loves her son – is not supposed to know everything about them, even if the money they provide in order to care for them is suspect. As described, to an Argentinian man, his ideals of a woman belong to a kind of innocence, whereas she should not know the truth about the ways of the world, e.g., about her female friend's prostitution. Argentinian women have to be faithful, while their men do not have to; women's lot is to accept men's promiscuity (125, 128, 143, 215).

I Argentina är det inte kvinnans sak att vara svartsjuk. För då skulle ingenting fungera. […] Att män är män och kvinnans sak är att anpassa sig. (86)

[In Argentina it is not a woman's way to be jealous. Nothing would work if that were so. […] Men are men and it's up to women to adapt to them.] (63)

This dual morality is stressed by the fact that, regardless of Catholic sexual taboo, unmarried Argentinian women accept that they are hunted for occasional sex (173–174).

Even the Argentinian family is described as patriarchal and family life as conservative. On the one hand, a son who neglects to take care of his mother is despicable. On the other, all parents of respectable Argentinian girls, if they already have boyfriends, seek to arrange a marriage for them at the earliest opportunity. Parents, especially fathers, decide on the lives and even the sexual lives of their children. To live with someone who one is not married to, only engaged to, is impossible (84, 145, 176, 204).

The author is confronted with a situation when an Argentinian woman having come from her job, tired and suffering from a headache, is preparing a meal for the family, while her husband is watching TV and not helping her at all. A pattern of his own cultural background is unsustainable (240). A symptomatic situation arises when Lilita, Juan's fiancée and future wife, is staying in Finland. Having got used to showing herself naked in a sauna in front of men other than her husband, she can see that women in this land have a higher status, and that they are freer and have more possibilities. She would prefer to stay longer in Finland; nevertheless, the one who decides about her life is her beloved Juan. Lilita is totally in accord with him, his habits and wishes, and in the end also with his opinions. Her upbringing tells her always to express herself as his wife. If Juan wants to leave Finland and go home then she also wants the same, even though she held the opposite point of view in the beginning (170).

The pattern the text of *AMS* creates is thus similar as in the case of repression and human rights (see above): the conditions for women are better in progressive Finland, much worse in the patriarchal Argentina. The notion of the female and male aspects differs "mellan å ena sidan det upplysta Europa och å andra sidan det efterblivna Argentina" (193) ["between informed Europe on the one part and backward Argentina on the other" (136)].

Nevertheless, masculinity, the characteristic that Kihlman views as the most problematic one in Argentina and the whole of South America, is not a part of typical Oriental characteristics in the Western point of view, according to Said, who does not count it as symptomatic of the nature of Oriental people. The Argentinian masculinity cannot thus be viewed as Kihlman's oriental prejudice.

On the other hand, Kihlman considers the Argentinian dual morality as less mendacious than in Europe, as it is simpler and less intellectualised (174). The author's view of Argentinian family life is not exclusively negative: the parents and children have strong love and consideration for each other, the generation revolt is harmonic, and even small children are naturally included. The family is large, it consists of more persons than in the European sense, as cousins are as close as siblings, and family members often help each other. For them, there is nothing more important than to meet frequently together, usually around mealtimes – and the author himself feels that he is now being included as a member of Juan's large Argentinian family, which has also become his own (95, 211, 261, 264–265). In contrast, Kihlman calls the North European family institution nonchalant and insensitive (157).

Sensuality and Sexuality

Some of the most important characteristics that the Western world attributes to Orientals, sensuality, exotic sensuousness, an undifferentiated sexual drive[6] (Said 4, 72, 167, 190, 203, 205, 311, 345), can be viewed as interconnected to masculinity. In *AMS*, Juan is described as an extremely promiscuous person, whose self-understanding is "un artista

---

[6] For a much more thorough analysis of the relation between sexuality and the Third World in *AMS*, not limited to Said's concept from *Orientalism* (discussing the notion of sexual liberation connected in European culture with the Third World), see Carlson, "Poikarakkauden houkutus" and Carlson, *Paikantuneita haluja*.

sexual" (93), an artist in the field of sex, each moment defending his own masculinity, satisfying his need for women and being on the make all the time (136). On the basis of experience, he has a very strongly developed notion about "hans manliga charm" (34) ["his manly charm" (26)], his own handsomeness, irresistibility, not only in a sexual sense, but in the sense that women also tend to fall in love with him very easily (175). According to him, he can have any woman he wants to. There are even famous Argentinian women (such as Sylvie Vartan) whom he has slept with (33, 34, 128).

Juan became sexually mature very early, having had sexual intercourse for the first time at the age of eleven. He had his first sexual relationship at fifteen (92–93). He is used to sleeping with women several times a day (172). He has had and continues to have liaisons with hundreds of women as well. Older women even occasionally pay him for his sexual services (173) – and not only women, especially men: he had his first experience of selling his body to an adult male at the age of fourteen, and since his teens he has been used to providing sexual intercourse for men as many as five times a day (100–101, 117–8). Miguel and Sergio, Juan's "colleagues from his trade," whom the author also gets to know, do not substantially differ from Juan in this sense.

Having arrived in Europe and Finland, Juan suffers from sexual isolation. He wants to be provided with women by his host, or at least to get permission from him to bring occasional sexual partners to his home. He even starts to look for these within the host's family (157, 172–175, 177).

On the other hand, does Europe differ substantially from Argentina? It is necessary to realise that the sexual dimension of the author's and Juan's relationship was omitted in *AMS* (see note 3); therefore Kihlman's own picture can tend to be asexual. Nevertheless, in the text, even Europe is described as a world where a kind of commercial and extreme sexuality exists. Juan is once offered a job by a Danish pornographic magazine company. Staying in Stockholm, the author and Juan go regularly to pornographic clubs. The author describes having intercourse in a threesome, though. Juan is deeply hurt when a Christian in a sauna unexpectedly tries to make a pass at him. Walking through the streets in central Stockholm, Juan and the author come across the same lifestyle as Juan is familiar with in Buenos Aires: prostitutes offering themselves to their clients, disappearing for a while and afterwards standing again in the same place – a world Kihlman did not know before (104–106, 147, 167, 184, 221).

Implicitly, an "undifferentiated sexual drive" is thus in *AMS* not typical for only the strange world outside Europe.

Unreliability and Lies

Accuracy is, as is claimed, abhorrent to the Oriental mind (Said 38, 205). The habits of inaccuracy could be seen in *AMS* in the fact that the Argentinians have a different notion of time than the Finnish. Juan does not count days, nor by any means weeks; the author counts days, sometimes even hours (8). Also as a result of this, throughout his stay in Argentina, Kihlman comes across the fact that Juan and other people do not keep their word concerning meeting agreements. They come late, sometimes by several hours, sometimes they do not come at all. In this sense they are sometimes expedient in that they arrive on time only if it is favourable for them (see, e.g., 37, 56, 220, 236–237).

An interrelated matter is lying. According to Said, Orientals are viewed in the West as given to intrigue, cunning, and directly as inveterate liars (38–39). During the very first meeting with Juan, the possibility of deceit, connected immediately with criminality, occurs to the author:

Å andra sidan räknade jag hela tiden med att allt vad han berättade var lögn. […] Han var en lögnare. Han väntade på ett lämpligt tillfälle att bestjäla mig på mina pengar. Han var falsk och opålitlig. Han var som alla sydlänningar. Så hade jag lärt mig hemma. […] Jag var europé och nordbo och borgare och protestant. Han var katolik och sydlänning och… ja, gatpojke. I mitt blod hade omärkligt och trots medvetet motstånd från min sida ympats min miljös alla sociala föreställningar och vanföreställningar. Juan var charmfull men opålitlig. Var på din vakt! (15)

[On the other hand, all the time I was assuming that everything he was telling me was a lie. […] He was a liar. He was waiting for an appropriate moment to steal my money. He was false and untrustworthy. He was like all southerners. I had learnt that back home. […] I was a European and a northerner and bourgeois and Protestant. He was a Catholic and a southerner and … well, a street-boy. Imperceptibly, and despite conscious resistance on my side, all the social concepts and distortions of my own upbringing had been inoculated into my blood. Juan was charming but unreliable. Be on your guard!] (12)

This lordly attitude can be seen as proper Orientalism, but conscious of its roots. Nevertheless, the author's mistrust of Juan continues. On a car trip in La Pampa, the author does not believe Juan even as he tells him the Spanish names of various flora, trees, and bushes, suspecting, that he has made them up himself (23–24). His behaviour is suspicious: he meddles with the author's papers in his hotel room, he makes notes secretly when he thinks the author is not watching, he is curious about the author's friends (61).

Tillsvidare var jag säker på att han ljög. […] Kanske för att sydländska ynglingar alltid ljuger? Kanske för att hela rasen är lögnaktig och opålitlig? Mina europeiska eller nordiska fördomar stack som nålar i medvetandet. (62)

[But, at the time, I was sure he was lying. […] Perhaps because southern youths always lie? Perhaps because the whole race were liars and untrustworthy? My European or Scandinavian prejudices stuck like pins in my mind.] (46)

Nevertheless, longer experience in Argentina leads the author to reflect much more thoroughly about what a lie is and what it is not. Sometimes this happens in a bit of a humorous way: a taxi driver asks him for a sum of 3000 pesos instead of 300 pesos, but the suspicion that the driver has taken him to a completely different place than he wanted to go to happens to be an invalid one. The peculiar Argentinian mixture of devotion and calculation starts to be too irresistible for him (57, 259).

In many cases, the author considers Juan's contentions concerning his lover's life as extremely exaggerated, but in the end he realises that the boy's life experience is very unusual by European standards (see further) and that he in fact is not lying. In the beginning, the author thinks that Juan is unable to prove that anyone has ever heard about his career as a singer, but subsequently there is confirmation that he was telling the truth (61–62, 64): "Jag tror inte på honom. Men det är sant ändå, framgår det senare" (34) ["I don't believe him. But nevertheless it turns out to be true" (26)]. This is a pattern that repeats itself several times in the text (see, e.g., 15, 209, 244).

Gradually, the author comes to the conclusion that the notion of a lie in Argentina and that of the European North is not the same. Juan made a difference between pious lies and speculative lies. Pious lies are justified when they do not harm anybody on a large scale and when being used in the struggle for survival – e.g., taxi boys do not tell their families how they make their living in order not to cause them distress. This dual morality can even be seen as a moral quality. Shopping in Montevideo, Juan lies to the author concerning his own date of birth, knowing that Kihlman was ready to buy him a shirt he needed in any case. The author then decides to accept Juan's lies under some conditions, knowing that there are lies of different types and some of them can be motivated – while the European North, based on Protestant Puritanism, claims an absolute truth everywhere and every time, regardless of context (136–137, 142, 243, 244, 246–247).[7]

The people in the milieu in which Juan also moves are always on the borderline of crime. This supposes a kind of extremely flexible morality (125). However, there are some limits to their immorality: nobody from the group of Juan's friends has ever committed a burglary, mugging, blackmail, or murder. Grave criminal acts are to be avoided but, when hungry, shoplifting is conceivable. Juan and his friends also have experience with selling smuggled liquor, drugs, and forbidden porn films. Their notion of law and order is different from that of the author's. The laws are absurd since they are made by the rulers to defend their own interests against powerless poor people. They then consider that swindles and frauds are legitimate means in their struggle against the contemptible upper-class, bourgeoisie, and capitalists (109, 117, 137). Juan is proud of himself for having once managed to provide a police superintendent with a bottle of smuggled Chivas whisky – this being seen as the best sort – and yet before the handover replaced the contents with the cheapest Old Smuggler (138–139). His father, Marcelo, when young, earned his livelihood as a card sharp, cheating the inexperienced sons of rich families and foreigners; this made it possible for him to survive (87).

On the other hand, a parallel question of the Europeans' propensity to lie can be raised as well. It shows that even Juan, not trusting foreign middle-aged tourists, considers some of the author's promises as empty talk. The author himself realises how carelessly he approaches Juan's and his Argentinian friend's attitude towards shoplifting, now performed in Stockholm, under circumstances that the persons stealing are his friends. He is even ready to provide his room as a warehouse for the stolen goods. In Finland, Juan is invited to play in a South American festival by a Christian community in northern parts of the country – nevertheless, he is cheated, having obtained a laughable

---

[7] Another proof of the fact that misunderstanding can follow from language use is the word 'obligación.' As 'förpliktelse' it has a positive content for the author. Juan, although ready to help other people with problems when he feels a necessity to do so, nevertheless understands the word as a bourgeois formality which in no way binds him to anything (*AMS* 244–246).

honorary remuneration of eleven Finnish marks, which do not even cover the cost of travel expenses (61, 166–167, 189).

The author himself makes an admission that even he sometimes lies (247). The final conclusion concerning the question of cheating in the relationship between Europe and Argentina is presented at the very end of the book:

> Det är skillnaden mellan Argentina och Europa. Spekulation i det lilla, hederlighet i de stora sammanhangen för kreolernas del. Medan för Europas del hederlighet i det oväsentliga för att dölja den utstuderade spekulationen på väldighetsplanet. 'Hur man än gör lurar de en ändå alltid till sist.' Det är inte så. Tvärtom. Hur de än gör så lurar vi dem ändå alltid till sist. En argentinare kan aldrig lura en europé. Han trodde han var smart. Jag är fan så mycket smartare. (255)

> [That is the difference between Argentina and Europe. Speculation in the small things, honour in larger issues on the side of the Creoles. While on the part of Europe, honour to inessentials, to conceal the studied speculation on the level of enormity. 'Whatever you do, they always cheat you in the end.' That is not so. On the contrary. Whatever they do, *we'll* always cheat them in the end. An Argentinian can never cheat a European. He thought he was clever. I was bloody cleverer.] (183)

Juan in Europe

Between the author's two stays in Argentina, Juan and later also his wife Lilita visit Europe, including Finland and Sweden. In this way the author's view of Argentina, as well as Juan's view of the two Nordic countries are presented. At the same time, Juan goes through an experience that is a reminder of a traditional immigrant's experience, including hard and painful immigrant symptoms, mental stress and suffering:

> Hans problem var trogna avbildningar av en europeisk invandrarproblematik, som berörde miljoner människor i hela den högt industrialiserade delen av vår världsdel. (158)

> [His problems were faithful reflections of European immigration policies affecting millions of people all over the highly industrial countries of our hemisphere. (112)]

Not knowing foreign languages in order to be able to communicate with Finnish or Swedish people, he tends to seek contacts only with other Argentinians who are in the same situation (158, 188). In any case, some of Juan's commentaries on Finland and Sweden resonate as proper Orientalism, although in an opposite manner: characteristics found by Europe in the Orient are now also found in Europe. Juan is especially critical of the Swedish youth from the streets of Stockholm, using drugs and alcohol. He considers the young generation as lost. Swedish young people are unprincipled, aggressive and too loud, spoiled, and abandoned, left to their fate – but also childish, infantile, immature, and degenerate – characteristics, which according to Said (40, 184) Orientalists also see in the Orient. In Sweden, there is a breakdown in communication among generations, politeness to older people does not exist, and the family institution, important in Argentina (see above), is destroyed. The material standard – for Juan only a means that can possibly lead to happiness, not happiness itself – is too good, which leads to destructiveness, disorientation, and irresponsibility. In his own case, it was the opposite: poverty taught him responsibility for himself and his family. Swedish youth are not even able to feel responsibility for themselves (181–185). The Orientalists found negative sides of splendour in the Orient (see Said 4, 345), Juan found features of it in Europe.

One of the stereotypical Oriental characteristics is fierceness (Said 168, 290). Nevertheless, Juan also sees it in the Nordic drinking tradition, which is totally alien to him, since in Argentina one never drinks to become drunk. As the author cannot accept Juan's sexual habits (see above), Juan cannot accept the author's drinking habits: they make the Argentinian feel disappointed, hopeless, and even afraid. Drunkenness is something inhuman for him, especially if it concerns very young people in Sweden and Finland (171–172, 222, 223).

Another "typical Oriental" characteristic is cruelty (Said 4, 168, 345). Juan finds that in Europe as well, having seen drunk and even sober people in Stockholm fighting each other. This kind of violence is, according to him, completely unmotivated, since it is carried out by people who should help each other – but in reality, the so-called Welfare Sweden is full of personal aggression, suspicion, egoism, and envy. He realises that he has never come across something like this in Buenos Aires. On the one hand, he knows that in Argentina people are being tortured every day: they disappear and are found again as crippled, dead, or are not found at all; on the other hand, it is a violence driven from above and it is politically motivated. At the same time, in Argentina common people spontaneously help each other out of trouble, without being asked and without entitlement to remuneration, feeling loyalty to either class or humanity as a whole (181–185).

Two Possibilities for Approaching One's Life

The project of the certainly gifted Juan's career as singer, guitar player, and actor in the North of Europe, planned for him by the author, does not succeed. Yet in the unpleasant hard climate, he is away from his own natural social milieu, he does not understand taciturn Northerners and feels an unsustainable loneliness (157, 161). As an "Oriental," he is perhaps too phlegmatic, lax, and falls prey to inordinate melancholy (Said 119, 168). Nevertheless, in a more thorough analysis of the reason for this failure, the question of differing values and mentality is more important.

As mentioned above, the life conditions, paths, and experience for the author in Finland and for Juan in Argentina have been vastly different (50, 108).

Människorna är annorlunda. […] Det finns en trygghet att känna på det mänskliga planet i Argentina, som försvunnit i den europeiska nordens utomordentliga sociala organisation. (200)

[The people *are* different. […] In Argentina one feels a security on the human level, which has now vanished in the excellent social organisation of Scandinavia.] (141)

85

The European North is thus grounded in social organisation, Argentina in human relations. The author is "van [...] vid nordisk ordning och den nordiska välfärdens tusen och ett reglementen" (122) ["familiar [...] with Scandinavian orderliness and its thousand and one welfare regulations" (87)]. Juan, having become mature very early, has a completely different life experience. With the hard conditions for people living in poverty he was exposed to, it taught him that the members of the lower class have to have solidarity with one another. His life in the huge and inhospitable city would not be possible without daily help from other people, who have their own bitter experience with the same conditions. He got to know thousands of people from many levels of society, especially the lowest one, and he was able to use all of these contacts in his struggle for survival. By his own experience, Juan learnt infinitely more about man, his conditions, and about surviving, but almost no practical things to be used in a professional or working life in society; for example, he is not able to use a dictionary. A class society was something he knew from his own experience, feeling loyalty and solidarity to "his equals." The rich people were for him mostly immoral and the poor were good – but he knew class society theoreticians very superficially, he had no interest in reading books or newspapers, and no genuine interest in politics at all (13, 60, 108, 119, 125, 135, 136).

In long passages the author reflects on the so-called "European inheritance" visible both in North America and in Europe: the competitive spirit, happiness understood as honour and glory, and the notion that "life is what you make it." Power, a European trauma, plays an extraordinarily important role in the world of its ideas. No wonder then, that with Finland belonging to Europe, people become mutual enemies and not comrades as in Argentina (162–164). On the contrary, Juan from Argentina is very "non-European" in this way: he has no desire to gain power, he is not frustrated in his social ambitions. He does not want to become something great, his happiness is of another, easier kind than the European one: love, friendship, a roof over his head, food for the day, and the freedom to do what he wants to within a relatively unambitious social frame. The basis for his life is sobriety; he is content with having little, mainly wanting to survive (115). His notion of freedom is connected with a kind of immaterialism: "Friheten är tusen gånger mera värd än trygghet och välstånd. Lyckan finns inte i materiella ting utan i ett gott samvete" (93) ["Freedom is a thousand times more valuable than security and prosperity. Happiness isn't found in material things, but in a clear conscience" (68)]. Kihlman comments:

Min filosofi var en framgångsfilosofi: att lyckas. [...] Hans filosofi var en annan än min: att leva och låta leva. (151)

[My philosophy was a philosophy of progress – to succeed. [...] His philosophy was different from mine – to live and let live.] (108)

There is yet another surprising difference the author finds between himself and Juan: Kihlman is having a good time being abroad, not staying at home, and likes to learn new things about Latin America, thanks to his "finlandssvenska rotlöshet, bildning, medfödda nyfikenhet" (252) ["Finland-Swedish rootlessness, [...] education, [...] inborn curiosity" (181)]. He knows that through his recognition of this he can gain more power, necessary, for example, to his literary career. "Kunskap är makt? Okay, i varje fall över sitt eget öde. Kunskap är ett livsinnehåll. Vetandet som livsmål. Nyfikenhet som drivkraft i livet" (162) ["Knowledge is power? OK, over one's own destiny, anyhow. Knowledge is a factor in life. Curiosity is a driving force in life" (115)]. But Juan's existence and mobility is only a local one, possible only in Buenos Aires, impossible even in nearby Montevideo (159). Unlike the author, Juan is not adaptable to another environment, he suffers from not being in his milieu among a million people. In fact, he does not have any interest in travelling (158, 161) – similar, according to Orientalists, to the Orientals (Arabs) who do not like travelling either (Said 237). When abroad, Juan does not try to learn anything about Sweden and Finland, he has no enjoyment in exploring as Columbus had: "Han var i varje fall inte europeisk i ordets expansiva mening" (159) ["Anyway, he was not European in the expansive meaning of that word" (113)].

With this background, with lacking the desire to gain power, and with his life philosophy to live and to let live, Juan thus does not see any point in educating himself as a professional musician upon which his future career in Europe could be built. His career would strip him of his own freedom, although a limited one, and that is why he refuses it. Not to be obliged to submit to the conditions set by the rich, exactly in the same way as he did when he finished his previous career as a musician in Argentina. He prefers not to serve the upper class, only to exploit it (135), so that he could be "fattig men stolt" (20, 26) ["poor, but proud" (16, 21)]. He is willing to live in freedom as he did before, even if it may sound paradoxical in view of his former experience as a homosexual prostitute. "Jag vill inte bli rik {*alt.* berömd}, jag vill bli lycklig" (26, 126, 130, 133) ["I don't want to be rich {*alternatively* famous}, I want to be happy" (21, 90, 93, 95)] is Juan's slogan, several times repeated in *AMS*.

It seems that the author wanted to "colonize" Juan through a plan to force something completely unnatural upon him; he wanted to act in an educative way similar to Professor Higgins in *Pygmalion* (see 251).[8] The author conquered Argentina at least symbolically: being equipped with a certain education, he was able to write a book about it. Juan did not conquer North Europe since he was not interested in doing so. This time Kihlman was yet again not able to keep his promise of help, given in the beginning (see above). The author thus understands his own mentality as being colonial, while Juan's mentality is completely different. Kihlman seems to have understood this – and at the same time have refused his own way of thinking – at the very end of the book: "Jag är Europa och Europa är ägaren, men jag äger inte. Inte Juan. Inte jorden jag trampar. Jag äger ingenting" (273) ["I am Europe and Europe is the owner, but I do not own. Not Juan. Not the earth I tread on. I own nothing" (195)].

In this way Kihlman presents two alternatives to approach one's life. "Hans mål i livet: att vara lycklig. Mitt mål i livet: att bygga en katedral" (255) ["His aim in life: to be happy. My aim in life: to build a cathedral" (183)]. Even if a parallel to this observation could be: "The West is an actor, the East a passive reactor" (Said 109), it is not stated that one approach is more valuable. They are parallel, one accepted by the other and vice versa. The non-European approach does not represent any aberrant thinking and mentality

---

8   Concerning possible neo-colonial features in *AMS* in connection with homosexual literary tradition, see Carlson, *Paikantuneita haluja* 118.

in *AMS* as represented for the Orientalists analysed by Said (see 38–40, 48–49, 205). On the contrary, the author is often critical of his own approach. He both admits being under the influence of colonial thinking himself – and he lets the counterpart be different. The fact that he neither wants to force his own values on Juan nor considers them as universally valid can be interpreted in a way that his final perspective is not an Orientalist one.

Conclusion

It is perhaps symptomatic that throughout the text Kihlman uses the words North and South to define the differences between Finland (or Sweden) and Argentina; e.g., "Jag var europé och nordbo och borgare och protestant. Han var katolik och sydlänning" (15) ["I was a European and a northerner and bourgeois and Protestant. He was a Catholic and a southerner" (12)]. As late as page 272, of the 284-page book, he writes: "Det är Europa och det är Argentina och att öst är öst och väst är väst och det inte är så" (272) ["It is Europe and it is Argentina and east is east and west is west and that's not how it is"[9] (194)]. For the first time here, nearly at the end, Kihlman uses the terms *east* and *west* as they are used in Said's vocabulary. A possible interpretation could be that the author admits he was reflecting in this way all the time – and now rejects his former way of thinking, viewed as colonial.

As described, *AMS*, the story about "[g]ossen från gränden och den fine herrn" (254) ["the boy from the back alley and the fine gentleman" (182)], includes a complex and at many times ambivalent structure as far as colonial thinking is concerned. The application of Said's concept is a productive means of interpretation. The conclusion could be that only two years after the first issue of *Orientalism*, Kihlman, most probably not knowing about the existence of the book, presents a thorough negotiation of the topics discussed by Said, even if not all of Kihlman's topics can be related to Said (as indicated, the notion of masculinity, found as deserving of the author's critique, is taken from other concepts). Although Kihlman has not become one of the Argentinians (274) and despite being under the influence of Orientalist prejudices himself, he recognizes how the Orientalist thinking functions, deconstructs many aspects of it, and learns that "typical Oriental characteristics" can easily occur also in Europe and be seen as such by "Orientals," exactly in the opposite way (especially as the description of Juan's stay in Europe shows). And, as has been discussed, the values and mentality of the Argentinians are often seen as more positive than their European opposites.

The book can be said to be an alternative Finnish or Finland-Swedish "pocket" *Orientalism*, which became possible, on the one hand, thanks to Kihlman's former social radicalism from the 1960s and 1970s, on the other hand, thanks to the love for the young Juan that also helped the author to overcome his former way of thinking, in which the Orientalist patterns were indisputably identifiable.[10]

---

[9] I had to change the official translation here by adding the word "not." The official translation unfortunately reads "that's how it is," which is the exact opposite of what is in the Swedish original.

[10] This work was supported by the European Regional Development Fund project "Creativity and Adaptability as Conditions of the Success of Europe in an Interrelated World" (reg. no.: CZ.02.1.01/0.0/0.0/16_019 /0000734).

Works Cited

Alhoniemi, Pirkko. *Isät, pojat, perinnöt. Christer Kihlmanin ja Bertel Kihlmanin kirjallisesta tuotannosta.* Helsinki: Suomalaisen Kirjallisuuden Seura, 1989.

Carlson, Mikko. "Mahdollisuuksien kaappi. Seksuaaliset vapaudet ja kulttuurien välinen tila Christer Kihlmanin omaelämäkerrallisessa teoksessa *Kaikki minun lapseni.*" *Säännellyt vapaudet. Tulkintoja toiseuden tuottamisesta.* Eds. Marko Gylén and Marianne Liljeström. Turku: UTU, 2014. 61–84.

Carlson, Mikko. *Paikantuneita haluja. Seksuaalisuus ja tila Christer Kihlmanin tuotannossa.* Nykykulttuurin tutkimuskeskuksen julkaisuja 114. Jyväskylä: Jyväskylän yliopistopaino, 2014.

Carlson, Mikko. "Poikarakkauden houkutus ja vieras maanosa. Homoseksuaalisuus, poikaprostituutio ja sosiaalinen tila Christer Kihlmanin romaanissa *Kaikki minun lapseni.*" *Naistutkimus/ Kvinnoforskning* 2 (2007): 16–30.

Dlask, Jan. "'Knihy o Argentině' finského Švéda Christera Kihlmana jako nový typ sociálně angažovaného románu?" *Kontinuita a diskontinuita vývinového procesu poézie, prózy a drámy. Premeny estetického kánonu. Koncepcie literárnych dejín.* Eds. Soňa Pašteková and Dagmar Podmaková. Bratislava: VEDA, 2007. 197–207.

Kihlman, Christer. *Alla mina söner.* [Helsingfors]: Söderström, 1980.

Kihlman, Christer. *All My Sons.* Trans. Joan Tate. London/Washington, DC: Peter Owen, 1984.

Kuhalampi, Anja. "Muiden kapina – toiseus Christer Kihlmanin tuotannossa." *Me ja muut. Etnisyys, identiteetti, toiseus.* Ed. Marjo Kylmänen. Tampere: Vastapaino, 1994. 57–67.

Said, Edward W. *Orientalism.* London: Penguin, 2003.

Tarkka, Pekka. *Författare i Finland.* Trans. Gunilla Cleve. Helsinki: Tammi, 1990.

Toiviainen, Seppo. *Christer Kihlman ja hänen maailmansa.* Tutkijaliiton julkaisusarja 32. Jyväskylä: Gummerus, 1984.

Westö, Mårten, and Kihlman, Christer. *Om hopplöshetens möjligheter. En samtalsbok.* [Helsingfors]: Söderström, 2000.

6. Playing with Identities: Variants of Biography and the Sylleptic 'I' in Bronisław Świderski's Migration Novels

Sylwia Izabela Schab

The theme of autobiographies and their variants frequently recurs in Bronisław Świderski's literary output as well as in his essayist reflections. In one of his interviews, for example, the writer refers to Günter Grass's understanding of (auto)biography as an alternative, an open structure, which involves the need to select a variant of memory. Addressing the question concerning the difference between an (auto)biography and a novel, Świderski claims that there is none (*Kiedy mogę zabić?* 119). Following the existentialists, he formulates the idea that man is "możliwością, projektem usytuowanym w przyszłości" (ibid.) ["a possibility, a project situated in the future"]. The author also admits to his deceptive play with autobiographical conventions, autofictionalizing his novels to develop his biography and enable him to feel "coraz bliżej siebie" (*Kiedy mogę zabić?* 134) ["closer and closer to himself"]. Therefore, he emphasises and considers the intricate correlations between the novel material, expressed through a protagonist-narrator, and the author's (his own) life. At the same time, Świderski points to the filter he applies to the constructions of the 'self,' i.e., the existentialist philosophy of Søren Kierkegaard, with epistemological uncertainty inscribed in it, with the primacy of doubt, and the exercise of multiplication and repetition.

In fact, the biography of Bronisław Świderski – intellectual, Kierkegaard researcher, journalist, and writer – abounds in ambiguities and complexities, escaping any attempts of simple classification or labelling. Świderski was born in Poland in 1946. As a student at the Faculty of Sociology and Philosophy of the University of Warsaw, he learned about his Jewish origins during a wave of anti-Semitism in Poland in the late 1960s. In the aftermath of the campaign against Jews, he was forced to emigrate; since 1970 he has lived in Denmark. History enters Świderski's life (and the lives of his characters) as an external force that "narzuc[a] coś obcego, narusz[a] nawet to, co Ja najgłębiej odczuwa jako swoje" (Gosk 64) ["imposes something strange, violates even what I feel most deeply as my own"]. Świderski was for many years an associate of the Søren Kierkegaard Research Centre from which he was dismissed, as he admitted, for publishing a text on Kierkegaard's anti-Semitism. His literary output flourishes in Denmark – he has published two novels (written in Polish and published in Poland): *Słowa obcego* (1998, The Stranger's Words), and *Asystent śmierci* (2007, Death's Assistant), nominated for one of the most important Polish literary awards (Nike Award), and an earlier mini-novel *Autobiografie* (1981, Autobiographies), published in London (in Polish). These works, which lay the foundations for this analysis, have not been translated into Danish (or any other languages). Świderski continues to reside in Denmark, where he has lived for fifty years, unrecognised as a creator of fiction and thus not classified as one of the Danish migrant writers. Although Polish literary and academic critics treat him more graciously, the native reception of this intellectually intriguing writer seems to be limited to a narrow circle of readers and experts.[1]

In the essay "Doświadczenia emigranta" (1990, Experiences of an Emigrant), Świderski formulates the idea of an emigrant's condition as a "wieczny tłumacz" [eternal translator], forced, in the process of mediation between cultures, to 'constantly translate himself.' (*Kiedy mogę zabić?* 111). He also poses the question of how to "pozostać sobą, zachować przeszłość i budować przyszłość" (112) ["remain yourself, preserve the past and build the future"] and gives a reply: it is a consequence of the inability to maintain the desired harmony of the past with the present and the future. Thus, he points to the need for "utrat[y] biografii, życio-rysu" (ibid.) ["the loss[es] of a biography, of a life-story"]. The "multi-biography," which is being built anew in multinational settings, draws on "niegramatyczność społeczna" (ibidem) ["social ungrammaticality"] – an emigrant becomes a mistake because his existence eludes national grammars: "Pozostanie bez historii, bez biografii społecznie zaakceptowanej w jakimkolwiek języku" (ibid.) ["He will remain without a history, without a biography socially accepted in any language"]. At the same time, by making a mistake, he confirms himself (113), defending his individuality and integrity. The writer confesses the specific condition of his identity – "he is possessed by" (and not *he possesses*) three different ethnocultural identities: Polish, Jewish, and Danish (*Kiedy mogę zabić?* 114). However, they do not form a stable system – not only towards each other but also within each of them. The answer to the existential question of how such a position affects his humanity is sought by Świderski in one of his "saviours" – Søren Kierkegaard, from whom he learned to "mówić we własnym imieniu" (118) ["speak for himself"] and to consider as his own the words he identifies with himself, regardless of the language in which they are uttered. He, therefore, speaks out in favour of individualism, against the oppressive norms of national grammar (including the norms of national languages), against communitarian political practices – against the adjustment to a predetermined and socially acceptable pattern.

The protagonists (and narrators) of Świderski's novels share with him the fate of characters located on the verge of worlds, and this position accentuates the issue of the subject's identity. It concerns individuals with an unstable/blurred sense of identity, who exist in a fluid world of change; individuals who are characterised by difficulty in formulating a self-definition both in individual and social dimensions. A determinant of their identity is indeterminacy, or, as the author puts it, "bycie nikim" ["being nobody"] – "jedyna pozycja społeczna godna pisarza" (*Kiedy mogę zabić?* 419) ["the only social position worthy of a writer"]. They are isolated from the space-time continuum of both the homeland and the foreign land. This sense of disorientation and not being settled in the world not only connects them with other protagonists of Polish modernist and postmodernist literature but also with the condition of the contemporary man in general (cf. Gosk 101). Świderski's protagonists pursue Witold Gombrowicz's strategy of

---

[1]   See Zduniak-Wiktorowicz; Dąbrowski; Borowczyk; Larek; Sawczuk; Winiecka, "Prawdy;" Bukowski; Schab.

alienation/strangeness marked as "always be a stranger" – having freed themselves from the constraints imposed by the community, they not only gain insight from a distance but also receive an impulse to make the effort of self-creating (Gosk 103).[2] "Być nikim i móc wszystkich krytykować, a przede wszystkim siebie: oto według mnie cechy autentycznego pisarza" (*Kiedy mogę zabić?* 420) ["Being nobody and being able to criticise everyone and above all myself: these are, in my opinion, the qualities of an authentic writer"]. This statement elucidates how Świderski defines his position in the world and follows this vision as an author.

In Świderski's novels, the construction of characters (protagonists and narrators) undoubtedly exhibits features of the sylleptic 'I.' Syllepsis is a trope originating in ancient poetics, which refers to the understanding of the same expression simultaneously in two ways – both literally and figuratively. Nowadays, this trope has been revisited as an analytical category, among others, by Jacques Derrida and Michel Riffaterre (see Winiecka, O sylleptyczności). In Polish literary reflection, syllepsis has been revisited by Ryszard Nycz (1997), who refers to the duality, ambiguity, and integration of opposing meanings into one figure/instance. In the contemporary view, the trope also involves a reference to the double coding of text "as contextual and intertextual meaning, as meaning and as significance, and finally as mimesis and semiosis" (Riffaterre read by Nycz 96; cf. Winiecka, O sylleptyczności 137ff; Gosk 108). The syllepsis model might have, as emphasised by Elżbieta Winiecka (O sylleptyczności 144), "zastosowanie wszędzie tam, gdzie życie styka się z literaturą, autentyk zmaga się z fikcją, prawda ze zmyśleniem" ["an application wherever life meets literature, the real contends with fiction, the truth with inventiveness"]. The sylleptic 'I' is therefore understood as both: real and invented, empirical and textual, authentic and fictional or novelistic (Nycz 96). Literature becomes part of life; the one-way relationship is replaced by feedback, also with regard to the type of subjective identity: "the empirical 'I' and the textual 'I' interact with each other and exchange their properties," and the subject "embraces its own fragmentation" (Nycz 98). Nycz encapsulates the concept of subjectivity in the words "we write with ourselves" (99), borrowed from the Polish writer Wiktor Woroszylski. Following the Polish modernist poet Bolesław Leśmian, Nycz emphasizes that an individual who realises such a pattern is usually one who is self-reliant and chooses self-realisation in accordance with his own inner nature, also at the price of irreconcilability with the rules of social reality (101). This manner of constructing protagonists as well as the type of subjectivity can be identified in Świderski's prose.[3]

Świderski's novels are migration texts[4] also in the direct sense that they explore the migration experience associated with the departure of the author-narrator protagonist

---

[2] The author advocates this mode of being an emigrant in his essayistic texts and in interviews (cf. Świderski, *Kiedy mogę zabić?*).

[3] It should be noted that other syllepsis-related concepts include the category of autofiction (Serge Doubrovsky), double contract (Poul Behrendt), and performative biography (Jon Helt Haarder), which may also be applied to Bronisław Świderski's novels.

[4] Or, as Mieczysław Dąbrowski (87ff.) considers them, intercultural texts, which, in a similar vein, move away from the biographical determinism underlying the notion of "migration" instead of "emigration" presented by Søren Frank.

from Poland to Denmark.[5] It is primarily a cultural experience mediated by language(s),[6] which becomes a catalyst for asking questions about one's own identity/identities and thus about one's biography (both one's own and one's parents' – see, e.g., three versions of the biography written by the protagonist-narrator's mother cited in *Asystent śmierci*). Therefore, we are dealing with a "podmiot w procesie" (Dąbrowski 90) ["subject in the process"], whose attitude is characterised by distance to the world (here Denmark and Poland) and to himself: the subject looks at himself from a distance and criticises "above all himself" (to return to the author's previously quoted words). At the same time, Świderski's novels contain strongly voiced criticism of the organisation (and mentality) of society – especially of the emigrant's host country, even though the images of Poland are equally far from idealised. Following Kierkegaard's thought, Świderski's criticism is directed at democracy (and the Danish version of the Welfare State), which is, on the one hand, a unifying system, and on the other, a system in which an immigrant – as an outsider not equipped with the proper cultural and linguistic idiom – is doomed to non-existence, marginalised and ignored in his otherness. This otherness, though, according to the author, might be an asset and a potential source of creativity. Świderski, therefore, contests the Danish understanding of equality as being the same as others and, consequently, accepting Janteloven's principles as a social decalogue (cf. one of the Law of Jante's commandments: "Do not think that you are better than us"). A motif which links the three novels is also silence/being mute as a necessity, imposed by the process of socialisation in childhood (see Mother's silence as a recurring motif in the novels) as well as the communist system[7] (see Świderski, *Autobiografie* 47). However, it also pertains to silence as a conscious choice, used as a strategy of resistance against levelling out differences ("moje milczenie jest – właśnie moje" Świderski, *Słowa obcego* 236 ["my silence is – precisely mine"]) as well as a strategy of understanding and accepting otherness.[8] The author's inspiration with Kierkegaard is also evident in this aspect.[9]

Finally, some examples of how the sylleptic 'I' manifests itself in each of Bronisław Świderski's novels will be provided. In all three of them, the protagonist/narrator is an emigrant with a threefold (Polish-Jewish-Danish), though, as mentioned earlier, unstable identity, who lives in Denmark and struggles with betrayal, rejection, strangeness/otherness, and inability to express himself in his non-native language: "jestem nie do końca Żydem i w całości wygnanym Polakiem, i w znacznej części odrzuconym Duńczykiem!" (Świderski, *Asystent śmierci* 335) ["I'm not a complete Jew yet a completely exiled Pole,

---

[5] Their migration (in the sense proposed by Søren Frank) can also be found in language – its linguistic impurity (heteroglossia), on the level of composition – in its multidimensionality and rhizomatic character, in the digressive character of the narrative, in the deconstruction of national images, and in the understanding of identity as a network of roots that will never stabilise.

[6] Cf. the category of "eternal translator" by Świderski which has been mentioned in the first part of my article.

[7] "Taught since childhood to be silent, how eloquent I was in silence! This Polish silence was heard in the country [...] But in Denmark nobody understood my silence!" "As a mute person, I could not enjoy democracy (...)" (Świderski, *Autobiografie* 49).

[8] "Only silence, accessible to everyone, can connect us. Only silence means the purest self-restraint in relation to another person who does not want to be drowned out by the sound of his own speech." (Świderski, *Słowa obcego* 243).

[9] See Świderski's essay on repetition (*Czepiam się Kierkegaarda* 66) in which silence is advocated as "most recommendable."

and a largely rejected Dane!"] His position in the world can be described as marginal, as being at the "zero point of culture." It can be summarised through the prism of language, which is one of the main identity keys: "Ojczysty język zapomniał emigranta, nowy – nie posiada dostatecznie precyzyjnych pojęć, by ująć jego indywidualne przeżycie" ["His mother tongue has forgotten the emigrant, his new one does not have precise enough concepts to capture his individual experience"], as Świderski writes in his essay "Doświadczenia emigranta" ("Experiences of an Emigrant," *Kiedy mogę zabić?* 112). The cover page of his first novel *Autobiografie* features "Jan i Bronisław Świderski" as its author (a singular form of the surname instead of the plural 'Świderscy,' as one might expect in Polish). The first-person narrator is a similarly split entity: B. and his *alter ego* Jan, physically alike and emotionally close but fulfils a different version of his biography, separating from him, betraying him, denying him, denying his past, giving up his assimilation in Denmark.

In *Słowa obcego* (1998, The Stranger's Words), the protagonist (along with the stranger mentioned in the title) is B., a lecturer of Polish at the University of Copenhagen. B. makes reference both to the text and to the empirical world, with the latter having a clear autobiographical dimension, parallel to the author's life experience. However, the narration is carried out in a different way compared to the other two novels – i.e., in an auctorial mode. The metaphorical figure of the stranger can also be read as a sylleptic feature. The stranger in the novel is an alien (perhaps from another planet), not speaking the local language and incomprehensible because he is not like the others (i.e., the Danes): he is a creature deprived of a biography, untranslatable, because of his muteness and otherness unsuitable for life in the Danish democracy, and thus ultimately rejected – the novel ends, in fact, with a scene of the stranger's deportation.

Asystent śmierci, where the narration takes place in the first-person mode, is his novel in which the sylleptic 'I' is the most strongly emphasized. After losing his job at the Søren Kierkegaard's Research Centre, the narrator-protagonist is employed as a caregiver of a dying person with an unknown identity (which is a parallel to the figure of stranger from *Słowa obcego* – due to his anonymity, inability to communicate, his status as an undesirable element in the Danish society). The task of the caregiver imposed by an institution representing the Danish state is to accelerate his death. The assistant accompanies the dying man at night during which he tells him about his life in Polish, including the biographies (their different versions) of his parents, beginning with the following statement: "Nazywam się Bronisław Świderski" (*Asystent śmierci* 62) ["My name is Bronisław Świderski"]. The novel refers to the two previous novels also in other ways, e.g., through Jan who appears as an immigrant in Denmark. Finally, the postscript to the novel, formulated as "Postscriptum Bronisława Świderskiego, autora i narratora powieści" (501) ["A Postscript by Bronisław Świderski, the author and narrator of the novel"], contains a list of consulted sources and references to the ideas contained in the novel, which have already been formulated in the author's earlier journalistic and essayistic texts.

The characters in these novels are woven from fiction and fact and their relatedness trespasses the boundaries of the novels – i.e., they can be read in the intertextual sequence of Świderski's work, and they resonate both through biographical and positional references (exclusion, strangeness) and attitude (defence of individualism). The truth in Świderski's novel becomes a "fikcyjna prawda" (Winiecka, "O sylleptyczności" 140) ["fictional truth"], the speaking 'I' intertwines with the spoken 'I,' being at the same time autobiographical and fictional – as a new space with an inconclusive, ambiguous status. Świderski's protagonist is in the position of one who has lost/is losing everything, whose world is fragmented, ruled by unpredictability, absurdity, grotesque, paradox, alienation, and exclusion. He has lost his biography and is losing the ability to interpret/translate himself between different cultural (and language) systems. He defends his integrity with individualism – linguistic and cultural ungrammaticality or silence.

The construction of the biographies in the novel is not about creating a coherent story at the end of which the Sense emerges, but about showing at the same time the splitting of 'I,' the instability of certainty ("truths") and self-confidence (of one's own right),[10] as well as about confronting Kierkegaard's work – taking "a venture in experimental psychology." The narrator of *Asystent śmierci* echoes the Danish philosopher: "Tożsamość nie polega na identyfikacji z poprzednimi pokoleniami, z ich językiem i ziemią, ale zależy od tego, co jednostka zrobi ze sobą – właśnie, aby być jednostką, a nie bladą kopią przodków. Jednostka to wiele postaci" (430) ["Identity is not about identification with previous generations, with their language and land, but it depends on what the individual will do with himself – precisely, to be an individual, not a faint copy of his ancestors. An individual is a lot of characters"].This multiplication, repetition,[11] toying with identities, an open structure, asking questions rather than providing answers, expressing doubts, is also not meant to find a recipe for the inability to say "we."[12] It is rather a road to 'I,' situated in an unknown future, a route to being "closer and closer to himself" (*Kiedy mogę zabić?* 134), which is supposed to help the individual reveal his own individual face and not just bear the "znami[ę] narodu" (Świderski, *Asystent śmierci* 407) ["nation's mark"].

Translated into English by Emilia Wąsikiewicz-Firlej

Works Cited

Borowczyk, Jerzy. "Przeciw tyranii porządku. O prozie Bronisława Świderskiego." *Czas Kultury* 3 (2013): 126–131.

Bukowski, Piotr de Bończa. "Der Fremde im Königreich der Dänen. Das Wort, der Diskurs und die Fremdheit in Bronisław Świderskis Roman *Słowa obcego.*" *Folia Scandinavica Posnaniensia* 24 (2018): 25–38.

---

[10] Świderski compares Nietzsche, Kierkegaard, and Gombrowicz and concludes that all three assign an important role to uncertainty. He concludes that "[wydaje się bowiem, że w naszym współżyciu z innymi niepewność daje nam więcej korzyści niż zuchwałą i pozorna pewność." [(Świderski, *Czepiam się Kierkegaarda* 233) ["therefore it seems that in our relationship with others, uncertainty offers us more benefits than bold and apparent certainty"].

[11] The Kierkegaardian notion of repetition is to be understood as signifying a higher degree of self-awareness (Świderski, *Czepiam się Kierkegaarda* 55).

[12] "nigdy nie będzie mi dane z przekonaniem powiedzieć "my." (Świderski, *Asystent śmierci* 123) ["I will never be able to say "we" with conviction."]

Dąbrowski, Mieczysław. *Tekst międzykulturowy. O przemianach literatury emigracyjnej.* Warszawa: Elipsa, 2007.

Frank, Søren. "Hvad er migrationslitteratur?" *Kritik* 203 (2012): 2–10.

Gosk, Hanna. *Bohater swoich czasów. Postać literacka w powojennej prozie polskiej o tematyce współczesnej. Wybrane zagadnienia.* Izabelin: Świat Literacki, 2002.

Haarder, Jon Helt. "Hullet i nullerne. Ind og ud af kunsten med performativ biografisme." *Passage* 63 (2010): 25–45.

Kierkegaard, Søren. *Powtórzenie. Próba psychologii eksperymentalnej Constantina Constantinusa.* Preface and translation: Bronisław Świderski. Warszawa: Fundacja ALETHEIA, 1992.

Larek, Michał. "Apostrofy Świderskiego." *Czas Kultury* 3 (2013): 119–125.

Nycz, Ryszard. *The Language of Polish Modernism.* Trans. by Tul's Bhambry. Frankfurt am Main: Peter Lang, 2017.

Turczyn, Anna. "Autofikcja, czyli autobiografia psychopolifoniczna." *Teksty Drugie* 1–2 (2007): 204–211.

Sawczuk, Mateusz. "Słowa i milczenie w prozie pisarza emigracyjnego Bronisława Świderskiego." *Facta Simonides* 1 (2016): 245–261.

Schab, Sylwia Izabela. "Migrationserfaringen i de polsk-danske forfatteres værker." *Folia Scandinavica Posnanienia* 23 (2017): 92–105.

Schab, Sylwia Izabela. "„…alle de ting hvis tab stadig giver mig amputationssmerter" – om migrationserfaringens sproglige og oversættelsemæssige aspekt." *Tijdschrift voor Skandinavistiek* 36.2 (2018): 243–249.

Świderski, Jan i Bronisław. *Autobiografie.* Londyn: Poets and Painters Press, 1981.

Świderski, Bronisław. *Słowa obcego.* Kraków: Wydawnictwo Znak, 1998.

Świderski, Bronisław. *Asystent śmierci. Powieść o karykaturach Mahometa, o miłości i nienawiści w Europie.* Warszawa: Wydawnictwo W.A.B., 2007.

Świderski, Bronisław. *Kiedy mogę zabić? Dyskusje o kulturze i przemocy.* Jerzy Borowczyk, Michał Larek (ed.). Poznań: WBPiCAK, 2012.

Świderski, Bronisław. *Czepiam się Kierkegaarda.* Warszawa: Fundacja Augusta hrabiego Cieszkowskiego, 2015.

Winiecka, Elżbieta. "O sylleptyczności tekstu literackiego." *Pamiętnik Literacki* 95.4 (2004): 137–157.

Winiecka, Elżbieta. "Prawdy, w które wierzymy." *Czas Kultury* 3 (2013): 112–118.

Zduniak-Wiktorowicz, Małgorzata. *Współczesny polski pisarz w Niemczech – doświadczenie, tożsamość, narracja.* Poznań: Wydawnictwo Poznańskie, 2010.

7. "Det här är en märklig plats": Space as a Reflection of Identity in Golnaz Hashemzadeh Bonde's Novel *Hon är inte jag*

Radka Stahr

Space, Migration, and Identity

Spatial representation is one of the basic components of the fictional exploration of reality. As is well known, in literary texts, space is not just the place of action that surrounds the characters, but it also participates strongly in unlocking the meaning. The special potential of spatial analysis was brought to the fore during the famous *spatial turn* in the late 1980s, which took place across the arts and sciences. Space began to be considered as important as time in the unfolding of human affairs and primarily regarded as a "social construction relevant to the understanding of the different histories of human subjects and to the production of cultural phenomena" (Warf and Arias 1).[1] The new conceptualization of space was especially influenced by the French philosophers Michel Foucault and Henri Lefebvre and formulated in Edward Soja's influential study *Postmodern Geographies*.[2] Space slowly got more attention from narratologists and has gained a central position in narrative texts. Today's literary analyses in this area concentrate primarily on the study of conceptualization of space in fictional works, be it a concrete or metaphorical representation. Literary scholars focus, among other things,

---

[1] As the German literary scholars Wolfgang Hallet and Birgit Neumann (and many others) point out, the studies of space in literature were well established long before the proclamation of the spatial turn. Space has always played a central role in all European philosophy, and in the early 20th century it became a constituent part of cultural theory. Relevant contributions to the spatiality of literature also appeared in literary studies before the turn; for example, the aesthetic spatial models of Ernst Cassirer, Jurij Lotman, and Mikhail Bakhtin. However, it is undeniable that the spatial concepts of the second half of the 20th century were fundamentally remodeled, even if they built on the tradition of older approaches (Hallet and Neumann 12–16).

[2] Foucault understands space as a set of relationships in which one lives. The space is therefore in itself heterogeneous, and a position can be described as a search for a set of relationships that can be used to define that location (331). The basis for Foucault's spatial theories is the social constitution of space, which is also a central theme in Lefebvre's approach. According to Lefebvre, the category of space does not exist universally but is socially and mentally produced and can only be understood in the context of a given society. The social space works, therefore, as a tool for the analysis of society (34). Starting from Foucault and Lefebvre, Soja demands balance in the relationship of time and space in humanities and (as the subtitle of his study suggests) calls for "The Reassertion of Space in Critical Theory." He is thus opposed to an essential and purely physical understanding of space, to thinking of space as an "environmental 'container' of human life" (79), and advocates the constitution of space as a product of social transformation and practice (80).

on the linguistic and textual means of creating space, on an author's selection of spatial information, or on the connection between space and characters.[3]

Spatial concepts play a major role in migration literature because crossing borders and entering a new, unknown space significantly contributes to the theme of cultural conflict. At the same time, it should be noted that increased migration is changing the relationship of Western society to space. Moving between cities, states, and continents has ceased to be a luxury; people have become more mobile, and their connections to place appear to have diminished in importance (Taylor 1).[4] According to the anthropologist Toon van Meijl, contemporary migration is fundamentally different from migration in the past, especially in relation to the reasons for movement: "A search for employment no longer seems to be the main reason to cross national borders, but people migrate more and more for a whole range of other reasons, including cultural reasons associated with differences in lifestyle as disseminated by multiple global media" (73). Globalization and current migration within Western society has undeniably led to the weakening of the relationships between humans and a particular place. Nevertheless, it should be emphasized that forced migration as an escape from war zones or because of religious or political beliefs represents a completely different matter. In this case, the relationship to the birthplace and home country is especially strong and emotionally coloured. This fact is often reflected in classical migration literature, which focuses on migration as a necessity rather than a decision that has been made freely. The connection to the lost home is a central motif in this literature, and the building of a new identity in the new country is strongly influenced just by the place itself. Literary analysis of space in migration texts can thus be considered an interesting key to understanding and interpreting the characters.

Not only in the case of migration is space an important formative factor in creating human identity. Over the past fifty years, the concept of *place-identity* has established itself primarily in sociology, psychology, and integrative geography.[5] The beginning of place-identity research falls into the field of cognitive psychology. In the early definition formulated by Proshansky and others in 1983, place-identity was described as

> a sub-structure of the self-identity of the person consisting of [...] cognitions about the physical world in which the individual lives. These cognitions represent memories, ideas, feelings, attitudes, values, preferences, meanings, and conceptions of behaviour and experience [...]. At the core of such physical environment-related cognitions is the 'environmental past' of the person; a past consisting of places, spaces and their properties which have served instrumentally in the satisfaction of the person's biological, psychological, social, and cultural needs. (Proshansky, Fabian and Kaminoff 59)

---

[3] For various possibilities of analysing fictional space, as well as for further secondary literature on the topic of spatial representation, see, e.g., article by Ansgar Nünning (primarily 39–46).

[4] It was not only the relationship of people to place that has changed in recent years. According to city planners, the place itself has also changed significantly. Under the influence of globalization, the centres of many cities are losing their uniqueness and cultural markers that made them instantly recognizable (Sepe iii).

[5] It should be noted that the term "place identity" has different meanings in different disciplines. While in psychology, sociology, and other humanities, it refers to the identity of a person, in geography and urban planning, it concerns the specific characteristics and appearance of a particular place (for more on "place identity" in urban planning, see Sepe).

Although Proshansky's conception was later criticized by other researchers (Taylor 40), he significantly contributed to further research on the relationship between man and space in the humanities. In today's interdisciplinary studies, place-identity refers in general to the meaning and significance of places for their inhabitants and users, as well as how these meanings contribute to the individuals' conceptualizations of self. Scientists from all disciplines assume that self-identity is not a static one but evolves through social interaction (Jackson 740). A person's identity reacts to changes in the pattern of established life, whether it be meeting new people, entering new cultural space or fundamental life events that force people to redefine themselves. In the case of migration, these factors seem to act simultaneously. But it is precisely the change of space that we can consider to be a starting point for the involvement of other constitutive factors. This chapter examines the close association between space, migration, and identity. Based on the analysis of a work of migration literature, the importance of changing place for the shaping of migrant identity should be emphasized, along with the literary means examined that the author uses to spatially represent the characters' development.

Hon är inte jag

Golnaz Hashemzadeh Bonde is a Swedish author, economic expert, and the founder and director of the non-profit organization *Inkludera Invest*.[6] She was born in Iran in 1983 and fled to Sweden with her parents as a young child. The family was forced to flee from their homeland for political reasons because the parents' viewpoints diverged from the regime that came to power with the Iranian Revolution, and they wanted to give their daughter a chance for a better life than that which awaited her in Iran. In most interviews, Hashemzadeh Bonde encounters questions about her identity and her relationship to the home country. Though she was a child when she left Iran, she carries a deep fascination for her native country and tries not to forget her heritage. At the same time, she admits that her "Iranian identity is very limited" (Markis) because of its distance from her new culture. With regard to our topic, it is interesting to note that Hashemzadeh Bonde's memories of her homeland are often spatially related: "Some of my first memories are just of bombs falling rapidly from the sky" (Markis), she explains in one of her interviews remembering the homeland. Of course, the earliest dramatic memories and experiences of escape significantly influenced the author's life and the way she views the world. This is evident in her two novels, which deal with migration and adaptation to a new culture and which contain strong autobiographical features.

Hashemzadeh Bonde succeeded internationally with her second book *Det var vi* (2017; *What We Owe,* 2018) which describes a complicated relationship between a daughter and her mother fighting cancer. The Iranian family background plays an important role in the story, but it is not so much about the migration process itself as about the lasting impact of this decision on several generations. This article, however,

---

6   *Inkludera Invest* is a non-profit organization which invests in social development. They back social entrepreneurs by giving them "a professional business perspective, helping them to develop and consolidate their enterprises" (Nordic Council of Ministers 175).

focuses on the author's debut novel *Hon är inte jag* (2012; *She Is Not Me, 2015*). The semi-autobiographical story begins in Sweden in the 1980s where an Iranian family has reached safety after years in hiding. The protagonist is the family's little daughter, a young girl who grows up in a grey factory town outside of Stockholm. The story takes place over several years; the character undergoes a long development and the reader witnesses various events that strongly influence identity of the adolescent girl. Not only is the emergence of the girl's new identity discussed, the change in the rooted identity of her parents is also reflected. Migration itself but above all the different ideas about their new life intensify the contrast between the two parents. Driven by the frustration of an unfulfilled existence, the father becomes even more violent towards his wife, and the parents separate after a few years of living in Sweden.

An important topic in the novel is racism in 1980s Sweden, which manifests itself in the family's everyday life but especially in the girl's education. They live in an almost exclusively white and middle-class society where it is not enough for a foreign girl to be good at school. In particular, according to her father, she must be better than all her Swedish classmates. But even though she works extremely hard, she is not accepted as the talented student she is, and the teachers tell her that she will never achieve the highest grades because of her "handicap": her origin. While she does everything in her power to transform herself and become an excellent student (by the end, she is accepted at the most prestigious university in Sweden), she actually becomes what others want her to be and creates a false identity for herself. At the same time, her obsession with hard work and self-discipline leaves traces on the girl's personality and leads to social anxiety and eating disorders. However, she manages to overcome her psychological problems and, at the end of the novel, we see a girl finding her own freedom – not political freedom but the freedom to be herself and realize her own plans for life.

There are three main characters in the novel: the mother, the father, and the daughter. After a few years in Sweden, the parents have a son, but his identity in relation to space is not well-developed; therefore, he will not be given much attention in the following analysis. We are not told the names of the characters; the heterogeneous narrator simply calls the girl "she" or "the girl" and the parents "mother" and "father." This anonymity can be understood as a generalization, as the novel does not only deal with this specific family but also represents the general problems of migrants in a new country. The absence of names also weakens the traditional connection between name and identity in the sense of "nomen omen;"[7] the reader cannot proceed from a concrete name to understanding the character and must derive his assumptions from other factors. The absent names can represent the cold relationships in the family, because even the mother refers to her daughter by the impersonal "she" when she talks about her.

Although the narrator exists outside the narrated world and seems relatively omniscient, there is a clear focalization on the figure of the girl, so that the reader mostly sees

---

[7] In her book *"Why Ask My Name?,"* Adele Reinhartz analyses anonymity and identity in biblical narrative and points out that the absence of a name in a text should not connote the absence of character's individuality, because "identity hovers in the encounter between character and reader and is demanding of both" (4). Her research shows that anonymity contributes to our effort to construct our reading of the characters and their stories. The proper name may ascribe stability and individuality, but the anonymity of the name calls these aspects in question and makes the figure more mysterious to the reader (188).

the events through her eyes and receives all information filtered through her experience of them. The mother comes shortly to the fore as the second female voice, namely in letters that she writes to her sisters in Iran and that are quoted in the novel. The characterization of the father can only be inferred through dialogues, his behaviour and – as this chapter sets out to prove – through his movement in space.

The relationship between space and identity in the novel can be analysed from two main perspectives. On the one hand, there is the role of space for the formation of the characters' identities – that is what the theory of place-identity mostly deals with. On the other hand, it is interesting to observe that space serves as a projection screen for the characters' identities. This means, for example, how the characters perceive a room and how they move in it because of their personality. Both aspects are, of course, interrelated and complementary, so their analysis is mutually conditioned.

Space Forms the Identity

The influence of space can be felt statically or dynamically. When a person has been in a particular space for a long time, he ceases to perceive it so strongly. The influence of space does not diminish, but the place-identity can be considered fixed. The person's relationship to place has grown to the point that he starts to identify himself with it. It concerns both the larger scale, such as nation and city, and the smaller scale, which includes neighbourhood, room, school, or workplace (Qazimi 306). Another situation occurs when we enter a new space, which automatically activates our senses, and we are more aware of its influence. Staying in a new space inevitably affects our relationship to the original space, which serves as a basis for comparison. It is not just a matter of marvelling at the unusual space (be it landscape, weather, or the appearance of buildings) but even things such as sounds and smells. Over time, however, the new space gradually becomes familiar and an integral part of our identity (307).

This dynamic moment of shaping place-identity is especially interesting to examine. In the analysed novel, it manifests primarily at the beginning of the story when the family comes to Sweden and the characters are directly confronted with the new location. In general, one can say that the new place in the novel is constructed as a contrast to the old one. It is not about specific local differences, as one would expect, but about the sensory perception of the place. The first descriptions of Sweden emphasize the prevailing calm, the strong light, and the lack of scents. All this is set in contrast to the loud market with spices that was situated on the street in front of their small dark flat in Iran.[8]

---

[8] The difference in the sensual perceptions of the two places is put in contrast right at the beginning of the story: "Hon var van vid nya dofter i varje gathörn: saffran på nyångat ris. Rått lammkött. Manssvett och upphettad olja. [...] Hon var van vid bildäckens gnisslande mot ojämn asfalt, gatuhandlarnas sånger, vid sirenerna [...]. Här var utomhus något annat. Det var tyst ute. Hon hade aldrig hört en sådan tystnad. Det var så tyst att det dunkade i öronen." (Hashemzadeh Bonde 7–8). ["She was used to new scents at every street corner: saffron on freshly steamed rice. Raw lamb meat. Men's sweat and heated oil. [...] She was used to the creaking of car tires against uneven asphalt, the songs of street traders, to the sirens [...]. Here the outdoors was something else. It was quiet outside. She had never heard such silence. It was so quiet that it thumped in her ears."] All translations of the examples from the novel are mine.

All three characters have different reactions to this contrast. The mother only sees the negative sides of the comparison, while the father, on the contrary, is uncritically enthusiastic about everything Swedish. Only the daughter is objective in the perception of the new place, thanks to her undetermined identity. The characters' initial relationship to the new location also reflects their relationship to the previous location. The mother is strongly bound to her Iranian identity, the father tries to deny this part of his past completely and the daughter is open to both because her place-identity is not as fixed and it is still being built. This is a good example of the heterogeneity in a migrated family with regard to their place-identity, which can often be seen in migration literature.[9]

In *Hon är inte jag* the parents fled Iran because of persecution, so it was a rational and necessary decision. However, it is revealed in time that the default place-identities of the mother and the father are opposite each other. Although the mother is aware of the need for migration, she is hostile to Sweden during the first months. Right at the beginning of her first letter, she writes about Sweden: "Det här är en märklig plats" (9) ["This is a strange place."] It is not a positive encounter with Swedish culture for the mother because she does not want to change anything about her rooted Iranian identity. Her negative attitude to the new place peaks when the family moves from a refugee camp in their first apartment. She describes it as follows: "Den är liten och mörk. Taket ligger inte långt ovanför våra huvuden, ibland känns det som att det ligger i mitt bröst" (13) ["It is small and dark. The ceiling is not far above our heads, sometimes it feels like it is on my chest"]. The mother's perception of the place does not constitute an objective description but rather the subjective reflection of her own attitude. The apartment may be small, but it is still an excellent place compared to the flats where the family had to hide in Iran.

The mother refuses any contact with her new surroundings and constantly complains to the father that there are no similar immigrants in the area. Incidentally, this is one of the main reasons for the father's enthusiasm for the place. During the move, he explains to his daughter:

Det bor bara svenskar i Fabriksorten, så du kommer få svenska kompisar, och äta svensk mat, och leka svenska lekar. Du kommer börja prata svenska direkt. (11)

[There live only Swedes in the factory town, so you will make Swedish friends and eat Swedish food and play Swedish games. You will start to speak Swedish immediately].

As has already been mentioned, the reader has no insight into the father's thoughts. His comments on the space are not specific to individual components of the place and do not evaluate its appearance at all. He is only focused on the meaning of the place. In his eyes, having their own place in Sweden is an important step on the way to assimilation. Although one can see from his behaviour that he is not satisfied with the apartment, he does not show his disappointment. The only thing he says after seeing their small flat for the first time is the theatrical statement "Hemma" (12) ["At home"].

---

[9] In Swedish migration literature, compare, e.g., the novel *Tätt intill våra liv* (2006, Close to our Lives) by the Kurdish-Swedish author Mustafa Can, which in many ways resembles Hashemzadeh Bonde's second novel *Det var vi*.

The change of place has a substantial impact on the identity of both parents and causes significant transformation in their behaviour. In this respect, the story demonstrates the fact that identification with the new space cannot take place day-by-day and that each person reacts differently. In the father's case, it should be pointed out that his rapidly changed place-identity is actually feigned. Because of the new surroundings, he apparently suppresses everything Iranian in himself and admires everything Swedish with an uncritical perspective. On this count, the place affects him negatively: the denial of his own identity and the forever optimistic mask he puts on lead to frustration, which ultimately impacts his behaviour and results in domestic violence against the mother.

Regarding the character of the mother, the new place markedly shapes her personality, too. At first, the unknown environment contributes to preserving and even strengthening her Iranian identity. But over time, she opens up and gradually becomes familiar with the surroundings. The result of her transformation is independence, she manages to get a job in a field she loves (though unfortunately not in the position she deserves) and to become independent from her violent husband. In this regard, the place forms the character rather positively.

Space Manifests Identity

It is evident that space, specifically its change, fundamentally affects the development of its inhabitants. However, it is also interesting to focus attention on how the characters' qualities can be deduced from their approach to the actual place and how this is represented by movement of the characters in a room. Remaining with the parents, their location in the literary space indicates above all the subject of gender.

In recent years, the research on place and identity has increasingly taken account of gender, especially in relation to the division of gender roles in space. In these cases, place-identity is complementary to and partially overlaps with the concept of feminist geography.[10] The British geographer Linda McDowell claims in her book *Gender, Identity and Place* that "a spatial division – that between the public and the private, between inside and outside – plays a central role in the social construction of gender divisions" (32). There are geographically defined places associated with a particular gender and constructed in binary opposition to each other. Thus, for example, outside, public and work are traditionally considered to be male space, while inside, private and home are associated with the female principle (McDowell 33). The debates about gender and space reflect not only the relationship of a particular sex to space that is (un)reserved for it but often also involves the issue of migration and gender diversity overcoming this

---

[10] Feminist geography emerged in the 1970s as a multidisciplinary research field, responding to the contemporaneous rise of feminist theories. Feminism penetrated geography at the same time as other humanities, but the new discipline was slower in developing, and it took more time for geography to embrace feminist scholarship (Nelson and Seager 2). The earliest feminist geographical work focused on mapping the spatial constrains facing women (3). In general, feminist geography deals with gender specificities in a geographical space and is very closely connected with sociology. Current research focuses on diverse topics, the most popular are issues such as the significance of gendered spatial divisions or gendered constraints manifested by limited spatial opportunities.

fundamental spatial change. According to McDowell, movement (in terms of migration) "is almost always associated with the renegotiation of gender divisions" (15). Some researchers point out that the change of contemporary society and its relation to place have had a more significant impact on women than on men (Taylor 39). In this respect, we can assume that the migratory change of space will primarily affect the gender identity of women. And this is something we can clearly observe in Hashemzadeh Bonde's novel.

In the beginning, the characters of the mother and the father move in different spaces, which correspond to the typical gender spaces: the mother's location is in the flat, she only moves within these four enclosed walls. The father is outside of home during the day: first, he explores the surroundings and then he gets a job as a bus driver, which means he is either gone or sleeping in the closed bedroom. The locations of the characters in this broader literary space correspond to the typical gender division.

The place-identity of the characters is also demonstrated in the more specific layout of the space, inside the flat itself. The fundamental place of the mother is the floor of the room. She spends her first weeks in Sweden sitting or lying on blankets which the family brought from Iran. Her position on the floor is mentioned several times by the narrator, for example:

[Hon] valt att stanna på filtarna med ryggen åt doften av lagerlokal, plast och en värld som borde ligga långt borta men som plötsligt gjorde anspråk på att vara verklighet. (19)

[(She) chose to stay on the blankets with her back to the smell of warehouse, plastic, and a world that should be far away but that suddenly claimed to be reality.]

The placement of the character in the room manifests two features of her identity. First, it represents the mother's strong connection to her Iranian home. Persian culture is closely related to carpets, and the mother's sitting on the floor reflects her desire for home and her aversion to the habits of the new place. The daughter even compares the blankets to a magnet, which pulls the mother to her Iranian roots.[11] The mother also typically sits with her back to the door, which demonstrates her dislike for the Swedish world behind the four walls.

Secondly, the mother's placement on the floor can also be interpreted as her subordination to men. The situation escalates when the father begins to act violent. Her position in the room makes it easy for him to attack her physically – sitting on the ground, she becomes an easy prey. But the attack causes a change in her, which is manifested by her following movement in space. The daughter reflects on this change as follows:

Monstrets födelse gjorde något med mamma. Den fick henne att resa sig från golvet och skapa sig ett hörn i den röda sammetssoffan. (19)

[The monster's birth did something with the mother. It made her rise from the floor and create a corner for herself on the red velvet sofa.]

---

[11] "De var som en magnet, de där filtrarna" (19) ["They were like a magnet, these blankets."]

This is a crucial moment for the change in the mother's identity and it is presented on the basis of space. The mother's symbolic rise from the floor represents her detachment from her Iranian past and it is the first step in her emancipation from the violent man. At the same time, as the mother opens up to the new space, her gender identity changes as well. She becomes more independent and an equal partner in relation to the father, which culminates in her departure from home. In this regard, there is a close link between space and gender in the identity formation and spatial presentation of the character.

The gender identity of the father is not as elaborate in relation to space as in the case of the mother. In terms of the spatial layout of gender roles, the character is represented traditionally because he dominates the space outside the home at the beginning of the novel. As already mentioned, he vents his anger and frustration at home, where he resorts to domestic violence against his wife. At first, he is upset because she does not want to assimilate. However, once the mother opens up to the new surroundings and discovers life behind the walls of the apartment, the domestic violence only intensifies. The mother now moves in his space and threatens his gender role as the breadwinner. Father's violent reaction demonstrates the fundamental problem of his new identity: the two-facedness. His enthusiasm for Sweden and for Western society in general proves to be a mask because, in his home, the original division of gender roles must prevail. After the mother leaves, the father also spends time on the floor. His position suggests mourning and grief for the mother, who was associated with this space. At the same time, he recalls suppressed Iranian memories for which sitting on the carpet is best suited. In a short time, however, he rises from the ground and returns to his traditional space and thus his social role in the family. This moment suggests the sensitive side of the father's identity; he is not just a violent aggressor but also an unfortunate, lonely person in whom the environmental change of life has awakened a monster.

The Girl's Place-Identity

While the changing identity of the mother and the father is influenced mainly by the initial migration change of space, and therefore mostly evolves at the beginning of the novel, the ambiguous identity of the daughter becomes evident rather late in the story. Like a typical child of migrants, her identity is torn between the current place she considers to be her home and the country of her family's origin, which she herself cannot recall very well.

With regard to the importance of the new space for the characters' identity, it is interesting to note the girl's first impressions of Sweden. As already mentioned, she is the only one who perceives the place relatively objectively and without any positive or negative emotional colouring, unlike her parents. Although she is very young at the beginning of the novel, her identity already seems to project in her approach to the new space. She is naturally enthusiastic and open to new impulses. It is this openness and boundlessness she primarily reflects when she encounters the new place for the first time. Her first comment on the place, concerning the first room into which the family is brought, is as follows:

Det lilla rummet var mindre än alla lägenheterna de hade flyttat mellan därborta. [...] Men rummet kändes större. Det kändes oändligt. [...] Den vita marken sträckte sig så långt ögat kunde se. (7)

[The small room was smaller than all the apartments they had moved between over there. [...] But the room felt bigger. It felt endless. [...] The white ground stretched as far as the eye could see.]

Her perception of space is objectively shaped and put in contrast to the space she had known until now. The biggest difference is the window, which makes the room appear larger. In Iran, they had always covered windows with towels so that they would not be discovered. The window and the windowsill soon become the girl's favourite place. They symbolically represent her intermediate position between the mother and the father: The mother is situated on the floor; the father is outside, and the girl at the window is thus located between them. This intermediate spatial position corresponds to the position of the daughter in the family and is often explicitly mentioned in the novel. One of the first chapters is entitled "Mellanvärld" ["The middle world," or "The world in between"], which can be considered a keyword in relation to the place-identity of the girl. She moves between two cultures, which are, in addition, represented spatially by each parent respectively. She learns Swedish vocabulary with her father at the table and listens to Persian music with her mother on the floor. At the same time, she acts as a catalyst for violence between the father and the mother, as she physically stands directly between both parents to alleviate the father's anger and partially protect the mother.

It is not only the social or cultural intermediate world between the mother and the father (and thus between the Iranian and the Swedish) that the girl's position connotes. This first small room in a refugee camp in general acts as an intermediate station between the past and the future, and this topic is also indicated by the location of the girl in the room.[12] She spends time stretched on the windowsill, and if she is elsewhere in the room, she at least looks out of the window, such as in this example: "Hon föredrog att rikta blicken utåt, ligga med ryggen mot rummet, ryggen mot mamma och pappa" (8) ["She preferred to look outward, to lie with her back to the room, her back to Mum and Dad"]. The girl is fascinated by the big world and the possibilities that lie behind the window. But throughout the story, her character appears very careful, distant, and relatively

---

[12] The refugee camp itself represents a special literary place whose social role evokes Foucault's concept of heterotopia. In his article "Of Other Spaces," Foucault constructs heterotopia as the "effectively realized utopia in which [...] all the other real arrangements that can be found within society, are at one and the same time represented, challenged and overturned" (332). Heterotopia thus fulfils a specific social purpose and appears in different forms. Foucault distinguishes between "heterotopias of crisis" (333) that are reserved for individuals who are in crisis in relation to others (typical of primitive society, e.g., the old) and "heterotopias of deviance" where people whose behaviour deviates from the standard are placed (e.g., prisons). The depiction of refugee camps in literature often corresponds to the basic features and functions that Foucault attributes to heterotopia. Above all, a refugee camp sets up a critical mirror of the society that is often emotionally related to it. At the same time, this place reflects social structures and mechanisms and thus indicates their problematic nature (for refugee camp as heterotopia cf., e.g., Oddenino 77ff).

passive in contact with other people. She performs her duties well but strangely mechanically. Thanks to her huge success, she fulfils her father's dreams of a better life. However, she is not sure if that is what she wants herself; as if her own openness and belief in the future were limited by a symbolic window from the past. Only at the end of the novel, when she manages to go her own way, does she seem to have freed herself from this invisible partition. This need to be free from the unhealthy influence of the parents is already expressed symbolically in the scene cited above when the girl looks from the window and lies with her back to the parents.[13]

Finally, it should be noted that the position of the girl in this intermediate space – whether specifically in the room or abstractly in relation to the parents and to the future – refers to the two famous concepts of postcolonial studies: hybridity and third space, as defined, for example, by Homi K. Bhabha. To put it simply, Bhabha's view of hybridity is based on the rejection of the traditional notion of a closed and stable culture. Cultural hybridity enables new forms of blending and overlapping of divergent cultural sign systems to emerge, which are then realized in an intermediate space. The third space is therefore not a real physically existing place but a space of enunciation and the opportunity to create cultural difference (Bhabha 55). In relation to Hashemzadeh Bonde's novel, Bhabha's ideas seem to be present in the context of the topic. The hybrid creation of the new transcultural identity, the contrasting of oneself and strangers, and the building of the imaginary third space between the spaces of the bearers of different identities are the main motifs of the novel, as is also the case in classic migration literature. Through the explicit position of the girl in the so-called "Mellanvärld," the author accentuates the postcolonial concepts even more and creates a clear connection between the abstract thematic level and its concrete literary representation.

In the novel, however, the girl's place-identity is not only elaborated in relation to migration but also to other problems that a teenager faces. For example, her extreme self-control, which results in eating disorders, is spatially reflected in her fixation on a closed apartment. At one stage of her illness, she is even unable to leave the flat. She feels she is in control of things there, especially with regard to her planned study day and, above all, the allocated food rations. Fixing on an enclosed familiar space is an extreme manifestation of her place identity, which is disturbed by her father's exaggerated demands. The roots of the problem thus reach back to the initial migration experience, which fundamentally changed the identity of the characters.

---

[13] The window represents one of the essential symbols that accompanies the protagonist throughout the story. It refers to the traditional interconnection between the inner spaces of a house and the world outside and functions as a means of communication for the protagonist, too. It puts her in the role of an observer with whom she identifies herself from the beginning and translates it into real social intercourse. In the novel, we find a number of other examples where the girl's attention is fixed on the window: in one passage, she even calls the window in the preschool as her lookout to the world (24); when she has to do the extra tasks her father has prepared for her, she has to sit with her back to the window so that she doesn't lose concentration (35–36); or in the situation when she sits in the social workers' office and has to decide whether to be assigned to her father or to her mother after their separation, the view from the window serves as an escape from reality to her (45).

Place as a Metaphor for Social Status

This analysis focuses primarily on the interconnection of place and identity regarding a migration topic, but in the end, I would like to point out that there are other interesting roles that the literary space assumes in Hashemzadeh Bonde's text. The spatial representation of the layout of society is one of the most striking (and related to the main topic).

Class differences are especially reflected in the actual location of the character's homes. The first apartment of the family is located on the periphery of a factory town and is associated primarily with concrete as the basic building material. After a few years, the family advances up the social ladder so much that they can move into a new apartment closer to the centre of Stockholm where the concrete neighbourhood is replaced by red bricks. They are now in a "better society," but, at the same time, they are clearly confronted with people ranking even higher. The author again uses spatial locations to represent this motif; the inaccessible paradise is Saltsjöbaden, an area separated from their residence by a lake. A teacher from Saltsjöbaden confronts her pupils with the differences between their place and the world behind the water:

> I Saltsjöbaden bodde alla i villor, hade utsikt över vattnet, åt oxfilé till söndagsmiddag och åkte ner till Tyskland för att hämta hem stora bilar. Efter något år förstod klassen att Saltsjöbadens Samskola var en sådan *fiin* skola. Där fick man *fiina* betyg, skaffade sig en *fiin* utbildning och sedan tjänade man alla de där pengarna som behövdes för att kunna bo i saltsjöbadsvilla, titta ut över vattnet och äta oxfilé medan man körde hem sin tyska bil (36).

> [In Saltsjöbaden everyone lived in villas, had a view of the water, ate beef fillet for Sunday dinner and went down to Germany to get themselves big cars. After some years, the class realized that the Saltsjöbadens Samskola was such a *fine* school. There, they received *fine* grades, obtained a *fine* education and then they made all the money they needed to live in a Saltsjöbaden villa, look out over the water, and eat beef fillet while driving home in their German cars.]

In terms of social layout, the situation is different from the previous place of residence. There, as a migrant, the girl was alone against the other classmates; here, the class as a whole is confronted with fundamental social differences. This situation logically leads to the better integration of the girl because it connects the collective to another common "enemy." The social gradation is perceived not at the individual but at the collective level. This transformation is manifested in the tremendous dreamy views from the window of the water and the world behind it, cast this time by everyone in the classroom. However, the girl is soon confronted with the naivety of the notion that she is now part of a homogeneous stratum of society when she and her friend of better social-standing, Evelina, decide to change schools and enrol in the school in Saltsjöbaden. While Evelina, although a weaker student, is supported by the teacher and enters the new school, the girl receives a refusal with an explanation that "alla typer av människor passar inte in på Saltsjöbadens Samskola" (40) ["not all types of people fit in at Saltsjöbadens Samskola"]. The concrete space is thus again associated with a particular social status and implies criticism of the position of migrants in the society.

The girl succeeds in breaking her adversity when she is admitted to an elite university. Her social ascension is symbolically rounded off by a new location; after years of saving money, her mother decides to buy her an apartment in Östermalm, the central and elite part of Stockholm. Not surprisingly, the choice will eventually fall on a bright apartment with extra-large windows. The window becomes the girl's favourite position again, but this time her gaze is not just out but she also likes to observe the interior of her apartment, indicating that the desired goal has been achieved. The mother emphasizes the significance of the location of the flat with her last sentence when she hands over the apartment to her daughter: "Det viktigaste är att du är här. Att du inte är där" (110) ["The most important thing is that you are here. That you're not there"]. These sentences are pronounced without further specification or commentary, but it is clear to the girl (and to the reader) that the indefinite "here" and "there" are directed not only to specific locations but also to the associated social status.

In addition to the general interconnection of geographical locations with social status, there are some other examples of metaphorical spatial distribution in the novel. For instance, the father's ambitious plan for the girl's future is also spatially represented. When they leave for school on her first day, the father uses the location of the building to portray different versions of the future and the resulting social status. The school is located on a hill and consists of three colourful villas that remind the father of the children's story *Bullerbyn*.

"Det där är framtiden," hade pappa fastställt och pekat på Bullerby-husen. "Det där är att gå bakåt," hade han fortsatt och pekat ner mot fabriken. "Det här," hade han fortsatt och pekat tillbaka mot de färgglada villorna, gula, gröna, rosa, "ska hålla dig långt från det där." (6)

["That is the future," Dad stated and pointed to the Bullerby houses. "That is to go backwards," he continued, pointing down at the factory. "This," he added, pointing back at the colourful villas – yellow, green, pink – "shall keep you far from that."]

The girl receives a spatially expressed guide for what is expected of her: she must get as high as possible in her education. At the same time, the geographical location of the school at the top and the factory at the bottom reflects the social status of the buildings and its attendees.

The interconnection of space and social status also appears on the girl's first day at the prestigious university. The auditorium, where lectures are held, is hierarchically divided. This is clearly communicated to students by their older classmates who are to welcome them at the university. They may sit in the upper rows while new students are seated below them. During the first months, however, a hierarchy will also be created among new students: On the front right side, sits the real elite, the rich and clever for whom it is part of natural order of things to be in an elite school and whose life smoothly follows the scheduled course. On the front left, is the elaborate elite, those smart and eager who have managed to achieve the best grades and have evolved to the highest peak. Behind the front rows sit the part of the students who are smart but don't wear designer clothes, do not take the university so seriously, and are interested in questions that are not relevant to the exam. The middle part of the auditorium is occupied by

109

students who are diligent and hardworking but unable to apply knowledge to reality. The rear rows belong to those who mostly come late and whose studies are doomed to failure. The layout of the auditorium is described in detail in the novel and can be read as a miniature image of the whole society: the elite, the middle class, and the bottom. At the same time, however, this is not a division based solely on social status, as in the previous examples. The protagonist sits in the front rows, a position which she achieved through her diligence and intelligence. In this respect, the girl represents the hope that it is possible to break through the stable stratification of society, determined by geographical and social origin. This motif is accentuated by spatial representation, and the image of the girl in the first rows has a greater impact on the reader's imagination.

7. Conclusion

The analysis shows that Hashemzadeh Bonde's novel very strongly refers to the relevance of place-identity in migration literature. Space, and especially its change, is depicted as one of the basic factors for the personality development of the characters, which is illustrated mainly by the transformation of the mother and the father after their arrival in Sweden. At the same time, the author uses space to suggest the attributes of the characters because their perception of space can be read as a fundamental projection of their feelings: the mother's negative description of the first two lodgings refers to her fear of new things, while her husband's exaggerated enthusiasm reflects desperation and poorly concealed anger at the development of the situation. Their approach to the new place is also an important indication of their relationship to the original place, which plays a major role in shaping their new identity. In this respect, the text demonstrates not only the influence of space on the development of its inhabitants but also individuality and heterogeneity in response to spatial change.

An important literary means of rendering the theme is the movement of characters in the space from which the reader can deduce a lot of information about the characteristics and further development of the protagonists. The location of the characters in the space is closely connected to other basic motifs such as gender. As in feminist geography, specific spaces are associated with specific gender roles. At the same time, we can find more concrete examples for a gender-oriented interpretation of the text, such as the mother's movement in the apartment which corresponds to her gradual emancipation. The position of the girl in the interspace can also be interpreted in different ways, for example, in relation to cultural hybridity and the third space. Last but not least, the connection of residence to social status is used to demonstrate the social rise of the main character. In conclusion, we can say that the depiction of space in the novel becomes an important literary strategy for raising more general questions, mainly concerning migration, gender roles, and the social strata.

In the beginning, I pointed out the fact that people's relationship to place has changed. Nevertheless, space remains one of the main factors in shaping our identity, although this often happens unconsciously. In this respect, Hashemzadeh Bonde's book can be read as a literary demonstration of the importance of space and, at the same time, as the practical implementation of this idea.[14]

Works Cited

Bhabha, Homi K. *The Location of Culture*. London/New York: Routledge, 1994.

Foucault, Michel. "Of Other Spaces: Utopias and Heterotopias." *Rethinking Architecture: A Reader in Cultural Theory*. Ed. Neil Leach. NYC: Routledge, 1997. 330–336.

Hallet, Wolfgang, and Birgit Neumann. "Raum und Bewegung in der Literatur. Zur Einführung." *Raum und Bewegung in der Literatur. Die Literaturwissenschaften und der Spatial Turn*. Ed. Wolfgang Hallet and Birgit Neumann. Biefeld: Transcript, 2009. 11–32.

Hashemzadeh Bonde, Golnaz. *Hon är inte jag*. Stockholm: Wahlström & Widstrand, 2012. E-book.

Jackson, Ronald L., ed. *Encyclopedia of Identity*. Los Angeles: Sage, 2010.

Lefebvre, Henri. *The Production of Space*. Oxford: Blackwell, 1991.

Markis, John. "Author Who Fled Iran Writes Book to Dismantle Stereotypes." 10 Sep. 2019. *The Chronicle*. Accessed 31 Mar. 2020.

McDowell, Linda. *Gender, Identity and Place. Understanding Feminist Geographies*. Cambridge: Polity, 2004.

Meijl, Toon van. "Anthropological Perspectives on Identity: From Sameness to Difference." *The SAGE Handbook of Identities*. Ed. Margaret Wetherell and Chandra Talpade Mohanty. London: Sage, 2010. 63–81.

Nelson, Lise, and Joni Seager. "Introduction." *A Companion to Feminist Geography*. Eds. Lise Nelson and Joni Seager. Malden, MA: Blackwell, 2005. 1–11.

Nünning, Ansgar. "Formen und Funktionen literarischer Raumdarstellung: Grundlagen, Ansätze, narratologische Kategorien und neue Perspektiven." *Raum und Bewegung in der Literatur. Die Literaturwissenschaften und der Spatial Turn*. Eds. Wolfgang Hallet and Birgit Neumann. Bielefeld: Transcript, 2009. 33–52.

Nordic Council of Ministers: *Social Entrepreneurship and Social Innovation: Initiatives to Promote Social Entrepreneurship and Social Innovation in the Nordic Countries*. Copenhagen: TemaNord, 2015.

Oddenino, Ilaria. "Re-Drawing Heterotopias: Challenging Refugee Camps as Other Spaces in Kate Evans' *Threads: From the Refugee Crisis*." *Le Simplegadi* 16/18 (2018): 75–84.

Proshansky, Harold M., Abbe K. Fabian, and Robert Kaminoff. "Place-Identity: Physical World Socialization of the Self." *Journal of Environmental Psychology* 3 (1983): 57–83.

Quazimi, Shukran. "Sense of Place and Place Identity." *European Journal of Social Sciences* 1/1 (2014): 306–310.

Reinhartz, Adele. *"Why Ask My Name?" Anonymity and Identity in Biblical Narrative*. Cary: Oxford University Press, 1998.

Sepe, Marichela. *Planning and Place in the City*. Florence: Taylor and Francis, 2013.

Soja, Edward W. *Postmodern Geographies. The Reassertion of Space in Critical Social Theory*. London: Verso, 1989.

Taylor, Stephanie. *Narratives of Identity and Place*. London: Routledge, 2010.

Warf, Barney, and Santa Arias. "Introduction: The Reinsertion of Space in the Humanities and Social Sciences." *The Spatial Turn: Interdisciplinary Perspectives*. Eds. Barney Warf and Santa Arias. London: Routledge, 2008. 1–10.

[14] This work was supported by the European Regional Development Fund project "Creativity and Adaptability as Conditions of the Success of Europe in an Interrelated World" (reg. no.: CZ.02.1.01/0.0/0.0/16_019/0000734).

8. *Dulce de Leche:* Translingualism, Laughter and Sweet Stickiness in Veronica Salinas's *Og – En argentinsk au pairs ordbok*

Elisabeth Oxfeldt

In 2016, Argentinian-Norwegian Veronica Salinas (b. 1977) published *Og – En argentinsk au pairs ordbok* (And: The Dictionary of an Argentinian Au Pair). Written as a series of autobiographic free-verse poems, the text depicts Salinas's first year in Norway in the early 2000s, living with a family in Fredrikstad, attending Norwegian language classes, and reminiscing about her recent and distant past in Argentina. Her memories cover her reasons for leaving Buenos Aires as an economic refugee as well as her childhood summers spent in an Indian village in Northern Argentina. It is a narrative of melancholy and hope, tied to the project of developing a new hybrid identity in Norway.[1]

Referring to her work as an "ordbok" (dictionary, literally translated: word book), Salinas plays with the idea of how a foreign-language immigrant relies on dictionaries for communication. Gyldendal's Norwegian dictionaries are blue and used to resemble the cover of Salinas's book. Yet, in Salinas's case, an "ordbok" also refers to a *book of words* for defining herself. The dictionary trope is not unusual in what may be called immigrant, migrant, migration, or immigration literature.[2] With its emphasis on the topic of learning a new language, the book falls into the category of a "language memoir." It is a typical example of translingual literature, the first book (or one of the first books) written by an immigrant in her new language about 10 years after she has arrived. As Ingeborg Kongslien has pointed out in an article on translingual literature in Scandinavia, such texts express the ways in which their authors come to understand their background histories including their having to switch languages through the writing project itself (37). Initially, at least, they use their new language in a grammatically correct manner, presumably to gain access to publishing houses and the literary public (ibid.). Hence, their texts differ from those of authors like Jonas Hassen Khemiri and Maria Navarro Skaranger who are of immigrant background but have a Scandinavian language as their first language and experiment with immigrant idiolects and other non-normative forms in their hybrid writing.

Og is furthermore conceived as an easy-to-read book, financed by *Leser-søker-bok*, and is part of The White Ravens International Youth Library. Hence, it is an easy read, linguistically as well as narratologically. As explained in *Utrop* (a multicultural newspaper

---

[1] The Argentinian literary perspective on Norway is rare. As of 2019, 1071 Argentinian immigrants lived in Norway, out of a total 765 108 immigrants (Statistics Norway).

[2] Another example is Chinese-British Xiaolu Guo's *A Concise Chinese-English Dictionary for Lovers* from 2007.

for minorities in Norway), the book consists of short sentences and a good deal of blank space on each page. Shifts between present and past are clearly marked, and the words are relatively short, as are the "chapters" (Holte). The free-verse poems vary in length from one line (verse) in the beginning, like "H a r d u d e t b r a ?" (Salinas, *Og* 7) ["A r e y o u d o i n g w e l l ?"] to six-page long childhood stories from Argentina. Making for a straightforward reading experience, each poem is marked according to whether it depicts Norway or Argentina. About three quarters of the poems are set in Norway (73 in total) and one quarter (23 in total) depict Argentina. The Argentina flashbacks begin after fifteen Norway poems. They start out depicting life in Buenos Aires and providing a historical backdrop for the poet-narrator's emigration due to a financial crisis around the turn of the millennium (32) and then recount childhood summers that she and her sister spent with their Indian grandmother in the jungle while their parents stayed in the capital to work. At the end, the focus lands on the present, and the book concludes with twenty-five poems set in Norway. Hence, the work is framed by her first-year experience of living as an au pair in Fredrikstad.

Og is written from a position of translingualism on issues of language and identity in a multicultural setting, including not only the au pair's stay in a Norwegian family but also a language school experience with immigrants from all over the world. Later in her career, Salinas has taken a more radical step beyond the post-monolingual paradigm (Yildiz), writing or performing together with other authors similarly writing minority or multicultural literature. The text collage comprising her dramatic piece, *Vinduer* [Windows], for instance, is inspired by slam poetry, rap, children's poetry, and blogging, and experiments with dialects, slang, Sámi joik, metaphors, and vulgarisms (Bikset). On the national day of the Sámi (February 6) in 2016, she contributed to the drama *Vidas Extremas* [Extreme Lives] about genocides and disappearances among indigenous people, particularly Mayan and Sámi (the performance toured Norway afterwards). Other text contributors were the Norwegian Sámi author Sigbjørn Skåden and Guatemalan writers Rosa Cháves and Angel "Kame" Canas Ambrosio (Bjørdal). She also appeared with the Danish poet Yahya Hassan and Sámi joik musician Inga Juuso on Morsmåls-dagen [Mother Tongue Day] at Litteraturhuset [The House of Literature] in Oslo for a panel debate on language and identity (Castello). In her own words:

Jeg er også opptatt av de personlige omkostingene [sic] ved migrasjon, enten den er selvvalgt eller påtvunget, og virkeligheten av å bli forstått og å gjøre seg forstått. Jeg er opptatt av flytende identitet, etnisitet, fremmedgjøring, makt, avmakt og lammelse – det personlige og det politiske. (Salinas, "Jeg ble frarøvet" 2014)

[I am also concerned with the personal costs of migration, whether it is chosen or forced, and the reality of being understood and making oneself be understood. I am concerned with liquid identity, ethnicity, alienation, power, powerlessness, and paralysis – the personal and the political.][3]

What I find particularly interesting in Salinas's work is her careful use of words and images serving to explore notions of a changing identity. Given her three major linguistic restrictions – 1) having to gain access to a literary public by showing that she masters

---

[3]   All translations of Salinas into English are my own.

a grammatically correct Norwegian, 2) being commissioned to write an easy-to-read book, and 3) wanting to depict what it is like to be a linguistic newcomer – she carefully chooses simple Norwegian words, a few Spanish words, and finally one key linguistic transgression which she milks, so to speak, for all it is worth, playing with *dulce de leche* (literally: "sweet of milk") as a substance, a word, and an exceptionally rich metaphor.[4]

In this article, I will first turn to the titular "og" ["and"] and show the way in which the poet-narrator negotiates her hybrid identity through this conjunction. Significantly, her hybrid identity pertains not only to Norway but also to her Indian heritage in Argentina. I will furthermore suggest that Julia Kristeva's notion of being a subject "in process" aptly captures the poet-narrator's life-long journey through languages, cultures, and identities ("Fra én identitet"). I will then analyze the role played by laughter as a bodily response tying the au pair to her Indian grandmother and what is emphasized as a pre-linguistic and pre-symbolic realm. Finally, I will turn to *dulce de leche*, exploring it as a key metaphor through Sara Ahmed's notion of the stickiness of affect (*The Cultural Politics*). I will analyze *Og* as a narrative of melancholy and hope, tied to the project of developing a new hybrid identity in Norway through a verbal and conceptual play with sweet stickiness.

The Hybridity of "Og"

"Og" is a conjunction which is easy to pronounce but hard to live by. It is difficult to transcend established dichotomies and either-or thinking. Salinas's language memoir introduces this theme in one of the first poems:

Lyden til ordet «og» er lett.
Jeg kan si «og» uten problemer,
men hva kan jeg bruke «og» til? (Salinas, *Og* 12)

[The sound of the word "and" is easy.
I can say "and" with no problems,
but what can I use "and" for?]

This question sets a conceptual frame and is answered at the end of the book through what appears as a verbal performative: an incantation based on new hope. After nearly a year of unhappiness with her initial au pair family in Fredrikstad, the poet-narrator places an ad in the newspaper in search of a new position, and thirty-nine Oslo families immediately contact her. The au pair concludes her memoir on an optimistic note:

I begynnelsen var det bare lyden til ordet
«og»
som var lett.
Jeg kunne si «og» uten problemer,
men visste ikke hva jeg kunne bruke det til.

---

4 As a food product it refers to caramelized sweetened condensed milk.

I dag er det mange ord som er lette.
Men «og» er min favoritt.
OG.

Jeg liker «OG»!
[…]
«Og» istedenfor «eller»! (170)

[In the beginning it was only the sound of the word
"and"
which was easy.
I could say "and" without problems,
but I didn't know what I could use it for.

Today many words are easy.
But "and" is my favorite.
AND.

I like "AND!"
[…]
"And" instead of "or!"]

She gives examples of either-or questions that have been awkward for her to answer, insisting that she is from the province *and* the city, she is poor *and* rich, she is from here *and* there, she likes the ocean *and* the mountains.

Hele min historie er reisen til et ord:
OG
Ett ord:
OG
Og jeg er argentinsk.
Og jeg er. (171)

[My entire history is the journey towards a word:
AND
One word:
AND
And I'm Argentinian.
And I am.]

The "og" becomes existential as the poet-narrator can only exist in her hybridity. Linguistically this hybridity applies to bilingualism and being able to speak Norwegian as well as Spanish (13). Ethnically, however, it concerns being Argentinian. At the end of the memoir, she does not claim to be Norwegian, or Argentinian-Norwegian. The either-or questions that she transcends pertain to her Argentinian background, where her family is from here and there, rural and urban, rich and poor. Both her parents, it turns out, are half Indian and half Spanish. Her mother is a Guaraní and her father a Toba Indian. Spanish is their national language, but her mother also speaks Guaraní, which her father understands, while he does not speak any Indian language himself. They make sure that their children do not learn to speak an Indian language either:

> Mamma snakket guaraní til papa,
> men bare når Sisi og jeg ikke skulle forstå.
> Da snakket de veldig lavt,
> som om ordene skulle skjules i vinden.
>
> Vi fikk ikke lære guaraní.
> Det ville være enda en grunn til å diskriminere oss. (67)
>
> [Mom spoke Guaraní to dad,
> but only when Sisi and I were not to understand.
> They spoke very softly,
> as if the words were to be hidden in the wind.
>
> We were not to learn Guaraní.
> It would be yet another reason to discriminate against us.]

The sisters grow up like many oppressed indigenous peoples who are assimilated and forced into a national monolingual paradigm. Hence, *Og* negotiates a new Norwegian identity while it also works through an earlier memory of political violence and its traumatic effect on the "mother tongue."[5]

The parents moved to the capital so that their daughters can become well educated. Living in Buenos Aires, the sisters, although they speak Spanish, are subject to discrimination due to their Indian appearance. They are treated as human waste, the poet-narrator explains, something President Sarmiento called the Indians in the 1800s. Although she grew up in the 1990s, the attitude of the 1800s still reigned and the "dream" was to replace Indians and black people with white Americans and Europeans (67). In Buenos Aires they are called "cabecitas negras." The poet-narrator provides a literal Norwegian translation of the phrase ("svarte skaller") but then proceeds to repeat the derogatory term in the original Spanish. "Svarte skaller" (black skulls), presumably, is a case of a literal translation creating an alienating effect which does not properly capture the immediate violence of the original:

> Vi ble kalt cabecitas negras, svarte skaller.
> «Cabecitas negras» var vi.
> «Cabecitas negras» sa kroppene til foreldrene mine.
> De gikk med bøyd rygg, framskutte skuldre
> og de snakket lavt.
> Så lavt at jeg måtte lukke øynene for å høre.
>
> De mumlet (68).

---

[5] I borrow this perspective and wording from Yasemin Yildiz, who analyzes Turkish-German author Emine Sevgi Özdamar's *Mutterzunge* (1990) from that perspective (146). While Özdamar's work is marked by a radical strategy of literal translation, Salinas's includes only one pregnant example (see discussion below).

[We were called cabecitas negras, black skulls.
"Cabecitas negras" we were.
"Cabecitas negras" my parents' bodies said.
They walked with bent backs, shoulders pressed forward
and they spoke softly.
So softly that I had to close my eyes to hear.

They mumbled.]

In Yasemin Yildiz' theory on translingual authors' use of literal translation, there is a connection between literality and trauma. Following trauma theorist Cathy Caruth, she finds that since trauma results from an overwhelming experience, it returns in a manner that is "absolutely true to the event" (Caruth 5, qtd. by Yildiz 162). Literal translation, on the other hand, is a means of working through the traumatic event (163). In the above case, returning to, and repeating "cabecitas negras," can be seen as indicative of a trauma, experienced in the first place by her parents and secondarily by the poet-narrator herself. Had she proceeded with the literal translation, repeating "svarte skaller" instead of "cabecitas negras," she would have created the effect of linguistic alienation that would have counteracted her intention of bringing to mind the burning sense of shame and helplessness experienced by her parents.

At the same time, she could have translated the term less literally and simply used the Norwegian term "svartskalle"[6] (black skull, as one word) and thus avoided the linguistic alienation effect. It would, however, not have transported the reader to an Argentinian experience set in a certain time and place but rather opened up for connotations of Norwegian racism.

It is evidently important to the poet-narrator to work through her own personal history in the context of a greater Argentinian history. The text becomes what Yildiz calls "a means of working through traumatic (trans)national histories" (146), with the parenthetical "trans" suggesting that the story captures a personal history of moving from one nation (and one national language) to another as well as a national (here Argentina's) history of (linguistic) oppression. These two stories are thoroughly intertwined, and the poet-narrator cannot tell her story about migrating to Norway without also relating the Argentinian oppression of indigenous Indians. Conversely, she uses her *trans*national experience to come to terms with her national history, as it evolves in the Argentinian center and on the periphery.

Serving as a counterpoint to Buenos Aires, is a place the poet-narrator refers to as Lola's Paradise. It is a jungle in Northern Argentina where her maternal grandmother lives, and where being of Indian heritage is a source of joy, strength, and liberation instead of sadness, shame, and oppression. Located on the nation's periphery, it is a pre-modern site of nature where Lola washes her clothes in the lake (Salinas, *Og* 74), and the girls have to walk for an hour to get to the nearest store. It is also a place where nobody wears shoes. In Lola's Paradise, the most soothing feeling is walking barefoot through soft, cool "chicken poo" ["hønebæsj" 101] – this in contrast to Buenos Aires

---

[6] This is defined as a pejorative, offensive term meaning "dark-skinned person." https://www.naob.no/ordbok/svartskalle

where the poet-narrator has been told that she has "Indian feet" in need of orthopedics. Feet often stand in metonymically as a sign of a person's true identity (as in the tale of Cinderella); in *Og* they do so literally and figuratively:

Men hos Lola levde føttene mine et fritt liv.
Der fant de tilbake til sin opprinnelige form.
I dag kan jeg si at føttene mine får være som de er.
Guaraníen i meg kan ikke tas bort. (102)

[But at Lola's my feet lived a life of freedom.
There, they returned to their original shape.
Today I can say that my feet are allowed to be themselves.
The Guaraní side of me cannot be removed.]

The first two lines indicate that it is possible to reach a point of acceptance of her mixed Indian heritage at a temporal and geographical distance from Buenos Aires, at Lola's Paradise. The second two lines, evoking "today" and written in the present tense, furthermore indicate that this continues to be attained – and maintained – in Norway, and that from this vantage point, she can consider herself simply Argentinian. Returning to the final page of *Og*, we found her concluding "Og jeg er argentinsk" (171) ["And I am Argentinian"]. Yet, the sentence begins with "og," so Argentinian comes in addition to something else, now eclipsed, which could be Guaraní Indian. This is the book's penultimate sentence, and as quoted above, it is partly repeated in the final line: "Og jeg er" (ibid.) [And I am]. A word is subtracted, and a new meaning is added. The last line can be understood on an existential level, reflecting being in general. Depending on how one reads it (aloud), it can also emphasize life as a process, an unfinished sentence, opening up for more adjectives and life experiences being added. The word "Norwegian" could, for instance, be added to what she is.[7] The poet-narrator never arrives at a fixed identity but remains a Kristevan "subject in process" (Kristeva, "Fra én identitet").

Laughter and the Kristevan Semiotic

Julia Kristeva's theories on gender, subject formation, and language seem particularly apt for capturing the poet-narrator's understanding of herself. As she emphasizes her laughing heartily in the face of failed communication with her maternal grandmother, she evokes a feminine space tied, in Kristeva's terminology, to the semiotic, in opposition to masculine symbolic space. The realm of the semiotic is what all humans enter into before they develop a language that allows them to become "a speaking subject" and to develop a sense of identity. Clearly, having to express oneself in a new and foreign language is infantilizing and forces one into silence, into the Kristevan semiotic, and into having to become "a speaking subject" anew.

---

7   Today, Veronica Salinas is described as a Norwegian playwright and actress with an Argentinian background on Norwegian Wikipedia. https://no.wikipedia.org/wiki/Ver%C3%B3nica_Salinas (accessed 25 February 2020).

118

What distinguishes the Argentinian au pair's response to having to learn new codes, new languages, and new symbolic orders, is that she encounters it with laughter. This, for instance, sets her apart from her fellow au pair Monika, a student from Poland. Together the two friends bring the children they are taking care of to libraries and parks and communicate by pointing to words in their respective dictionaries. Neither speaks English. While good company in many ways, Monika is also a downer. Her first line in the book is "I n g e n t i n g   e r   l e t t" (Salinas, *Og* 11) ["N o t h i n g   i s   e a s y"]. Sitting in a park watching the children play, the Argentinian au pair smiles at them. Monika pulls out her dictionary and stops at the word "tristhet" (19) ["sadness"]. Tears well up in her eyes, while the poet-narrator forces her own tears back. The two au pairs appear as emotional opposites, with Monika being more of a sad melancholic: "Monika peker mye på det triste» (22) ["Monika often points to what is sad."] Monika's affect is contagious and sticky, as Sara Ahmed would put it, yet the poet-narrator tries to shake it off – literally through laughter vibrating through her body and becoming even more contagious than Monika's sadness.[8] The poet-narrator laughs in the face of absurdity, as when one day she wishes she could ask Monika to tell her about herself but finds that neither of them has the words necessary for such a conversation. Linguistically disempowered, they sit in silence, yet eventually the poet-narrator is overwhelmed:

Med ett begynner kroppen min å riste.
Jeg vet ikke om det er gråt eller latter.
Men så vinner latteren.
Som om kroppene tar over tilværelsen
og redder seg selv fra alt som er vondt.

Det er en merkelig følelse.
Vi ser på hverandre.
Og ler.
Og ler.
Og ler enda mer. (19)

[Suddenly my body begins to shake.
I don't know if it is crying or laughter.
But then laughter wins.
As if our bodies take over our existence
and save themselves from everything bad.

It's a strange feeling.
We look at each other.
And laugh.
And laugh.
And laugh even more.]

---

8   In *The Cultural Politics of Emotion*, Ahmed describes her project as tracking "how emotions circulate between bodies, examining how they 'stick' as well as move" (4).

119

Repeating the word "laugh" three times in separate lines, the poet-narrator empha-sizes the force and long duration of the laughter. Her laughter is furthermore depicted as euphoric laughter residing in her body. The body starts laughing to counteract what is painful. "Laughter is incompatible with emotion" (126), explains Henri Bergson, who has written extensively on the subject of laughter, adding "nothing disarms us like laugh-ter" (124). Yet, while Bergson insists on the intelligence of the comic ("Its appeal is to intelligence, pure and simple," 11), the poet-narrator's emphasis on laughter as a bodily experience situates her reaction to the comic beyond a sense-and-sensibility dichotomy. As indicated above, it seems rather to belong in the realm of the Kristevan semiotic, in the realm of the feminine and if not maternal, then grand-maternal.[9]

Laughter is closely tied to her childhood visits to Lola. We do not know what lan-guage they use for communication, since the sisters have not learned any Indian lan-guages, yet this is not problematized in the text; it is as if they live beyond the notion of language divides. Lola lives in the jungle, in harmony with nature. She herself comes across as a force of nature – she has birthed thirteen children, has the gift of laughter, and laughs even louder than the monkeys in the surrounding trees (Salinas, *Og* 75). The poems about Lola's Paradise contain several exotic, humorous stories about the sisters' encounters with domestic and wild animals whose patterns of behavior they are unable to decode.[10] One day Lola has sent them off for the first time to buy rice and pasta on their own. They have to pass through a forest and are told to avoid eye contact with the monkeys. When they cannot resist looking at them, they end up bombarded by mangos:

Apekattene skrek intenst,
og plutselig hørte vi et voldsomt dunk bak oss.
En mango suste ned fra treet.
I neste øyeblikk traff en diger frukt Sisi i ryggen,
og så traff en annen mango ryggen min.
Apene hylte i fryd.
Vi løp og snublet i mangoene
som regnet fra trærne. (79)

[The monkeys screamed intensely,
and suddenly we heard a fierce thunk behind us.
A mango whizzed down from the tree.
A moment after a giant fruit hit Sisi's back,
and then another mango hit my back.
The monkeys howled with delight.
We ran and tripped in the mangos
which rained down from the trees.]

---

[9] Kristeva links the semiotic disposition to the capacity for enjoyment: "Identifying the semiotic disposition means in fact identifying the shift in the speaking subject, his capacity for renewing the order in which he is inescapably caught up; and that capacity is, for the *subject*, the capacity for enjoyment" ("The System" 29).

[10] E.g., hens, frogs, cows, monkeys, snakes, and crocodiles.

On their way home from the store, the girls try walking a different path but are instead surrounded by hundreds of persistent cows that want their goods. Empty-handed they return home:

Vi fortalte alt mens vi gråt.
Vi skammet oss på gårdsplassen til Lola.
Hun så på oss, hørte på oss og lo.
Hun lo masse.
Sisi og jeg både lo og gråt. (82)

[We told everything while we were crying.
We were ashamed of ourselves in Lola's courtyard.
She looked at us, listened to us, and laughed.
She laughed a lot.
Sisi and I both laughed and cried.]

Lola's great laughter heals. It reflects a disposition that she and the poet-narrator appear to share, although it also seems to have skipped a generation. The poet-narrator's parents, toiling in the city and living through political and economic crises, are never depicted laughing.[11] Hence, Lola serves an atavistic, pre-modern grandmother function, which one often finds in migration narratives and language memoirs. As Yildiz points out in her analysis of Özdamar's work, the figure of the grandmother represents traditional folk wisdom and an era before the construction of the monolingual nation state (in Özdamar's case, Turkey). Whereas the mother becomes an ally of the state, even if reluctantly so, severing her daughters' ties to the Indian language and community and upholding the Argentinian state's monolingual paradigm, the grandmother "stands out as a subversive counter force" (Yildiz 153). Communication with grandmothers can evidently circumvent national linguistic boundaries and pertain more to the semiotic than to the symbolic realm.[12]

Yet, there comes a point when, in Norway, the Argentinian au pair is no longer able to laugh and starts crying. In a twelve-sentence long poem, she repeats that she cries twelve times, that is, all the time (Salinas, *Og* 123). She feels unhappy living with her host family whom she finds cold and distant, and she feels further rejected and belittled as she is forcefully thrown off a bus. Fellow passengers get angry with her for eating on the bus. When she does not understand what they are getting at, one tells her to go back to the country she came from, adding racist insult to injury, while the bus driver stops the bus, opens the doors, and two passengers literally carry her off the bus.

There is no indication whether this was a single encounter, or whether the poet-narrator has had other similar racist experiences. Yet, in the text, it becomes the straw that breaks the camel's back. Several incidents have led up to a point of extreme anger. Before the bus incident, the reserved and barely communicative host mother got furious

---

[11] The only exception is that her mother is depicted as laughing when cooking with her neighbor in the kitchen (88).
[12] We find an example of this also in Norwegian author Aasne Linnestå's long poem *Morsmål* (2012) in which the poet-narrator depicts a refugee bonding with her Norwegian language teacher's grandmother (Oxfeldt, "'Gebrokken'").

with her for not having noticed that one of the daughters got hurt in the park, something for which the au pair is sorry and apologizes profusely, but which the host mother regards as yet another sign of negligence since she has also "caught" her not changing diapers frequently enough. At this point, grief and confusion turn to rage in a five-page poem:

> Det føles som jeg er full av feil.
> Som om jeg er i veien.
> Jeg klarer ikke å være her lenger.
> Jeg vil hjem.
> Jeg vil bort fra dette kalde drittlandet. (141)

> [It feels like I'm full of faults.
> As if I'm in the way.
> I cannot stand being here any longer.
> I want to go home.
> I want to get away from this cold shit country.]

The words "dritt," "forbanna," and "jævla forbanna" ["shit, damned, and bloody damned"] recur in this poem which culminates in the poet-narrator's decision to leave. At first, it is Norway she wants to leave, but as she calms down and sees other options, she decides to leave the family in Fredrikstad for a new family in Oslo. Or rather, it is as if her body decides on her behalf: "Jeg har lyst til å finne en ny familie, sier munnen min" (152) ["I want to find a new family, my mouth says."] Her mouth says this to her Norwegian teacher, who helps her place an au pair ad in the paper. Hence, the hope for a happier future emanates from her body, which knows how to react in affect and make her life better; it knows how to survive. The reader is left on a positive note of hope for change, moving towards a position of future possibility in which hopeful anxiety is translated into anxious hope, as Ahmed puts it in *The Promise of Happiness* (183).

Sweet Stickiness: From *Dulce de Leche* to *Melkesyltetøy*

In *The Promise of Happiness* (2010), Sara Ahmed lists a series of disturbing social figures that seem to get in the way of the ordinary citizen on his or her path to happiness. These figures include the feminist killjoy, the unhappy queer, and the melancholy migrant. While others may wish to avoid such disturbing figures, such "affect aliens" (170), Ahmed identifies with them and finds them useful in her questioning of "happiness." Marginalized, in a position of clear alienation, the figures allow her to probe the false consciousness upon which common perceptions of happiness (or the promise of happiness) build (e.g. 165). She is interested in how "our" happiness always involves the suffering of someone else.[13] In *Og*, the happiness of the Norwegian Fredrikstad family,

---

13   Ahmed writes: "the promise of happiness depends upon the localization of suffering; others suffer so that a certain 'we' can hold on to the good life" (195). "So much happiness is premised on and promised by the concealment of suffering, the freedom to look away from what compromises one's happiness" (196).

for instance, seems to depend on the suffering of their au pair. Overall, Ahmed seeks out the politics of justice based on what she calls "the freedom to be unhappy."

In her chapter on the melancholic migrant, Ahmed bases her discussion on Freud's "Mourning and Melancholia" (1917) in which he describes mourning as a healthy process of grieving for a lost object, letting it go, and moving on. Melancholia, on the other hand, describes a condition of holding on to the lost object, even if it may be impossible to draw a sharp line between the two emotions. In Ahmed's optic, the melancholic migrant appears as a figure holding onto a lost object, a lost culture, a lost home country, and not getting over it (139). It is a figure who is stuck and unable to form new attachments and thus cannot become integrated into a new (national and linguistic) community. They remain unhappy and thwart the happiness of citizens of the new nation to which they have immigrated. Ahmed puts it this way:

> Integration remains a national ideal, a way of imagining national happiness. Migrants as would-be citizens are thus increasingly bound by the happiness duty not to speak [...] of attachments that cannot be reconciled into the colorful diversity of the multicultural nation. The happiness duty for migrants means telling a certain story about your arrival as good, or the good of your arrival. (158)

Besides telling a backstory about the Argentinian economic crisis of the early 2000s, *Og*'s poet-narrator tells the story of arriving in Norway with a suitcase containing the maximum allowance of 23 kilos. In addition to clothing and toiletries, she has brought a book by the Argentinian author Julio Cortázar,[14] pictures of family and friends, as well as three glass containers of *dulce de leche*. At this point the Spanish term appears unmarked in the text, as linguistic matter out of place, just as the sweet and sticky substance itself turns into matter out of place in the suitcase. "It runs something out of your baggage" (40), a woman warns the poet-narrator as she rolls her suitcase out of the airport. The poet-narrator explains:

> Glassene hadde eksplodert.
> Det rant dulce de leche ut av kofferten.
> Jeg dro en hånd langs lokket.
> Hånden ble klissete.
> Jeg tørket meg på bukselårene.
> Dårlig start, tenkte jeg (40)

> [The glasses had exploded.
> Dulce de leche was running out of my suitcase.
> I ran my hand along the lid.
> My hand became sticky.
> I wiped it on the thighs of my pants.
> Bad start, I thought.]

---

[14] Salinas refers to it as *Paradiset*, yet the Norwegian title is *Paradis*, a term for the game hopscotch, which in turn is its English title: *Hopscotch* (1963). The original title is *Rayuela*. As the idea of paradise as a site of unity and completion is a leitmotif in the book, as in "Lola's Paradise," Cortazar's book title may have been chosen precisely because it is *Paradise* in Norwegian.

Dulce de leche is a favorite item from Argentina, something the poet-narrator wants to hold on to. This is emphasized as a bad idea. It leaves the poet-narrator and her memories sticky, dirty, and impure. In the little room she is given by her host family, underneath the staircase, she opens her suitcase to find that there is *dulce de leche* everywhere: "Klærne og boken var klissete. / Alt tøyet fikk store, brune flekker" (44) ["My clothing and the book were sticky / All the clothing got big, brown spots."] And worse yet, her pictures are ruined:

Jeg løftet opp bildene.
Bildene var myke og rare.
Ansiktet til mor hadde forsvunnet.
Jeg kunne bare se kroppen hennes.
En liten kropp med en brun skygge over seg.
Min far hadde forsvunnet, og mine venner også.
De var bare brune skygger alle sammen (44).

[I lifted the pictures.
The pictures were soft and strange.
My mother's face had disappeared.
I could only see her body
A little body with a brown shadow above it.
My father had disappeared, and my friends, too.
They were just brown shadows, all of them.]

The au pair puts her parents and her friends in the garbage. The same goes for some of her clothes but not the Cortazar book where some parts are still legible. She then recalls her yoga instructor in Buenos Aires telling her that "en gang må du være villig til å miste alt" ["at one point you must be willing to lose everything"] and ends the poem with the question: "Var jeg det?"(45) ["Was I?"] In Ahmed's terminology, the question is whether the au pair will remain a melancholic migrant, facing the wrong way, towards Argentina and the past instead of her new Norwegian community. The au pair returns to the topic of *dulce de leche's* stickiness in the "angry poem" mentioned above when she becomes ready to leave Fredrikstad and start anew in Oslo. Ignored by her host mother, who watches TV and wants to "talk" tomorrow, the au pair goes to her room and opens her suitcase, observes the *dulce de leche* spots, and recalls the pictures and clothing she had to throw away. Anger remains her main affect, preparing her for change:

Jævla forbanna reise,
jævla forbanna liv,
jævla forbanna dulce de leche,
jævla hele dritten i Argentina
som dyttet meg til Norge.
Jævla forbanna Norge (142).

[Bloody damned journey,
bloody damned life,
bloody damned dulce de leche,

damn all the shit in Argentina
which pushed me to Norway.
Bloody damned Norway.]

She rages on at her past self, the idiot who brought the *dulce de leche* in the first place (143), who prioritized bringing pictures, a book, and *dulce de leche* over simply bringing more clothes (144). At the end of this poem, she has made up her mind, packed, and is ready to leave – ready to leave not only Fredrikstad, we may conclude, but also Argentina, or rather a state of melancholia towards Argentina.

As she calms down, she once again starts focusing on the positive, on "gode ting for meg i Norge" ["good things for me in Norway"], such as her Norwegian class and learning a new language. She fulfills "the happiness duty for migrants" which "means telling a certain story about your arrival as good, or the good of your arrival," as Ahmed put it above (158). Elaborating on the *dulce de leche* metaphor, she decides she has to find a Norwegian equivalent:

Jeg prøver å finne ting som kan holde meg oppe.
Akkurat som dulce de leche i Argentina.
Jeg prøver å finne mitt norske melkesyltetøy (Salinas, *Og* 149).

[I try to find things that can keep my spirits high.
Just like dulce de leche in Argentina.
I try to find my own Norwegian milk preserve]

Here, the poet-narrator invents her own translation and her own word.[15] The Argentinian au pair's translation "melkesyltetøy" ["milk preserve"] is strange and poetic. It demonstrates the dual perspective and "ostranenie" provided by the bilingual migrant.[16] Yet, it also calls attention to the metaphoric richness of the term, as it refers to milk, preserve, and the notion of preserving something in sugar.

Milk is food, something sweet that naturally passes from mother to child, creating a bond of affection and nourishment. It bears resemblance to our common conception of a "mother tongue," a language that naturally passes from mother to child. Yet, *Og* tells a much more complex story of silence, whispered languages, and an official monolingual paradigm oppressing indigenous people and their language. It is a story of thwarted assumptions, about a poet-narrator who thinks she can conserve, preserve, and maintain what is dear to her, as sweet memories, without rupture, leakage, and messiness. As

---

[15] *Dulce de leche* does not exist as a word you can look up in a Norwegian dictionary. It is, however, currently used in the labelling of Norwegian food products containing the product, and a Google search shows that it is also used on Norwegian cooking blogs and websites. On these sites it is defined as cream made out of sweetened condensed milk ("krem av søt kondensert melk") and as caramelized milk ("karamellisert melk"): https://www.nrk.no/mat/dulce-de-leche-_-krem-av-sot-kondensert-melk-1.14095699 (accessed 29 February 2020) and https://krem.no/hjem/nyhet-karamellisert-melk-endelig-i-norge/ (accessed 29 February 2020).

[16] As Steven Kelman points out in *The Translingual Imagination* (2000): "By using language that will not allow us to take anything for granted, the translingual author is fulfilling those conditions that the formalists established for aesthetic experience" (29–30, quoted in Kongslien 35). In other words, like other translingual authors, Salinas is naturally provided with an experience of *ostranenie* (defamiliarization) through which she can grasp and depict her new life conditions.

she works through her transition in her language memoir, she depicts a person literally holding onto *dulce de leche*, while she, as a writer, plays with the verbal signifier and ultimately translates it into Norwegian, enriching Norwegian language and imagination with a new concept. The Spanish word and its literal translation preserve and present something Spanish/Argentinian; the translation changes it, and works as a postmono-lingual writing strategy, reflecting a life-long experience of living beyond the mother tongue. Aesthetically, it suggests poetic language, a language of sweetness adhering to its own rules, within a Kristevan semiotic realm. And viewed from Ahmed's theory of affect, it works as a metaphor suggesting new national attachments – from Argentinian *dulce de leche* to something that could be considered Norwegian *melkesyltetøy*, something that does not yet exist but remains as hope and possibility for a happy future.

The end appears happy. Yet, as Ahmed reminds us, it also indicates compliance with a national happiness duty. The au pair, in fact, "sells" herself as sweet and happy, defining herself primarily as "blid" ["cheerful"]:

Blid, argentinsk au pair søker familie i Oslo.
Hun har studert norsk i nesten ett år
og er glad i barn (160 and 166).

[Cheerful Argentinian au pair seeks family in Oslo.
She has studied Norwegian for almost a year
and likes children.]

This is the ad that appeals to thirty-nine families. On the one hand, the language memoir lets us understand that the poet-narrator has grown up with a great sense of humor and the ability to laugh and shake off pain and suffering brought on by shame, fear, and humiliation. On the other hand, we are left with traces indicating how the immigrant has to comply with a national happiness ideal. I quoted Ahmed indicating that immigrants had a "duty" not to speak of attachments that would prevent them from integrating well into their new culture. Eclipsed in the quote above is Ahmed's claim that they are also not to speak "about racism in the present" (*The Promise* 158). While the au pair speaks clearly about the racism she has experienced in the past in Argentina, she barely touches upon the topic in her story about Norway. She mentions the passenger on the bus telling her to go back where she came from and leaves it at that. As mentioned above, she may not have encountered other incidents of racism, yet we are left with a picture of a resourceful immigrant whose cheerfulness, sense of humor, and laughter do not only reflect the community of laughers pertaining to her past, to her grandmother, to Monika, and other girlfriends at the language school, like Nilufer from Turkey, who is also poised to explode with her in laughter at the absurdity of learning a new language (Salinas, *Og* 119). As Bergson points out, laughter is social and connects the laugher to "other laughers, real or imaginary" (12). Ultimately, *Og* reaches out to the reader, seeking to establish a new community of Norwegian-speaking (and Norwegian-reading) laughers.

Conclusions on the Sweet Stickiness of Language, Culture, and Identity

This article discussed the way in which *Og*'s poet-narrator defines herself as a Kristevan "subject in process" whose identity is never fixed but ever ready to respond to new situations by defining itself anew in her current situation as well as retrospectively. The present, after all, affects one's memories of the past. For the Argentinian au pair in Norway, this concerns how she sees herself in Norway today as well as how she sees herself as part Indian in Argentina in the past, which is reconciled as simply Argentinian. The titular "og" is to be understood not only in terms of hybridity but also in terms of ongoing addition; there will constantly be new adjectives that one can use to describe her as she passes on her journey through life, "Norwegian" presumably being one of them.

Using Kristeva's approach, the au pair may be interpreted as using laughter as part of a semiotic reservoir of response as she is rendered speechless in a new language. Similarly, we can also see how the genre of the work itself – the free-verse poetry – allows her to tap into the realm of the semiotic and use poetic language as a suitable way of reacting to her predicament of being placed outside the symbolic realm of Norwegian language and cultural codes at large.

Finally, I have suggested that *dulce de leche* and the poet's play with a possible Norwegian translation of that term serve as a key metaphor in the text. It illustrates the poetically unique situation of the translingual writer, who can provide the reader with new ways of looking at the world. It also illustrates how melancholic attachments can be sticky and destructive, yet at the same time can open up the hope of a happy future. Ultimately, I have analyzed how the au pair uses her bilingual and bicultural perspective to invent new words and metaphors that describe her process towards developing a new hybrid identity in Norway through a highly original, verbal, and conceptual play with conjunctions and sweet stickiness.

Works Cited

Ahmed, Sara. *The Cultural Politics of Emotion*. 2nd ed. Edinburgh: Edinburgh University Press, 2014.

Ahmed, Sara. *The Promise of Happiness*. Durham: Duke University Press, 2010.

Bergson, Henri. *Laughter: An Essay on the Meaning of the Comic*. Trans. Cloudesley Brereton and Fred Rothwell. Copenhagen: Green Integer, 1999 [1914].

Biksett, Lillian. "Kontrastfylt om hva som opptar oss." *Dagbladet* 17. June 2017.

Bjørdal, Sondre. «Urfolkenes mørke urpremiere.» *Vårt land*. 6. Feb. 2016.

Castello, Claudio. "Jakten på morsmålet." *Utrop.no* 25. Feb. 2014 [accessed 25 March 2020].

Holte, Eva Alnes. «Fine bøker på lettnorsk.» *Utrop.no* 24. Sept. 2019 [accessed 25 March 2020].

Kelman, Steven. *The Translingual Imagination*. Lincoln: University of Nebraska Press, 2000.

Kongslien, Ingeborg. "Translingval fantasi: Nordiske forfattarar som skriv på andrespråket." *NORDAND: Nordisk tidsskrift for andrespråksforskning*, (2009), 1(4): 31–52.

Kristeva, Julia. "Fra én identitet til en annen," trans. Toril Moi and Arnstein Bjørkly. *Moderne litteraturteori. En antologi*. 2nd ed. Eds. Atle Kittang et al. Oslo: Universitetsforlaget, 2003 [1975]. 246–267.

Kristeva, Julia. "The System and the Speaking Subject." *The Kristeva Reader*. Ed. Toril Moi. New York: Columbia University Press, 1986 [1973]. 24–33.

Oxfeldt, Elisabeth. "'Gebrokken'. Refugees, Trauma, and Poetry in Aasne Linnestå's *Morsmål* (2012)." *Samlaren* (2017): 5–22. http://uu.diva-portal.org/smash/get/diva2:1187312/FULL TEXT01.pdf

Salinas, Veronica. «Jeg ble frarøvet mit morsmål.» *Utrop.no* 7. Mar. 2014 [accessed 25 March 2020].

Salinas, Veronica. *Og: En argentinsk au pairs ordbok*. Oslo: Cappellen Damm, 2016.

Statistics Norway. "Innvandrere og norskfødte med innvandrerforeldre." https://www.ssb.no/befolkning/statistikker/innvbef [accessed 3 March 2020].

Yildiz, Yasemin. *Beyond the Mother Tongue: The Postmonolingual Condition*. New York: Fordham University Press, 2012.

9. Migration and Loss of Identity in Linnea Axelsson's *Ædnan: Epos* (2018)

Petra Broomans

"I really understand why people abandoned the Sámi language."[1] This claim, made by Linnea Axelsson (b. 1980) in an interview, reflects one of the responses to forced migration and colonization of the protagonists in her epic poem *Ædnan: Epos* (2018). One of the recurring themes in the poem is forced migration of the reindeer-herding communities in northern Scandinavia, who were made to leave their territories at the beginning of the twentieth century. When Norway became an independent state in 1905, after the Union with Sweden was dissolved, the two states subsequently reached agreements about the reindeer-herding families who moved between the summer pastures in Norway and the winter pastures in Sweden. It was decided that the rights of these Sámi to utilize the land in Norway had to be regulated, and when a new agreement came into force in 1919, access to many areas was denied, meaning that many Sámi could no longer reach their summer pastures. As a result, Sweden selected a large number of families in the Karesuando area to be moved into more southern regions within the reindeer husbandry area in Sweden. Axelsson's family were among these forced migrants (Nord).

In this contribution, I will investigate how this forced migration, taking place within the twentieth century, is reflected in Axelsson's epic poem *Ædnan: Epos*. I will discuss the responses of the protagonists, who act as narrators and represent various generations within the poem.

Structure, Genre, and Content of *Ædnan: Epos*

Ædnan: Epos is a 760-page epic poem about Sámi families in the twentieth century. The poem begins in 1913, but there is no chronological order to the book. *Ædnan* meanders backwards and forwards in time, telling stories about several generations of two families, which reach into the present day (2016). It can be compared with a *yoik*, a typical form of Sámi song that often has no fixed beginning or a clear ending. The poem consists of three parts. The first is called "Ædnan," which means "land." In this part, the first forced migration, occurring in the first half of the twentieth century, is an important theme. In

---

[1] "Jag förstår verkligen att man övergav samiskan" (Josefsson). All translations in this chapter are mine unless stated otherwise.

the second part, "Ædno," meaning "river," the main theme is the second forced migration, which occurred during the second half of the twentieth century as a result of the
development of hydroelectric power plants and industrialization. The last part is called
"Ædni," the Sámi word for "mother." This part describes mobilization and the relearning
of language and cultural identity. Each part is divided into shorter sections, indicating
the place, the name of the narrator, and often the time at which the story is told. The
Girjas court case, which took place in 2016, functions to tie the historical events firmly
to the present.

As suggested above, the work can be labelled an epic poem. In the *Encyclopædia
Britannica*, an epic poem is defined as a long narrative poem about past heroic deeds,[2]
originating in the stories handed down through oral tradition. Famous examples are
Homer's *Iliad* and *Odyssey* and, from the late Middle Ages, Dante Alighieri's *Divine
Comedy* (1320). A little earlier, on the periphery of Europe, the Old Norse epic poem
Völuspá from the beginning of the *Poetic Edda,* considered to have been created in
the tenth century by an anonymous author, is the most famous mythological poem in
Nordic literary history. In the nineteenth century, on the wave of national romanticism,
Elias Lönnrot constructed the Finnish epic *Kalevala* (1849). Modern examples from
the twentieth century include Märta Tikkanen's *Århundradets kärlekssaga* (1978; *The
Love Story of the Century*, 2020) and Kerstin Ekman's *Knivkastarens kvinna* (1991, The
Knife-Thrower's Woman). These epic poems deal with eternal themes, such as war,
nation-building, and love.

Ædnan tells the story of Sámi families in the twentieth and at the beginning of the
twenty-first century. The reindeer-herding families are driven away from their territories
and the protagonists tell the story of the loss of land and assimilation, resulting in the
loss of culture and language. This changes when the last generation in *Ædnan* begins to
regain their language and culture. As Axelsson herself stated in an interview, *Ædnan* is
influenced by Sámi oral storytelling, especially by the *yoik*. She was particularly interested in their circular movement,[3] and, in *Ædnan*, her use of these circular movements
comes to the fore in the way the storytelling moves through a fluid time and space.

The Modern Sámi Literary Context

Scholars such as Vuokko Hirvonen, Anne Heith, and Kaisa Ahvenjärvi have described
aspects of Sámi literary history in a profound way. Hirvonen's seminal study on Sámi
women writers, *Voices from Sápmi. Sámi Women's Path to Authorship* (1998/2008) takes
a gender approach to foremothers, grandmothers, mothers, and daughters. Anne Heith
focuses on cultural heritage and the effects of colonialism on minorities in the North
such as the Sámi, while Kaisa Ahvenjärvi has analysed the works of modern Sámi writers such as Sigbjørn Skåden. Regarding modern Sámi literature, I propose a division of
Sámi writers into three groups based on the differing political perspectives that can be

---

2   https://www.britannica.com/art/epic Accessed on 30 March 2020.
3   "Linnea Axelsson tänkte själv på jojken, cirkelrörelsen, när hon skrev" (Nord).

observed. This will also be based on whom they address their stories to and on the aim of their literary works.

The first type includes authors such as Sigbjørn Skåden (1976), who reflect on and mirror both their own and the global world in their Sámi poetry. The second type intend to awaken their own people, who urge resistance and, at the same time, present the Sápmi homeland as a safe and isolated biotope, writers such as Hege Siri (1973). The third type are authors who want to inform their compatriots, the majority, about the position of the Sámi people and who write in the major language, as does Linnea Axelsson. All of these writers have to make decisions from the perspective of a minority writer.

Inspired by Iban Zaldua's essay, "Eight Crucial Decisions (A Basque Writer Is Obliged to Face)" (2009), I have previously demonstrated the decisions that Sámi writers have to make before they start writing (Broomans, "The Importance of Literature and Cultural Transfer" and "Minority Memories"). One of the decisions that many authors have to make concerns the language in which they will write: the minority language or the major language? Axelsson has stated that she "can understand and read a little Sámi";[4] however, there was no choice in this respect as she apparently does not have sufficient skills to write a literary work in the Sámi language.

The Twenty-First Century Historical Context

Ædnan: Epos was published in an era in which Sámi culture and history, as well as the colonization and oppression they were subject to, became more visible through literature and film. Axelsson was impressed by the film *Sámi blood* (2016), which, like *Ædnan*, includes references to scientific racism (Josefsson). This hidden story in Swedish history has been researched by scholars such as Lennart Lundmark. In 2015, a biography by Maja Hagerman called *Käraste Herman: Rasbiologen Herman Lundborgs gåta* was published, and, one year later, in 2016, Hagerman worked with Claes Gabrielsson on a film that explored Lundborg's aim to improve the Swedish race. In 1922, Lundborg became the director of the Statens institut för rasbiologi in Uppsala, the first State Institute for Race Biology.[5] Lundborg was against interracial relationships between the Sámi, the Finns, and the Swedes, arguing that this would result in degeneration (Lindskog 187).

While Axelsson uses the poetic form to describe the oppression of the Sámi in the twentieth century, it is also apparent that she has another aim – to make the forgotten history visible to her compatriots: "When the history teacher talked about colonialism, banishment, or such types of abuse, it was so clueless. Nevertheless, it is deeply tragic that only the Sámi people have the knowledge of that which is such a complex and serious part of the country's history" (Josefsson). The most important historical event in *Ædnan* is the forced migration of Sámi families with the focus on how it changed the lives of generations of Sámi (Vogel).

---

[4] "Och jag kan förstå och läsa lite samiska" (Nord).
[5] See also the documentary: https://vimeo.com/ondemand/66847.

Writing on Migration

The academic field of migration studies is enormous. It includes studies in the fields of history, psychology, sociology, nationalism, and post-colonialism, among others. Most studies focus on migration from one country or nation state to another. Migration is found in all eras, and while there are several types of migration, it usually refers to people being forced to leave their homeland for political or economic reasons as well as due to climate change.

The Encyclopedia of European Migration and Minorities: From the Seventeenth Century to the Present (Hoerder et al.) offers a collection of insights from migration studies. In the introduction, "Terminologies and Concepts of Migration Research," they set up a "typology of migrations," which encompasses the motive, distance, duration, length of stay, socioeconomic context, and economic sector (xxix). For the present chapter, the motives for migration are of particular importance. Migration can be forced, either "by human or ecological force," or it can be ideologically motivated in which case the migrant will usually be called a "refugee." Furthermore, economic reasons and migration related to the cultural sphere, such as the phenomenon of the Grand Tour, may also provide motives. Within the socioeconomic space, migration may occur from a rural environment to an urban space, with urbanization being "the best-known type of migration in European history" (Hoerder et al. xxix).

The migration of the Sámi, as depicted in *Ædnan*, concerns forced migration due to human and ecological elements as well as for economic reasons. In Hoerder *et al.*'s typology, "colonial" is also mentioned, but it is understood as an international phenomenon. For the Sámi, their forced migration experience was more intranational and transnational: migration to urban spaces took place within state borders, but to some extent Nordic borders were involved as well, if only to stop them from being crossed.

In Sweden, migration has been studied extensively as well. In the nineteenth century, many people from Sweden and other Nordic countries emigrated to Canada and the U.S. due to poverty and famine. In the twentieth century, migration from other countries to Sweden, especially after the Second World War, increased until 2015. One of the centres in Sweden for migration research is the Hugo Valentin Centre at Uppsala University. Harald Runblom, who was attached to the Centre (then called the Centre for Multiethnic Research), edited the volume *Migrants and the Homeland: Images, Symbols and Realities* (2000). This study addresses some of the questions that Hoederer et al. also dealt with. However, the focus is on the relationship between the migrant and the homeland and the question of what a homeland is. In the introduction, one of the topics Runblom discusses is the ideology of "the melting pot" – very similar to the post-colonial term "assimilation" – versus the idea of migrants maintaining ethnic characteristics of the left-behind homeland. As mentioned above, in these studies, migration is regarded as an international movement from one state to another. Furthermore, Westin states that international migration and the crossing of borders also means crossing linguistic and cultural borders. Thus, the national or state boundary is the most significant boundary to be crossed (Westin 38).

However, as the Sámi case demonstrates, migration also occurs within state borders, as the Sámi experienced when forced from the north of Scandinavia into regions in the east or southwards. Loss of language and culture was also experienced, despite this migration occurring within state borders. According to Westin, the migration movement is definitive, "unidirectional," and takes place over a "significant length of time" and a "significant stretch of space, across significant boundaries, or away from home" (41). Migrants have to adjust to the new situation, the new culture; they have to learn to communicate in the new language and they have to acquire a new repertoire of social skills.

The studies by Hoerder and Runblom, not to mention Westin, do not deal with how migration affected already existing historical, territorial, and ethnic minorities encompassed by modern nation states (Broomans, "The Importance of Literature and Cultural Transfer" 24). They also fail to deal with different notions of homeland. The Sámi homeland Sápmi is situated in an area that stretches across Norway, Sweden, Finland, and the Kola peninsula in Russia. In the case of the families in Ædnan, virtual borders between Norway and Sweden were crossed and subsequently closed. In this regard, the question "What is a homeland?" posed by Runblom in his introduction (10), is of relevance, as Runblom recognizes that "homeland and state are not the same" (ibid.). This is clearly the case for the Sámi people, and, as Ædnan shows, the concept of homeland can be connected to a cultural and linguistic space, with forced migration leading to the loss of mother tongue and culture.

A multigenerational perspective is also to be tackled here. The first-generation migrants have different memories and perceptions of the "homeland" to second or third-generation migrants. As I will demonstrate in the next section, in Ædnan, the first generation that was forced to leave the territories looks back in nostalgia; the second generation chooses the strategy of mimicry, assimilation, and forgetting the mother tongue; the third generation, choosing the strategy of activism, strives to regain their lost language, culture, and Sámi identity.[6]

Responses to Forced Migration in *Ædnan: Epos*

How do the protagonists in Ædnan respond to migration? Do they experience it as forced, do they lose their cultural and ethnic identity, or do they fight back? To address these questions, I will select some of the narrators in Ædnan who represent each generation.

Ristin and Ber-Joná, who represent the first generation, experience forced emigration first-hand. They are forced to move to Sweden and no longer permitted to follow the reindeer herds to the summer pastures in Norway. The second generation is represented by Lise, who belongs to another Sámi family, is assimilated into the Swedish society, and does not speak Sámi, while Sandra, Lise's daughter, represents the third generation. She becomes an activist who wants to defend the cause of the Sámi and marries a Sámi reindeer herder.

---

[6] For the notion of "mimicry," see Bhabha 82–95.

The first stanzas of *Ædnan* can be read as a love poem set in the times before Ber-Joná, the first-person narrator in the first part of *Ædnan*, and his beloved Ristin were forced to leave the summer pastures in Norway and migrate to Sweden due to the border politics between Norway and Sweden. He talks about their love, "your body and mine," and how they were born in the mountains but then reminds him that he must also follow the reindeer herd and therefore must free himself from her embrace.

> Där krafsar min hjord
> Och för oss från
> Land till land (Axelsson 10)

> [There my herd is grazing
> And leads us from
> Land to land]

In the following stanza, Ber-Joná recounts the birth of their two sons, Aslat, the strong, and Nila, who is physically weak. Thus, a new generation is born. The two-way migratory movement from the winter pastures in Sweden to the summer pastures in Norway is both cyclical and unconnected to nation-state borders in the sense that it takes place within the Sápmi region. At the time, the Sámi did not experience the border between Norway and Sweden as a hard border and their cyclical migrations belonged to the way of life of the Sámi reindeer herders, who were thus semi-nomadic.

Tragically, the strong son, Aslat, dies while climbing a rock, and afterwards another disaster befalls Ristin and Ber-Joná. In 1920, the governor visits them, bringing a message from the "three kingdoms" of Finland, Norway, and Sweden in which they are told that they must lead their reindeer herds to unknown lands. Far from their reindeer world, an unknown person has randomly selected those families who will be forced to migrate to other areas (Axelsson 135), away from the forests, the mountains, and the lakes.

> Flyttleder och sånger
> Måste förträngas
> Fördrivas ur minnet (Axelsson 136)

> [Travel routes and songs
> Must be repressed
> Expelled from memory]

Ber-Joná observes the impact of the migration on his family; they no longer wish to *yoik* or sing.

> Sjöng inte fram
> marken och
> minnena mer (Axelsson 87)

> [Sung no more
> Territories and
> Memories]

He also describes how the language of those in power colonizes their bodies:

Svenska ord
omöjliga att uttala

De trängde in
genom kläderna
la sig över huden (Axelsson 133)

[Swedish words
impossible to pronounce

They pushed in
through our clothes
coated our skin] (trans. by Vogel 2019)

In the winter of 1920, Ristin is confronted with the violence of scientific racism while the family is in Karesuando kyrkby (the parish of Karesuando).

Svenskens fingrar
i hela min mun (Axelsson 147)

[The Swede's fingers
all inside my mouth] (trans. by Vogel 2019)

The doctor investigates and measures her skull and body. Male artists make anatomical drawings of "the racial animal" (148). Ristin, the first-person narrator of this part, feels shame and humiliation because she is naked and the men in the room are laughing at her (150–151).

In the winter of 1921, they are forced to travel further south with their reindeer herds, but they do not know the way. Everything is strange for Ristin, Ber-Joná and the other families who have had to migrate. In the strange land, Ristin can no longer sing (*yoik*) (163).

In Chapter XIV, many years later, in 1945, Ristin and Ber-Joná are settled in a new environment and now describe the new landscapes and the unfriendly people who do not want to have the newcomers in their area because their reindeer trample the paths of their ancestors. In this respect, *Ædnan* also reflects the conflicts among the Sámi that were created by the forced migration. Ristin and Ber-Joná also talk about the "Swedes" who dam the rivers and how industrialization began with the building of roads and railways. Ristin starts to sell her handicraft to Swedish women while their husbands tame the rivers.

At the end of the first part, in 1946, Ristin and Ber-Joná live in an apartment where Ristin reflects on her "downed kingdom" (189). She thinks about her dead son, about the Norsemen, who closed the borders on one side, and the Finns, who closed the border on the other. Ristin and Ber-Joná are trapped in their apartment and she can only think about the past. Ber-Joná returns home with a relative who still lives in the area in which they once lived. He shows them a book that is about them: the Swedish doctor who had

135

visited them wrote a book about the Sámi. The book contains many pictures. They show a photo of a boy. It is their son Nila. The caption reads: "Insane man" (195).

The first part ends in Piteå, with Nila, who is now called the Swedish name Nils, in an asylum. The narrators are a nurse and Nila. She has taught him to speak and to say his own name. The town of Piteå is located in the Gulf of Bothnia where there are waves. Nila has returned to the sea.

The main protagonist in the second part of *Ædna: Epos*, called "Ædno" (River) is Lise. She belongs to another family and lives in an apartment where Ristin had lived before her. Lise recalls the Sámi newcomers who were forced to migrate to their area. She recognizes that these Sámi women were different, and she recounts details such as their different bonnets.

In many of the chapters in "Ædno," Lise recalls her youth and her mother who, although remaining faithful to her Sámi identity, sent her children, Lise and her brother Jon-Henrik, to a boarding school in Jokkmokk where they were not permitted to speak the Sámi language. Her mother tells her later that she was not surprised that Lise married a Swedish man. According to Lise's mother, she was ill-equipped and too impractical for the hard work of the reindeer herding profession. Lise had two children, Sandra and Per, with her Swedish husband Rolf. When Sandra gets older, she asks her mother to tell her about her childhood because she wants to write an essay on her mother's life.

Berätta hur det
Var på Nomadskolan
Mamma (Axelsson 274)

[Tell me how it
Was at boarding school
Mamma]

Lise does not want to talk about her past and claims she can no longer speak Sámi.

Och jag ville
Inte prata om det (Axelsson 274)

[I did not want
to talk about it]

Two other chapters in "Ædno" also emphasize this issue. Sandra continues to ask her mother to talk about her life because she feels that she must write about her history and her journey. Lise cannot explain to her daughter why the word "journey" is completely wrong (293). The traumatic event Lise remembers, and which we could perceive as changing the course of her life, is that she was forced to leave her mother as a seven-year-old girl and sent to a boarding school. We might also conceive of this event as a kind of forced migration that resulted in language and identity loss.

Dig ieddne när jag
Bodde på Nomman

Å vad jag saknade
Dig áhttje (Axelsson 313)

[O, how I missed
You, mama, when I
Lived at Nomman

O, how I missed
You, papa][7]

Lise remembers that she and her brother could still speak Sámi when they went to the boarding school. However, she was not able to keep her mother tongue alive. In Book X of "Ædno," which occurs in a time indicated as "Much later," Lise describes the process of losing the Sámi language. The Swedish language took over her thoughts and the Sámi language fell dormant in her body because she felt shame in her submission (337). On the next page, it seems that a third narrator takes over Lise's thoughts. The narrator argues that Sámi history is not part of the Swedish history, "as if we and our parents never existed" (338). This fragment reminds us of what Axelsson means in the statement from the interview quoted above.

Lise admits that she simply let the language disappear, and when Sandra asks her to answer in Sámi, she cannot speak: "Inte ett ljud får jag fram" (453) ["No sound comes to my lips"]. At the same time, however, Lise has saved the old bonnets of her aunts and her grandmother, waiting until one of her children wants to use them. She wonders why she listened to her aunt Ella talk negatively about the Sámi as being primitive people, and why she did not ask her why she spoke of her own people in that way (280). The attitude of her aunt Ella is an example of mimicry as a response to oppression.

Another theme in "Ædno" is the effects of the activities of Vattenfall, the company that builds dams, roads, and hydroelectric power plants. The landscape of the Sámi, their own migratory routes, and homes, are disappearing, which results in their further alienation. At the end of this part, we learn that Lise and her husband Rolf work for the company.

Later in her life, in a chapter reflecting the situation in 2015, the year in which Sweden opened its borders to refugees from Syria and other countries, Lise meets them in a "language café" and she recognizes something that reminds her of her own life: that they all had to leave something behind, something they did not want to lose (449ff).

In the last chapter of "Ædno," set at a Sámi school in Jokkmokk in 2010, the situation is different from the 1950s boarding school attended by Lise. Here, a teacher acts as the narrator, and this episode shows that the Sámi are regaining their language and identity. The teacher went to school with Lise and she remembers how beautiful Lise was, and how she would *yoik* for her behind the shed because it was not only forbidden to speak in Sámi but also to *yoik*. Now, she is the teacher of Lise's grandchildren, Sandra's children.

---

7   Nomman = Nomad school, Lise's boarding school. The words "ieddne" (see p. 74) and "áhttje" (see p. 55) mean "mama" and "papa" and are from the Lulesamiska dialect, the Sámi language variant that is spoken around the city of Luleå. See: https://www.sametinget.se/14885, retrieved on 15 April 2020. The dictionary *Lulelapsk ordbok*, compiled by Harald Grundström in 1946–1954 (13 volumes), was published as a pdf document on the website of the Sameting, see preface by Sortelius.

She hears the children speaking Sámi and witnesses the Sámi language being reborn (523). A spirit of hope is apparent in the last chapter of "Ædno." Sandra, described by her mother Lise as someone who fights for Sámi rights (272), is the main narrator in the third part of *Ædnan: Epos* called "Ædni," or "Mother." The story in this part covers the years between 1983 and 2016. Like the first two parts, the events are not told in chronological order. The year 1983 marks the death of Sandra's grandmother. In a scene set at the cemetery, Sandra promises her grandmother that she will wear the Sámi smock, as her grandmother had done. This is the moment that Sandra becomes an activist. However, this episode is only told at the end of the final part of the book.

Nästa gång mormor

Tanker jag ta på
mig kolten som du (Axelsson 751)

[Next time grandma

I will dress
in the smock like you]

The first chapter of the final part is set in 2016 and also starts with a reference to the smock. Sandra, the narrator, describes how she wears it with pride. Dressing in the colourful smock is a way for her to emphasize her Sámi descent, although her father Rolf is Swedish. The smock is her weapon: "Rustad med arv och liv" (535) ["Armed with heritage and life"]. Sandra also follows the progress of the Girjas court case, which occurred in 2015. Girjas is a village in Sápmi which instituted proceedings against the Swedish State in order to regain its rights to use the land for hunting and fishing. Sandra tells her mother Lise about the denigrating words used intentionally by the lawyer during the case, one of which is "Lapps" instead of the name Sámi. This lawyer also argues that written documents provided by the state are more credible forms of evidence than the oral Sámi storytelling tradition (577). As in the two previous parts of the poem, the colonization of the Sámi, and how they were dispersed across four countries, is mentioned as well as the claim that they are not part of the Swedish history.

Sandra's brother, Per, also acts as narrator in some of the chapters in the third part, as did her father Rolf in the second part. Per reflects on how a language could survive; he longs after something that is called the mother tongue but does not know the Sámi language. He regards his sister Sandra as a militant, taking action by learning the Sámi language with her children.

Up until the third part of *Ædna: Epos*, the focus is on the reindeer-herding Sámi community. Now, however, Sandra remarks that it was the Swedish state that also decided who could be labelled Sámi and who could not. This meant that the Sámi who did not belong to the reindeer-herding community – for example, the sea Sámi or the mountain Sámi – were not recognized as Sámi (664–665). As formulated in another chapter, the Sámi people were divided into categories unfamiliar to them and their way of life: they were labelled nomads, residents, or owners (673). The borders were not only drawn to define territories but also symbolically, thus denying the Sámi identity to many.

Per becomes aware of the fact that he was naive to think that everybody was equal in Sweden. On the contrary, he realizes the Sámi were forced to forget their language and culture. There is also a reference to his schooling in which he recounts how his history teacher taught him that all of the migrants who come to Sweden bring with them experiences that the Swedes do not have (672). Here, we are made aware that many Swedes do not know or have forgotten that this is also the case for the Sámi people.

In addition to the legal struggle between the Sámi and the Swedish State, as told through the eyes of Sandra and her brother Per, the last part of *Ædnan: Epos* reveals the destruction of the Sámi language, the natural environment, and the landscape of Sápmi as the Sámi have known it for generations by the Vattenfall company.

Kraftstationen
ett slott mitt i skogen

De hade ivrigt fått
röja bort laven
trampa ner språket
välta bort seiten (Axelsson 686)

[The power plant
a fortress amidst the forest

They zealously
cleared the lichen
trampled the language
annulled the sacred site]

At the same time, in the final part of the poem, Sandra personifies the resistance of the Sámi and reveals how they have begun to regain their language and thus their Sámi identity. Sandra has learned to *yoik*, to speak the language, and also to make a Sámi smock (709). She also discovers that her mother Lise can *yoik.* (729). It turns out that Lise, who apparently chose to accept colonization and assimilation, carried her hidden Sámi identity within her and was ultimately able to transfer it across generations.

Conclusion

Ædnan: Epos is a magnificent epic poem which relates to the reader the history and effects of forced migration on the Sámi families in the twentieth century. The structure of the poem is reminiscent of a *yoik*, which belongs to the oral tradition of the Sámi. The narrators all respond to the historical events in different ways, and they all make personal and political choices in the face of colonization and oppression. The description of the relocation of the Sámi community reminds us of the power to destroy a people, forcing them to give up their language, culture, and attachment to the homeland.

Ristin and Ber-Joná, the narrators of the first generation, who undergo forced emigration first-hand, respond with silence and sadness. Ber-Joná acts as a witness to the language and territory loss. Lise, a narrator of the next generation, personifies the struggle to remember and the desire to forget her language and culture, sometimes wanting only to identify with the dominant culture and being ashamed of her Sámi origin and heritage. Her daughter, Sandra, chooses to defend the cause of the Sámi; she wants to regain the rights to their territory and her Sámi identity by learning the language with her children and ends up marrying a reindeer-herding Sámi man.

In the first part, land and territory are lost; in the second part, language and culture are lost, the rivers are dammed, and the landscape destroyed. In the third and final part, Sandra might be regarded as personifying "re-emigration"; returning to her Sámi identity by relearning the language and culture.

In *Ædnan: Epos*, there is one silent, speechless, and invisible narrator: the weaker son of Ber-Joná and Ristin, Nila. However, throughout the generations he is never forgotten. He is remembered by his parents; by Lise, who heard Ristin's stories; and by Sandra and Per, who heard the stories from their mother. Nila's role in *Ædnan: Epos* might be interpreted as symbolic of the invisibility of the Sámi in Swedish history, of a people who became speechless in their own language. *Ædnan: Epos* is an impressive poetic experience but also a brilliant political manifesto of the author herself.

Works Cited

Axelsson, Linnea. *Ædnan. Epos*. Stockholm: Albert Bonniers Förlag, 2018.

Bhabha, Homi K. *The Location of Culture*, London/New York: Routledge, 2004 [1994].

Broomans, Petra. "The Importance of Literature and Cultural Transfer - Redefining Minority and Migrant Cultures." *Battles and Borders. Perspectives on Cultural Transmission and Literature in Minor Language Areas*. Eds. Broomans, Petra et al. Groningen: Barkhuis Publishing, 2015. 9–38.

Broomans, Petra, "Minority Memories: Lost Language, Identity, and In-betweenness in Two Crime Novels by Mikael Niemi and Lars Pettersson." Special Issue. Border Crossings, Rites of Passage, and Liminal Experiences in Contemporary Literature. Eds. Van den Bossche, Sara, and Sophie Wennerscheid. *Journal of Diversity and Gender Studies (DiGeSt)*, 2018: 45–62.

Hagerman, Maja. *Käraste Herman. Rasbiologen Herman Lundborgs gåta*, Stockholm: Norstedts, 2015.

Hoerder, Dirk, Lucassen, Jan, and Leo Lucassen. "Terminologies and Concepts of Migration Research." Eds. Bade, Klaus J., Emmer, Pieter C., Lucassen, Leo. and Jochen Oltmer. *The Encyclopedia of European Migration and Minorities. From the Seventeenth Century to the Present*. Cambridge: Cambridge University Press, 2010. xxv–xxxix.

Josefsson, Erika. "Linnea Axelsson om sitt samiska släktepos: "Jag förstår verkligen att man övergav samiskan." *Arbetarbladet*, 11–03–2018, https://www.arbetarbladet.se/artikel/linnea-axelsson-om-sitt-samiska-slaktepos-jag-forstar-verkligen-att-man-overgav-samiskan

Lindskog, Gerda Helena. *Vid svenskhetens nordliga utposter. Om bilden av samerna i svensk barn- och ungdomslitteratur under 1900-talet*. Lund: BTJ Förlag, 2005.

Lundmark, Lennart. *"Lappen är ombytlig, ostadig och obekväm-"* *Svenska statens samepolitik i rasismens tidevarv*. Umeå: Norrbottensakademiens Skriftserie nr. 3, 2002.

Nord, Malin. "Linnea Axelsson." 11–27–2018, http://www.samer.se/5657

Runblom, Harald. "Introduction: Homeland as Imagination and Reality." *Migrants and the Homeland. Images, Symbols and Realities*. Ed. Harald Runblom. Centre for Multiethnic Research, Uppsala Multiethnic Papers 44. Uppsala: Uppsala University, 2000. 9–30.

Sortelius, Nils-Olof. "Förord" *Lulesamisk ordbok*. Sametinget i Sverige, 2011. https://www.samet inget.se/14885

Vogel, Saskia. "An Interview with Linnea Axelsson." *WWB Daily*, 29–03–2019. https://www .wordswithoutborders.org/dispatches/article/an-interview-with-linnea-axelsson-saskia-vogel

Vogel, Saskia. "From Aednan." *WWB Daily*, 29–03–2019. https://www.wordswithoutborders.org /article/march-2019-swedish-from-aednan-linnea-axelsson-saskia-vogel

Westin, Charles. "Migration, Time, and Space." *Migrants and the Homeland. Images, Symbols and Realities*. Ed. Harald Runblom. Centre for Multiethnic Research, Uppsala Multiethnic Papers 44. Uppsala: Uppsala University, 2000. 33–42.

Yoshida, Atsuhiko. "Epic. Literary Genre." https://www.britannica.com/art/epic

Zaldua, Iban. "Eight Crucial Decisions (A Basque Writer Is Obliged to Face)." *Writers in between Languages: Minority Literatures in the Global Scene*. Ed. Mari JoseOlaziregi, Reno: Center for Basque Studies at the University of Nevada, 2009. 89–112.

10. "The Ugly Grey-White Blocks of Concrete": Class, Gender, and Ethnicity in Danish "Ghetto Literature"

Jon Helt Haarder

"When I close my eyes," Karina Pedersen writes in a book about her childhood in a Danish "ghetto," "I can see the neighbourhood quite clearly: the ugly grey-white blocks of concrete and the inhabitants" (Pedersen 7) ["Når jeg lukker øjnene, kan jeg se kvarteret helt tydeligt: de store grimme, gråhvide betonblokke og beboerne"]. Indeed, most of us probably can. Estates with modernist mass housing, built in concrete on the fringe of urban areas, have become a cultural topos, the depressing dwellings of the socially marginalized – "the underclass," as Pedersen calls the inhabitants of the area where she grew up: Korskærparken, outside of Fredericia, a relatively large provincial town in Denmark. In later years, such areas and their inhabitants have become synonymous with immigrants. The term "ghetto" signifies exactly this connection, and in Denmark the use of this offensive and disputed term is official. By now, however, Denmark also has literature about life in these areas. "The ghetto" writes back, as it were. The present article introduces us to this writing, focusing on intersections between place, class, gender, and ethnicity.

The notorious Danish "ghetto plan" firmly ties certain kinds of housing areas to immigrants with a non-Western background.[1] The plan is based on an official, annually updated list containing "udsatte boligområder" ["underprivileged housing areas"], meaning "almene boligområder" ["non-profit housing areas"] that meet criteria for crime rates and income, education, and employment levels.[2] If a non-profit housing area meets two of these four criteria it is considered an "udsat boligområde." A Danish ghetto is a specific form of "udsat boligområde" where the amount of "indvandrere og efterkommere fra ikke-vestlige lande" ["immigrants and descendants from non-Western countries"] is above fifty percent. Ghetto areas that have been on the list for five years are considered "hard ghettoes." The two kinds of ghettoes are the subject of the ghetto laws passed with a large majority in the Danish parliament in November 2018. The legislation, among other things, obliges housing associations to reduce the amount of social housing in areas defined as hard ghettoes to a maximum of forty percent – by demolition, if necessary.

---

[1] For an introduction in English, see "Danish Parliament passes contentious 'ghetto plan.'"

[2] For an introduction to the Danish specialty of "almene boligområder," see "The Danish Housing Sector." The important thing to know is that "almene boligområder" are *not* synonymous with social housing – though some of the flats in such areas will be social housing. The latest "ghetto list" and its criteria can be found in "Færre udsatte boligområder og ghettoområder på de nye lister."

The point of the present chapter is not to dispute the fact that some housing areas in Denmark have a high percentage of immigrants and descendants from non-Western countries, and though the official use of the ghetto term and the ghetto plan are certainly debatable, I am not going to discuss them at the general historical, political, or socio-logical level.[3] The issue is cultural interpretations of life in modernist mass housing, typically in the form of the satellite towns – built since the 1960s onwards out of at first promising and then somewhat disappointing material: concrete. Based on these interpre-tations, I would argue that the relation between these areas and immigrants is historically contingent rather than necessary. In other words: the Danish history of immigration is bound up with the larger and longer story of the attempt by the young welfare state to remedy class barriers through housing policy (Schultz Larsen).

My argument for using the highly problematic term ghetto in this context, some-times with and sometimes without quotation marks, is simply that it is there – in Danish political discourse as well as in cultural products, rap lyrics being a particularly strong influence. American hip-hop is in many ways a "glocalized" sense-making resource for young people in general (Danish youth being no exception) but with a special pertinence for young people from deprived housing areas, and the term ghetto is obligatory here (Krog, Krog and Stougaard Petersen, Haarder, "Tilbage over Atlanten med stil"). In a variety of ways, the term also turns up in the texts that I work with, often with a built-in distance. In Morten Pape's *Planen* (2015, The Plan), one of the most important nov-els which deal with growing up in a Danish housing estate, the grown-ups explain the multicultural "dance of war" in the local school with the fact that "it is located in the middle of a ghetto. That means that there is a lot of guest workers in a certain housing area." ["De voksne siger at det er fordi vi går på en skole der ligger midt i en ghetto. Det betyder at der er mange gæstearbejdere i et bestemt boligområde" (11).][4] The use of the term "guest worker" situates Morten's early childhood at a time before the issue of immi-gration became the decisive factor of Danish politics, and the child-like reflection – in present-tense narration – of an explanation given by grown-ups sets up a distance around the ghetto term itself.

"Danish Ghetto Literature"

I have shown how the cultural prehistory of present-day ghetto conceptions elicits two points that are highly pertinent, even on a general political level (Haarder, "The Precariat as Place"). Firstly, judging by cultural representations, present-day Danish "ghettoes" are anything but parallel societies. Historically, satellite towns with modernist mass housing were the realization of the egalitarian ideals of the Danish welfare state in its

---

3 See Schwartz 2019 for the full history of the term "ghetto" and Wacquant 2008 for the influential *Compar-ative Sociology of Advanced Marginalization*. Wacquant dismisses the use of the term "ghetto" in a contem-porary European context: ethnically heterogenous, with permeable boundaries and high levels of welfare state presence; European suburban areas of modernist mass housing are, in fact, *anti-ghettoes*. Wacquant 2014 sums up his studies and arguments.
4 All translations of quotes from the Danish in this article are my own.

prime (see also Kjældgaard). These utopias underwent a massively dystopian reinterpretation after 1970 (Høghøj). This dystopian turn had to do with a gradual up-concentration of people with social problems in some of the housing estates. At the same time, the new housing areas as such and the very material with which they were built turned into symbolic containers for the general hungover atmosphere of the 1970s and an unease with modernity, not least with the very same welfare state. In a contemporary context, even a superficial reading of, say, Yahya Hassan's unprecedentedly successful collection of poetry *Yahya Hassan* (2013) will note the presence of the welfare state in his life as well as the ghetto (his word) where he grew up. Welfare state personnel removed him from his violent family, contained him in facilities for young criminals, and taught him to read and write. Coming of age in an officially defined ghetto in Brabrand Vest on the outskirts of Aarhus involved the welfare state to a much larger degree than in the case of an average youth in other areas. Both in Geeti Amiri's *Glansbilleder* (2016, Picture Perfect) and Ahmad Mahmoud *Sort land* (2015, Black Land), schoolteachers and librarians are decisive agents in their *Fortællinger fra Ghettoen* [Narratives from the Ghetto], the subtitle of Mahmoud's book. Such narratives take place near the very heart of late-modern welfare states.

Secondly, social segregation precedes and intersects with ethnic segregation. Signifying the above-mentioned dystopian interpretation of Danish housing estates, the term ghetto was used before Denmark had any immigrants to speak of (Høghøj, Freiesleben). Likewise, Pape's *Planen* suggests that the all-too visible conflict between "kartofler" ["potatoes" = ethnic Danes] and "perkere" [roughly equivalent to the British slur "Pakis"] hides the deeper fact of a common social marginalization, invisible to both the inhabitants of the housing area *in* the novel as well as the reviewers *of* the novel (Freiesleben Lund).

The point of the novel is not, in my view, that ethnic differences are but an ideological cover-up of the real issue of class, but rather that class and ethnicity are entangled in ways that tend to show only one side. This is a form of partial racialisation, one might say, which can, should one so wish, be related to the official ghetto politics of the state of Denmark with its focus on non-Western immigrants and their descendants. The social problems of the housing areas on the ghetto lists are very real. The question is whether an anti-ghetto strategy based on criteria where ethnicity figures as a social problem in itself contributes to, rather than counters, ghettoisation, i.e., enhances the official as well as vernacular localisation and racialisation of social problems of a more general nature. Leading ghetto sociologist Loïc Wacquant speaks of "territorial stigmatisation" (2008). A more local source uses the metaphor of "gebyr" ["fee"]: young brown men from multi-ethnic areas of Copenhagen have the feeling that they 'pay a fee' for their address as well as for the colour of their skin (Soei, *Omar og de andre*).

In what follows, I will focus on place-specific configurations of class, place, ethnicity, and gender in Danish cultural representations of the "ghetto," not least in the corpus of literary texts that make up what I – for lack of a better term and with all fingers crossed – will call "Danish ghetto literature." I use the term "configuration" in the manner theorised by Ricœur: as the poetic processing of a world already full of meaning. Buildings of concrete and Danish modernist mass housing areas are in themselves densely packed with history, meanings, and emotions. Using the full arsenal of literature (and, to some extent, other art forms) "Danish Ghetto Literature" configures this "pre-figuration of the practical field," it organises already existing patterns of meaning in new poetic forms, such as narratives or poems, by way of the reader's efforts. "What is at stake," says Ricœur, "is the concrete process by which the textual configuration mediates between the prefiguration of the practical field and its refiguration through the reception of the work" (51).

"Danish ghetto literature" consists mainly of those literary texts from the mid-1960s to the present that deal with the history, construction, and habitation of modernist mass housing, organised under the Danish laws for "almene boligområder" ["non-profit housing"] and presently scrutinized for signs of ghettoisation. The distinction between fiction and non-fiction is of less importance here. What I am interested in is the textual configuration of relations between a specific housing and planning paradigm and questions of class, gender, and ethnicity, primarily in a contemporary context. I will focus on three configurations: pink concrete as a symbolic container for a class-specific form of femininity and two *forms* of crisis-ridden patriarchy. The social categorisations of ethnicity, class, and gender turn out to intersect not only with each other but also with place: the configurations can be mapped on the social cartography of present Danish class society. The three figurations are interesting in themselves, but they do point out the more general fact that speaking about class is always also speaking about gender, ethnicity, and place (cf. Skeggs).

My corpus has an overlap with but is decidedly not homologous with other loose formations one could mention, such as "migrant literature" (Frank, Larsen) and "underclass representations" (Albertsen). The levels of ethnic minorities are highly variable in both real-life housing areas and more or less fictitious renderings of them, and historically such areas were less class-specific than they appear in the common imagination of today. "Danish Ghetto Literature" is decidedly not a "perkerkanon" ["Paki canon"], as Lone Aburas has termed the facile grouping together of authors by minority ethnicity in an angry dismissal of the automated association of ethnic minorities and worn-out concrete blocks (19-20). "Danish ghetto literature" also differs from the treatment of the old working-class areas in inner cities – a much longer story with roots in the 19th century and Jonas Bengtsson's novel *Submarino* (2007, film 2010) offers a more contemporary example – because of the focus on the specific kinds of concrete buildings and the clearly delineated areas that are made up of them. I use a broad concept of "texts" by including song lyrics, TV, and film since the tropes I am interested in can be found in many different cultural products. However, the main focus is literary.

The Danish situation, on the one hand, is specific because of Danish housing policy – historically and, with the "ghetto plan," even more so in a contemporary context. On the other hand, the universal or social democratic model of welfare is common for all of Scandinavia – indeed, it is also referred to as the Nordic welfare model. Not least, Norway and Sweden have a comparable and relevant literature dealing with areas of modernist mass housing. In all three literatures, the kind of areas that only the Danes call "ghettoes" often function as symbols of the welfare state itself. This time around, I will have to make do with the mere mentioning of Zeshan Shakar's *Tante Ulrikkes vei* [2017, named after a specific street in Oslo East] – told by two young men, one using standard Norwegian, the other the local multiethnolect – and Elisa Karlsson's *Klass* (2017, Class) set in the quintessential Swedish "ghetto" of Rinkeby.

Pink Concrete in Block Land

In 2016, The Danish Broadcasting Corporation (DR) aired a highly successful documentary about a group of young women living in Copenhagen suburban high rises.[5] The very title *Prinsesser fra blokken* [Princesses from the Block] establishes a connection between the block as a class and place-specific form of habitation and certain conceptions of femininity. The introduction juxtaposes interview snippets, pictures of concrete high rises, and hand-held footage of rave partying outside, as well as home life from inside the apartments. In the pictures, the blocks have been coloured slightly pink, the same goes for the very word "blokken" ["block"] in the title. Following this title, we get various scenes connected to make-up and statements concerning the importance of appearance. Siri, aged 25, for one, explains: "Vores skønhedsidealer på Vestegnen, det er jo fake. Jo falskere jo bedre. Vi er pjattede med silibabser herude" ["Our beauty ideals in Copenhagen West… well, they are fake; the faker the better. We are crazy about sili-boobs out here"]. (*Prinsesser fra blokken* I, 1:30). The four 30-minute episodes are organized in smaller sections, named after the areas where the girls live – some in Copenhagen West, some on the island of Amager, all of them locations on the class segregated city map of Copenhagen.

The default symbolic and emotional content of the material of concrete and the houses and areas built out of it was codified in the 1970s. In TV shows, pop songs, and novels, the areas of modernist mass housing were depicted as the depressing dwellings of an underclass marred by crime, unemployment, and divorce: "Enlige mødre og andre uden job / bliver stuvet sammen til kvarteret er fyldt op" ["Single mothers and others without jobs / are crammed together until the neighbourhood is packed"], as Jomfru Ane Band had it in "Asfaltballet" (The Asphalt Ball), a successful 1978 song. The conditions of children's and young people's life raised specific concerns, as is obvious in both Michael Buchwald's experimental novel *Blokland* (1975, Block Land) and Bent Haller's young adult novel *Katamaranen* (1976, The Catamaran). Haller's grim and graphic story about violence and very early experiences with sex among boys living in the "betonlort" [concrete shit] (as the protagonist's father calls the estate to which they have moved) raised what was arguably the largest round of controversy in Danish literature of the 1970s.

When the producers of *Prinsesser fra blokken* some 40 years later colour the grey high rises pink, this is a re-signification of a well-established cultural topos. The traditional atmosphere of concrete – hopelessness and marginalisation – is a subsonic drone under the young women's energetic presentation of themselves as carelessly partying school-dropouts and ardent devotees of make-up and plastic surgery. As the series unfold, this drone becomes more audible as we learn more of the troubled background of (and less than promising prospects for) the princesses. In line with the indirect framing of the young women's self-presentation, director Eva Marie Rødbro never distances the viewer from them by using, say, an authoritative voice-over. The princesses are, however, aware of the way they are looked at, or the way they imagine they are looked

---

5   According to DR, the series unexpectedly turned out to be their biggest ever streaming success. See "DR3's Vestegnsprinsesser slår streamingrekord."

at. "Jeg har lange negle, og jeg er megabrun og sådan lidt overdrevet. Jeg elsker det!" [My nails are long, and I am extremely tanned – it's kind of excessive. I love it!"] – says Simona, aged 16 (*Prinsesser fra blokken* I, 1.44). Their realization of Copenhagen West beauty ideals – artificiality and excess – presupposes an imagined norm they can refuse, an interpellation from middle class perceptions of "correct" femininity they can reject (Haarder, Simonsen, and Schwartz). In spite of, no doubt, the best of intentions, the series does to some extent reinforce a traditional (middle) classist conception of working-class women as excessive – a constantly made point in the work of English sociologist Beverley Skeggs. And, another point of hers, this "excessive" working-class femininity can be mapped geographically as well as, I would argue, located in the areas of modernist mass housing that Danes happily refer to as ghettoes.

As in quite a few other contemporary Danish narratives from these housing areas – one example being Karina Pedersen's *Helt ude i hampen: Mails fra underklassen* (2015, Far Out: Emails from the Underclass) – and in line with the quintessentially Danish lineage of "almene boligområder," ethnic minorities are absent in *Prinsesser fra blokken*. Under their "extreme" tans, the princesses are very white and very Danish. This codes the class- and place-specific princess femininity of the pink concrete in ethnic Danish terms, even if this coding is done in the negative, so to speak. A comparison with the gender norms that Geeti Amiri in her 2016 autobiography *Glansbilleder* had to rebel against as a young woman with Afghan parents (epitomized in her mother's disappointed aspirations for her daughter's grand Afghan wedding) clearly brings this out.

The Crisis-Ridden White Patriarchy

The third episode of *Prinsesser fra blokken* deals with the family background of the young women, not least the absence of their fathers, and the sorrow this absence has caused them. The documentary refers to the typical family backgrounds in the areas where the women live, but the relation between housing estates and single mother families is also a cultural motif articulated in the dystopian turn in the conception of estates, taking place in the 1970s – as is obvious in the song by Jomfru Ane Band quoted above.

In Morten Pape's autofictional coming-of-age-in-the-concrete novel *Planen*, the title is a vernacular reference to "Urbanplanen," a large housing estate in Copenhagen but may also refer to the larger plan behind it, the welfare state itself. Little Morten is very anxious that his parents will divorce. He knows that this would align his own life with what he sees all around him:

> Når jeg besøgte mine andre venner i Planen, var der én ting der altid slog mig – der var stort set aldrig nogen fædre hjemme. Det var et kvarter fyldt med enlige mødre, enker og børnepenge hver måned (29).

> [When I visited my other friend in The Plan, I was always struck by one thing – there were never any fathers present. It was a neighbourhood filled with single mothers, widows, and child support every month.]

147

The fact that this family type is ethnically specific is clear from both Morten's own background and the names of the friends he refers to here: Palle, Samuel, og Steffen.

For Morten, the single mother family structure is marked by emotional truncation and social decline. After the divorce has come, despite little Morten's efforts, he has a conversation with his mother. She asks him what it is that he is so afraid of: "Jeg frygter at alle bare bliver ligeglade med hinanden. Sådan er det gået i alle de andres familier" (101) ["I fear that everyone will be indifferent to each other. That's how things have gone down in all the other families"]. He then lists all the children he knows to whom this had happened and very tellingly adds: "Alle dem med danske efternavne, i hvert fald" (ibid.) ["all those with Danish surnames, at any rate"]. His mother reassures him that his father is different, he is a good man, he will always care for Morten and his siblings. Alas, Morten is right, and the rest of the novel is very much a story of betrayal. Morten's father is unable to live up to even the most minimal obligations of fatherhood. Neither is he able to sustain a home and a life for himself. For him, the divorce is also a fall out from the working class and into the precariat, whereas Morten's mother manages to keep the single parent family on the brink of such social decline. It does get ugly, but they do get by.

With reference to the ethnically Danish coding of this configuration and the feeling of fatherly lack (rather than matriarchal presence), I have termed it "the crisis-ridden white patriarchy." This form of patriarchy is related to "implosive masculinity," a form of masculinity characterized by the absence and erosion of qualities traditionally associated with breadwinner fatherhood: reliability, authority, and providing for the family.

In Morten's case, the implosion of his father's masculinity is distinctively related to his body. The divorce accelerates decay, both in the form of increasing neglect of personal hygiene and in the form of physical deterioration (some of this goes for Morten's mother as well, but to a lesser extent). This process is part of the very composition of the novel. In fact, *Planen* is a literary patricide, comparable to the one in Karl Ove Knausgård's *Min kamp* (2009-2011) but set in the very different surroundings of a Danish "ghetto." When we meet Morten's father in chapter one, he is in front of the family TV alternating between scratching his balls and picking his nose. This non-compliance with not only the basic hygienic divisions of different zones of the body but also of divisions between private and common zones of home intensifies after the divorce (122ff). Morten and his siblings visit him in his new apartment. He has only one bed where all of them have to sleep, but one night, sleepless, Morten watches his father fart and masturbate while watching porn on TV. In the morning, he has to take his morning leak down a dirty toilet full of his dad's yellowy semen. In the very last scene, Morten watches his father appear in front of the big window of the take-away where he is having a kebab (558f). The father is in an advanced state of decay. Obese, dirty, and wearing both a large leg bandage and greasy hearing aids, his sad figure disappears down the street, out of this well-staged scene and the life of his son, a script-writer-to-be who is clearly on a class journey away from The Plan.

The Crisis-Ridden Brown Patriarchy

Taken together, the poems of *Yahya Hassan* amount to a coming-of-age-in-the-concrete narrative, and just like in *Planen*, the father-son-relationship is a central motif. The family father, however, is all too present, and his masculinity explosive rather than implosive. The collection opens with the poem "BARNDOM" ["Childhood"]:

FEM BØRN PÅ RÆKKE OG EN FAR MED EN KØLLE
FLERGRÆDERI OG EN PL AF PIS
VI STIKKER SKIFTEVIS EN HÅND FREM
FOR FORUDSIGELIGHEDENS SKYLD
DEN DER LYD NÅR SLAGENE RAMMER
SØSTER DER HOPPER SÅ HURTIGT
FRA DEN ENE FOD TIL DEN ANDEN
THE PISS A WATERFALL DOWN HER LEGS

[FIVE CHILDREN IN LINE AND A FATHER WITH A CLUB
POLY- WEEPING AND A POOL OF PISS
IN TURNS WE STICK OUT OUR HANDS
FOR THE SAKE OF PREDICTABILITY
THAT SOUND WHEN THE BLOWS HIT
SISTER JUMPING SO QUICKLY FROM ONE FOOT TO THE OTHER
THE PISS A WATERFALL DOWN HER LEGS][6]

The father counts the blows: "ET SLAG ET SKRIG ET TAL 30 ELLER 40 TIL TIDER 50" [A BLOW A SCREAM A NUMBER 30 OR 40 SOMETIMES 50]. Meanwhile, the mother – out of frustration and sorrow, one imagines – smashes dishes in the stairway, making it obvious in what surroundings this takes place. A reference to Al Jazeera, transmitting from the West Bank, makes it tempting to think we also know who "we" are, roughly. However, the poet deftly finishes this gruesome and instant classic of contemporary Danish poetry with these lines where this question of identity is turned into an aporia, specific for these five battered children (and children like them):

I SKOLEN MÅ VI IKKE TALE ARABISK
DERHJEMME MÅ VI IKKE TALE DANSK
ET SLAG ET SKRIG ET TAL

[AT SCHOOL WE ARE NOT ALLOWED TO SPEAK ARABIC
AT HOME WE ARE NOT ALLOWED TO SPEAK DANISH
A BLOW A SCREAM A NUMBER]

---

[6]   Like a number of notable predecessors from the history of Danish poetry (e.g., the expressionist Rud Broby and Michael Strunge with a relation to punk), Yahya Hassan uses only capital letters.

In a later poem, the father tries to strangle the mother. The family is dispersed by the authorities, and we follow the lyrical *I* through various institutions and crime forms: theft, violence, and drug dealing. He is taken on by the leading publishing house in Denmark at a very young age, but the finishing "LANGDIGT" ["LONG POEM"] is decidedly not the last station in an edifying tale of maturity and class journey. Written in a self-consciously multiethnolect Danish, the poet makes no secret of the fact that he is by now both a hardened criminal and a promising poet.

There are certainly exceptions, but patriarchal violence is widespread in the sub-group of "Danish ghetto literature" that deals with growing up in a Danish family with an immigrant background. Aydin Soei's autofictional novel *Forsoning: Fortælling om en familie* (2016, Atonement: Tale of a Family) is an attempt to understand a father who became a murderer. In *Sort land*, Ahmad Mahmoud tells the story of how he escaped his violent father and older brother. In *Glansbilleder,* following the death of their beloved father, Geeti Amiri's older brother takes over with measures so extreme that she ends up in a domestic violence shelter. Sara Omar's two bestselling novels (2017, 2019) both deal with systematic and extreme violence, mainly but not exclusively domestic.[7] In my corpus I call this figuration "the crisis-ridden brown patriarchy" and relate it to an "explosive masculinity" characterized by unpredictable and recurring domestic violence.

Three Explanations

All of the texts that I mention here are concerned with understanding violence in the crisis-ridden brown patriarchy. I see three frames of interpretation, overlapping in their presentation of co-determination but distinguishable. The first one pertains specifically to families with diaspora experiences of exile, refugee camps, and war. "HVORNÅR VAR I SIDST I SIKKERHED" ["WHEN WAS THE LAST TIME YOU FELT SAFE"], the poet of *Yahya Hassan* asks his parents (12), "KRIGEN ER STADIG I JER" ["THE WAR IS STILL IN YOU"]. This is Mahmoud:

> Volden, vi oplever, er i bund og grund en bivirkning ved krigstraumatiserede forældre. Deres land blev stjålet fra dem, de levede i flygtningelejr, kom til Danmark for at få et bedre liv, men magtede ikke opgaven selv. Med tiden blev hjemmet til en ny flygtningelejr, hvor volden opstod uden varsel og forsvandt lige så hurtigt. (30-31)

> [The violence we experience is basically a side effect of war traumatised parents. Their country was stolen from them, they spent their life in a refugee camp, arrived in Denmark to get a better life but could not handle it on their own. In time, home became a new refugee camp where violence erupted without notice and disappeared just as quickly again.]

---

7   The link between patriarchal violence and Danish "ghettoes" is not in the center of attention for Sara Omar, but having rescued her young protagonist Frmesk out of systematic sexual abuse and violence in Kurdistan, she does locate her in the familiar surroundings of blocks, stairways, and apartments (see *Skyggedanseren* [The Shadow Dancer] 35ff) where the violence and abuse continues.

The second frame of interpretation concerns a strained relationship between brought-along masculinity ideals and the ruling conceptions in Denmark. Typically, this conflict is described as enhanced by marginalisation, not least in the form of unemployment. This is how Aydin Soei voices his mother's explanation of the fact that her husband ended up murdering a friend:

> Vi kvinder ville uddannelse og arbejde og kæmpede for det, mens mændene passivt så os lykkes med vores projekter. Det betød, at kvinderne ikke længere gad de her mænd, der sad hjemme og forsøgte at bestemme over dem. Mange af mændene var idioter, men de var jo ikke dumme, og jeg tror, at mange af dem tænkte: Hvornår bliver det min tur? (*Forsoning* 438-9)

> [We women wanted education and work and fought for it, while the men passively watched us succeed with our projects. This meant that the women lost interest in these men sitting at home and trying to exert power over them. Many of these men were idiots, but they were not stupid, and I think many of them thought to themselves: when is it going to be my turn?]

Geeti Amiris story in *Glansbilleder* revolves around the loss of an illusion. For a long while, her brother's violence seemed to be the unrelated opposite of the kindness of her plaster-saint father, but she later realizes that her father, in fact, through passivity, had severely neglected his son and left him to find his own bearings as a man out on the street. In a radio documentary, after the reconciliation between the siblings, Amiri's brother explained his violence as desperate attempts at fulfilling impossible expectations as the man of the house (*Zakias datter*).

The third frame of interpretation is Islam. Yahya Hassan is highly critical of the form of Islam he encountered while growing up in a certified ghetto in Aarhus West; according to him, a form of religion characterised by ignorance and hypocrisy. While the explicit nature of this criticism earned Hassan fame and countless death threats, just as it necessitated 24/7 police protection (a situation and a life he relates in *Yahya Hassan 2*), Hassan does not describe the violence of his father as specifically linked to Islam. In this, he differs from Sara Omar. Her novels describe violence towards women as an all-pervasive function of Islam, or, to quote a specification by her grandfather, the only non-evil male in the universe of her two novels: "den del af islam, der er kvindeundertrykkende" (Skyggedanseren 42) ["the part of Islam that is oppressive to women"].

Convergence

Judging by these texts, the ethnically Danish children of the "ghetto" often grow up in the crisis-ridden white patriarchy with absent and/or imploded father figures, while children in immigrant families often grow up in the crisis-ridden brown patriarchy with all too present violent fathers. One can reasonably surmise that this is a kind of initial position. In a long-term perspective, the two configurations will show a tendency to converge. The facts of mainstream Danish ways of life, not least high divorce rates, will affect ethnic minority families. Even the "brown" father figure will implode, but without necessarily withdrawing from the violence; the quote from Aydin Soei's *Forsoning* given above says as much.

In his sociological studies of angry brown men and what he calls "modborgerskab" ["counter-citizenship"] Soei sheds more light on the specifics of divorces in "brown" families and their effects on, not least, the sons: the divorce rate in ethnic minority families are almost as high as in ethnically Danish families, but often the process is much more dramatic, both before, under, and after the divorce (Soei, *Omar og de andre* 52ff).[8] Soei's point is that many of the angry young men he follows have grown up with a lethal mixture of domestic violence, absent father figures, and very strained relationships between divorced parents.

Cultural representations, fictional and/or autobiographical, seem to tell similar stories. In *Når støvet har lagt sagt sig* [When the Dust Has Settled] – a multi protagonist fictional TV series about a terrorist attack in Copenhagen running on DR in the spring of 2020 – we follow Jamal from a Copenhagen ghetto (a word used in the series), among many others. His father has abandoned the family and gone back to the refugee camp, an older brother has taken over as the breadwinner and patriarch. He is less violent than the brother in Amiri's *Glansbilleder*, but the motif is basically similar. In Sara Omar's *Skyggedanseren*, Frmesk's mother divorced her violent husband after their arrival in Denmark, but he frequently makes his way up the stairway of their block to eat, terrify, and abuse her and their children (the mother is, in fact, not much better, but less physically violent).

While ethnic differences continue to matter, even in times of convergence, it is worth remembering that much of the landscape drawn up by these texts has to do with class and place-specific circumstances that affect young men whatever their ethnic background. Morten Pape's second novel, *Guds bedste børn* [2018, God's Best Children], takes place in the streets near Urbanplanen, the site of his first novel. The novel is comparable to Soei's sociological work in that Pape, by means of literary fiction but building on real events from 2009, tries to map the background of two ethnically Danish young men, one of them decidedly a psychopath, who randomly kills a brown man out of racism. Their white supremacist ideology and tendency towards violence are explicitly anchored in a macho criminal underclass culture that is, ironically, comparable to the one in which some of Soei's young men live. Backed up by the use of real-life statements from both the then prime minister and the head of the homicide department, Pape's larger political claim is that the racist background of the killing of Zeki (Deniz Uzun was his real name) was systematically hushed up by the authorities.

---

[8] One of Soei's sources is the survey *Skilsmissebørn med etnisk minoritetsbaggrund* [Children of Divorced Parents with Ethnic Minority Background] (Ottoson, Liversage and Olsen 2014). Most of the young men later get their act together, so to speak, some remain criminals and a few resort to terrorism. Omar Abdel Hamid El-Hussein, who killed two people on 14–15 February 2015, is the most infamous. He was killed by the police after the second attack, on a synagogue in Copenhagen.

Disgust as Coping

An interesting example of partial convergence can be found in the comparison of *Yahya Hassan* and *Planen*, more specifically in the relation between the narrating sons and their crisis-ridden fathers. The basic feeling in Morten's early childhood, as it is narrated in *Planen*, is anxiety. And little Morten has every reason to be anxious. His parents divorce and he is systematically bullied at school by "*perker*" boys. This micro-sociological level of anxiety is discretely linked to both an atmosphere of general deterioration of the area and maybe even the welfare state as such in the course of the 1990s, and to the build-up of global tension epitomized by 9/11 – an event that had bad consequences for people like Morten (and Mo in Zeshan Shakar's *Tante Ulrikkes Vei*) who try to find a third way in the increasingly binary ethnic landscape of the "ghetto." However, Morten's anxiety gradually gives way to stronger self-confidence stemming from a growing sense that he will be able to leave "Planen" and thus perform a class journey. This is by no means without complications and ambiguity, but the very construction of the novel as a *Bildungsroman*, with an authoritative first-person narrator who tells his childhood story from somewhere else, testifies to the stability of a grown-up middle-class identity.

In a sense, the long novel is narrated from the kebab joint where Morten takes leave of his father. "Min kynisme kommer bag på mig" (559) ["My cynicism takes me by surprise"], he says of his own attitude. The final framing of his father as a disgusting bum must be seen as the completion of the wounded child's necessary dissociation from a deceitful parent (destructive and dangerous in spite of, or rather because of, his weakness), while the writer-to-be can compose his narrative around three scenes where this disgust, and thus the dissociation, is articulated. Class or rather class difference, maybe even class shaming, is part of the process: the establishment of a difference between the bum out on the street and the upcoming writer on the inside.

The basic atmosphere of *Yahya Hassan* is harder to characterize because of the fragmented and polyphonic discourse of the poems, but *horror*, rather than the milder anxiety of *Planen*, is certainly one feeling pervading the poet's early childhood in an extremely violent home, enhanced by the ironic deadpan attitude with which many of the atrocities are told. Interestingly, disgust plays an important role even for this survivor. His father's acts speak for themselves, but he is also compared to a gorilla, and the son's resentment for his father's combination of religious hypocrisy and primitive cruelty is recurring.

Disgust as an ugly felling "is never ambivalent about its object," says Sianne Ngai and continues: "Whereas the obscuring of the subjective-objective boundary becomes internal to the nature of feelings like animatedness and paranoia, disgust strengthens and polices this boundary" (335). This observation certainly seems to be in line with the experience of the two survivors Morten and Yahya: disgust reduces the notorious complexity of any parent-child relationship, troubled relationships being only more complex. Disgust establishes both distance and a difference stabilising the frail identity of the survivor. This policing of the subject's boundaries by way of disgust is the main strategy of another survivor, Karina Pedersen. In *Helt ude i hampen* her disgust for her addict mother and criminal brothers is explicitly linked to both the ghetto of Korskærparken and what she consistently terms "underklassen" ["the underclass"]. The second chapter of this collection of allegedly authentic emails between Karina and a friend opens like this:

> "Når jeg lukker øjnene, kan jeg se kvarteret helt tydeligt: de store grimme, gråhvide betonblokke og beboerne – samfundets mindst succesrige individer – der aldrig kan holde sig på dydens smale sti :-)" (7).

> [When I close my eyes, I can see the neighbourhood quite clearly: the big ugly grey-white blocks of concrete and the inhabitants – the least successful individuals of society – who can never stay on the narrow path of virtue :-)]

From there, the passage continues with a long description of the repulsive body of her addict mother. Disgust, class, place, and a destructive parent are condensed into one and held at arm's length, keeping a threatening ambivalence at bay. This is certainly less than sympathetic but perhaps understandable, given the childhood Karina seems to have had. Had Pedersen accepted the advice of her publishing house and called her text a novel, the empirically less than accurate allegations concerning the people in Korskær-parken would have been less of a problem, and we would possibly find it easier to apply an empathic but also potentially patronizing reading of the email-writing protagonist (Haarder, Simonsen, and Schwartz).

Tolerated Ambivalence

Ambivalence is not suppressed in *Planen* and *Yahya Hassan*. The narrator of *Planen* insists on the complexity of his relationship with his disgusting father as well as the feelings of guilt associated with the literary patricide of the book itself. In *Yahya Hassan*, it is hard to forget such poem as "FAR MIN UFØDTE SØN" [FATHER MY UNBORN SON] where both the endless violence, the loss of a normal child's life, *and* the inevita-

bility of attachment is articulated in 5 lines:

> JEG SPILDER TYVE LITER MØRKE
> OG EN BARNDOM OP AD VÆGGEN
> EN STENALDERHÅND EN PAPERBACK-KORAN
> MÅSKE VILLE JEG HAVE ELSKET DIG
> HVIS JEG VAR DIN FAR OG IKKE DIN SØN (103)

> [I WASTE TWENTY LITRES DARKNESS
> AND A CHILDHOOD UP THE WALL
> A STONE AGE HAND A PAPERBACK KORAN
> I MIGHT HAVE LOVED YOU
> IF I WAS YOUR FATHER AND NOT YOUR SON]

The father's combination of religious ignorance, hypocrisy, and primitive violence is condensed in one short line – the stone age hand plus the paperback Koran – and the conclusion successfully creates a formula containing both distance and tolerated ambivalence.

Very near the end of "LANGDIGT," and thus the book, the poet turns up at the publishing house "MED DEN ANSIGT DER LIGNER MIN FAR/VISER DEN FREM/ MED LIVLIG PIK OG SEKRETÆR I TANKERNE" (166) ["WITH THE FACE THAT LOOKS LIKE MY FATHER/SHOWING IT OFF/ WITH LIVELY DICK AND SEC-RETARY ON MY MIND"].[9] It seems that the poet engages himself in a game of sexual attraction where he self-consciously plays on his likeness with his father. This likeness is both a physiognomic and a psychological fact and a fact of racialization, the stereo-typical way he is looked at by others. The poet seems painfully aware of both, but his self-awareness also makes it possible for him to manipulate others. This is a recurring motif in the book on the level of narrative, but it is also related to the very words and sentences of the poems. The first part of the book is written in, as he terms it himself, "MANIPULERENDE GODT DANSK" (139) ["MANIPULATINGLY GOOD DAN-ISH"], whereas the finishing "LANGDIGT" consistently and self-consciously applies the 'authentic' multiethnic Danish of his 'authentic' ghetto background as a highly effec-tive poetic device – mastering standard Danish is a prerequisite for his multiethnic Dan-ish rather than the other way around.

The fact that he looks like his father, not least in the eyes of others looking at him (such as the people of the publishing house), does to some extent direct disgust back in his own direction. There are several instances of less than pleasurable looks in the mirror, and in "LANGDIGT" he shapes the self-directed disgust in the startling image of himself as a cripple with his own penis in his mouth (138). Morten from *Planen* does not in the same way feel that he carries the face of his disgusting father around, and the relation between where he came from and what and where he wants to be is much less troubled than it is in *Yahya Hassan*. It is worth considering, whether this difference has to do with the fact that Hassan's face marks him as other, as 'belonging to' the ghetto, at least when he is outside of the ghetto, such as in the offices of the publishing house Gyldendal.

Coda

"The worst thing is, though," writes Karina in continuation of the passage I quoted in my introduction and the section above, "that it is not just me who can see my childhood neighbourhood; it can also see me – or rather – it has my number" ["Det værste er dog, at det ikke kune r mig, som kan se mit barndomskvarter; det kan også se mig – eller rettere – det kan mit nummer"]. The point of this passage is that her mother rings her all

---

[9] I apologise for the standard English translations of the lines from "LANGDIGT." I found no way of trans-lating the multiethnolect traits of the poem, in this case the non-standard grammatical gendering of nouns.

the time, and Karina does not have the heart to tell her not to. In fact, the content of the phone calls is what makes up almost all of the emails in the book. We hear almost nothing about Karina's own life. Whether this is for protection, out of discretion, or because it is so very different to break away from "my childhood neighbourhood," we do not know.

In this article we have also picked up the phone and listened to stories about, among other things, childhoods in Danish 'ghettoes.' We may learn quite a bit about the aspects of life in Danish non-profit housing areas that confirm, challenge or, run counter to the official stories, but in the end such stories are not about alien "parallel societies" and disgusting "underclass" people, as Karina Pedersen insists, but about everyone and society as a whole. The ghettoes of Danish literature are also mirrors. The entanglement between class, gender, and ethnicity *takes place* everywhere, and ghettoisation is the general process in which we laboriously separate ourselves from the people we believe are different.

Works Cited

Primary Sources
Aburas, Lone. *Det er et jeg der taler (Regnskabets time)*. Copenhagen: Gyldendal, 2017.
Amiri, Geeti. *Glansbilleder*. Copenhagen: Lindhardt og Ringhof, 2016.
Brüel, Sanne/Claus Flygare (Jomfru Ane Band): "Asfaltballet." *Rock me Baby*. LP. Elap Music. 1978.
Buchwald, Michael. *Blokland*. Viborg: Arena, 1975.
Haller, Bent. *Katamaranen*. Copenhagen: Borgen, 1976.
Hassan, Yahya. *Yahya Hassan*. Copenhagen: Gyldendal, 2013.
Hassan, Yahya. *Yahya Hassan 2*. Copenhagen: Gyldendal, 2019.
Mahmoud, Ahmad. *Sort land: Fortællinger fra ghettoen*. Copenhagen: People's Press, 2015.
Når støvet har lagt sig. DR. 2 Feb. 2020. https://www.dr.dk/drtv/serie/naar-stoevet-har-lagt-sig_164395 (30 March 2020)
Omar, Sara. *Dødevaskeren*. Copenhagen: Politikens forlag, 2017.
Omar, Sara. *Skyggedanseren*. Copenhagen: Politikens forlag, 2019.
Pape, Morten. *Planen*. Copenhagen: Gyldendal, 2015.
Pape, Morten. *Guds bedste børn*. Copenhagen: Gyldendal, 2018.
Pedersen, Karina. *Helt ude i hampen: Mails fra underklassen*. Copenhagen: Gyldendal, 2016.
Prinsesser fra blokken. DR TV. 30 Nov. 2016. https://www.dr.dk/drtv/episode/prinsesser-fra-blokken_47336#!/00:00 (30 March 2020)
Soei, Aydin. *Forsoning. Fortælling om en familie*. Copenhagen: Tiderne skifter, 2016.
Zakias datter. DR Radio. 8 June 2017. [no longer available online]

Secondary Sources
Albertsen, Anita. "Det sociale teater. Underklasse-repræsentationer og symbolsk grænsearbejde i *På røven i Nakskov* og *Helt ude i hampen*." *Spring* 42 (2018): 156–174.
"Danish parliament passes contentious 'ghetto plan'" on *Thelocal.dk*. 2018: https://www.thelocal.dk/20181123/danish-parliament-passes-contentious-ghetto-plan (30 March 2020)

"DR3's Vestegnsprinsesser slår streamingrekord" *DR*. 5 Dec. 2016. https://www.dr.dk/nyheder/kultur
/dr3s-vestegnsprinsesser-slaar-streamingrekord (30 March 2020)

Frank, Søren: "Hvad er migrationslitteratur?" *Kritik* 203 (2012): 2–10.

Freiesleben, Mikaela. *Et Danmark af parallelsamfund*. PhD thesis, University of Copenhagen.
Downloaded from: https://curis.ku.dk/ws/files/160573902/Ph.d._2016_Freiesleben.pdf%20(13
2016 (30 March 2020)

"Færre udsatte boligområder og ghettoområder på de nye lister" 2019: https://www.trm.dk/nyheder
/2019/faerre-udsatte-boligomraader-og-ghettoomraader-paa-de-nye-lister/ (30 March 2020)

Høghøj, Mikkel. *Between Utopia and Dystopia. A socio-cultural history of modernist mass housing in Denmark, c. 1945-1985*, PhD thesis, University of Aarhus, 2019.

Haarder, Jon Helt. "Tilbage over Atlanten med stil. En importhistorie om dansk rap." *Aktualitet. Litteratur. Kultur. Medier.* 4.2 (2010): https://tidsskrift.dk/aktualitet/article/view/112801 (30 March 2020)

Haarder, Jon Helt. "The Precariat as Place. Literary History of the Danish Ghetto." *Scandinavica* 59.2 (2020): 29-50. https://www.scandinavica.net/article/18832-the-precariat-as-place-a-literary -history-of-the-danish-ghetto

Haarder, Jon Helt, Peter Simonsen and Camilla Schwartz. "Hvem kan tale for prekariatet – og hvorfra? In the Ghetto med Kristian Bang Foss, Morten Pape, Yahya Hassan, Karina Pedersen og prinsesserne fra blokken." *Edda* 3 (2018): 185-202. https://www.idunn.no/edda/2018/03 /hvem_kan_tale_for_prekariatet_og_hvorfra (1 April 2020)

Kjældgaard, Lasse. *Meningen med velfærdsstaten: Da litteraturen tog ordet - og politikerne lyttede*. Copenhagen: Gyldendal, 2018.

Krog, Mads. "Assembling Aarhus West: "Glocal Rap, Genre and Heterogeneity." *Popular Music History* 10.3 (2005): 280–296.

Krog, Mads and Birgitte Stougaard Petersen. *Hiphop i Skandinavien*. Aarhus: Aarhus University Press, 2008.

Larsen, Peter Stein. "Dansk identitet i moderne lyrik." *Passage* 31.75 (2016): 7–26: https://tidsskrift .dk/passage/article/view/25227/22154 (30 March 2020)

Lund, Nicklas Freisleben: "De fremtidsløse tager ordet. Klasse, prekariat og velfærdskritik i dansk samtidsprosa" i *Passage* 31.76 (2016): 27–29. https://tidsskrift.dk/passage/article/view/25229 (30 March 2020)

Ngai, Sianne. *Ugly Feelings*. Cambridge, MA & London, England, 2005.

Ottoson, Mai Heede, Anika Liversage and Rikke Fuglsang Olsen. *Skilsmissebørn med etnisk minoritetsbaggrund*. Copenhagen: Det nationale forskningscenter for velfærd. 2014: https://pure.vive .dk/ws/files/201694/1418_Skilsmisseb_rn_med_etnisk_minoritetsbaggrund.pdf (1 April 2020)

Ricœur, Paul. *Time and Narrative*. Vol I. Trans. Kathleen Mclaughlin and David Pellauer. London: The University of Chicago Press, 1984.

Schultz Larsen, Troels: "Kapitel 18. Fra ghetto til forsømte boligområder. Socialvidenskabelig refleksivitet som afsæt for en afvisning af ghettobegrebet i en dansk sammenhæng." *Grundbog i socialvidenskab – 5 perspektiver*. Ed. Bent Greve. 2nd ed. Copenhagen: Nyt fra samfundsvidenskaberne, 2015. 415–432.

Schwartz, Daniel B. *Ghetto. The History of a Word*. Cambridge, MA: Harvard University Press, 2019.

Skeggs, Beverley. *Class, Self, Culture*. London: Routledge, 2004.

"The Social Housing Sector" *BL. Danske Almene Boliger*: https://bl.dk/in-english/ (30 March 2020)

Soei, Aydin. *Omar og de andre: Vrede unge mænd og modborgerskab*. Copenhagen: Gads forlag, 2018.

Wacquant, Loïc. *Urban Outcasts: A Comparative Sociology of Advanced Marginality*. Cambridge, UK: Polity, 2008.

Wacquant, Loïc. "Marginality, Ethnicity and Penality in the Neoliberal City: an Analytic Cartography." *Ethnic and Racial Studies* 37.10 (2014): 1687–1711. https://www4.shu.ac.uk/research /cresr/sites/shu.ac.uk/files/marginality-ethnicity-penality-neoliberal-city.pdf (1 April 2020)

Notes on Contributors

Helena Březinová is Associate Professor of Scandinavian Studies at Charles University in Prague. Her research is mainly on Scandinavian Romanticism, Hans Christian Andersen, and Johannes V. Jensen. Among her recent publications is *Slavíci, mořské víly a bolavé zuby: Pohádky H. Ch. Andersena: mezi romantismem a modernitou* [Nightingales, Mermaids and Toothaches: Andersen's Fairy Tales between Romanticism and Modernity, 2018]. The book was awarded the 2019 Zlatá stuha [Golden Ribbon] in the category of the theory and criticism of children's literature.

Petra Broomans is Associate Professor with *ius promovendi* at the University of Groningen and Visiting Professor at Ghent University. She was awarded an honorary doctorate from Uppsala University in 2020, was a visiting professor in the University Immersion Program (UIP) at Sichuan University (2017–2019), and is coordinator of the U4Society network in Cultural Transfer Research and chief editor of the book series Studies on Cultural Transfer and Transmission (CTaT). She has published extensively on cultural transfer, the reception of Scandinavian literature and women's literature. Her research interests include cultural transfer, world literature, meta-literary history, minority literature. She is coordinator of the Dutch translators' dictionary (https://www.vertalerslexicon.nl/)

Jan Dlask is Assistant Professor of Finnish Literature at Charles University in Prague. He studied Finnish and Swedish Philology and specialized in Finland-Swedish literature. He defended his doctoral dissertation on the Tikkanen-Kihlman debate in 2010 (its main theses were presented in Swedish in *Historiska och litteraturhistoriska studier* 87). He has written the book *Dějiny finskošvédské literatury v perspektivě bourdieuovské sociologie* [The History of Finland-Swedish Literature through the Perspective of Bourdieusian Sociology; in Czech] (Červený Kostelec: Pavel Mervart, 2018). He has also published other articles and studies in Czech, Swedish, Finnish, and English.

Satu Gröndahl is Associate Professor of Finno-Ugric Languages at The Hugo Valentin Centre, Uppsala University. She has published widely about minority and migrant literature in the Nordic countries, especially Sweden. Gröndahl was one of the co-editors, together with Eila Rantonen, of *Migrants and Literature in Finland and Sweden* (Helsinki: Finnish Literature Society, 2018). She has been visiting professor in minority literature at Sámi University of Applied Sciences, Kautokeino, Norway.

Jon Helt Haarder is Associate Professor of Danish Literature at the Department for the Study of Culture at University of Southern Denmark (SDU). He has published numerous articles and book chapters, as well as books on a variety of subjects within the fields of Scandinavian literature and literary theory. He was part of the SDU project *Uses of Literature: The Social Dimensions of Literature* headed by Rita Felski, and currently leads the project "Reassembling the Ghetto," funded by Independent Research Fund Denmark 2021–2024.

Martin Humpál is Professor of Scandinavian Literature at Charles University in Prague. He has written the books *The Roots of Modernist Narrative: Knut Hamsun's Novels* Hunger, Mysteries*, and* Pan (Oslo: Solum, 1998) and *Moderní skandinávské literatury 1870–2000* [Modern Scandinavian Literature 1870–2000; in Czech, together with Helena Kadečková and Viola Parente-Čapková] (Prague: Karolinum, 2006, 2nd rev. ed. 2013). He has also published numerous articles in scholarly books and journals.

Annika Bøstein Myhr is Professor of Norwegian Literature at the University of South-Eastern Norway. Myhr holds an MA degree in Russian Studies and a Ph.D. in Comparative Literature and has published extensively on Russian and Scandinavian literature. She is the editor of *Twist* (2021), and co-editor of *Sårbarhet og litteratur* ['Vulnerability and Literature'] (2021, with Margareta Dancus and Silje H. Linhart), and of *Negotiating Identities in Nordic Migrant Narratives: Crossing Borders and Telling Lives* (2022, with Pia Lane and Bjørghild Kjelsvik).

Elisabeth Oxfeldt is Professor of Scandinavian Literature at the University of Oslo. Her research interests include postcolonial topics, such as Orientalism, travel literature, migrant literature, minority voices, feminism, and literary activism. Recently she has led a project on Scandinavian feelings of guilt vis-à-vis underprivileged global Others: "Scandinavian Narratives of Guilt and Privilege in an Age of Globalization" (SCAN-GUILT). She is currently leading the project "Unashamed Citizenship: Minority Literary Voices in Contemporary Scandinavia."

Sylwia Izabela Schab is Professor of Scandinavian Literature at the Department of Scandinavian Studies, Adam Mickiewicz University in Poznań. In 2018, she published her book on travel writing and representation *Palimpsest Polski: Reprezentacje Polski i Polaków w duńskich relacjach podróżniczych* [Polish Palimpsest: Representations of Poland and Poles in Danish Travelogues]. She has also published numerous articles in scholarly books and journals, mostly on Danish and Polish travel literature, the postcolonial aspects of Danish literature and Danish migration literature.

Radka Stahr is Assistant Professor of Scandinavian Languages and Literature at Charles University in Prague. She defended her PhD thesis on Karen Blixen and ekphrasis in 2018. In her research she focuses on the reflection of fine arts in literature and on spatial concepts in migration literature. She has also taught Scandinavian literature at Goethe-Universität in Frankfurt am Main.

Summary

Migration and Identity in Nordic Literature

This book focuses on migration as it has manifested itself in literature and culture in nineteenth, twentieth, and early twenty-first century Northern Europe, more concretely, in Denmark, Norway, Sweden, Finland, and Iceland. The authors examine the theme of migration in relation to the questions of identity, both national and individual. The basic premise is the idea that migration almost always leads to a disturbance of identity and creates a potential for conflicts between individuals, as well as between groups of people.

The book has two parts. The first discusses relevant theoretical and historical issues that form the conceptual background of the main theme. The second part of the book analyzes some concrete cases of disturbance, disruption, and hybridization of identity, as they are represented in literary works linked to the European North.